The early years of the 20th Century saw many advances in technology, for example aeroplanes were taking to the skies and wireless telegraphy becoming more available. There were also new war machines such as submarines and tanks. Additionally, pharmaceutical drugs and photographic components previously supplied from German manufacturers were no longer available during the Great War of 1914-18. Responding to some of the technical challenges, the Council of the Royal Society formed a War Committee, which in turn commissioned sub-committees concerned with chemistry, physics and engineering. Later, sub-committees relating to food, grain pests and the use of natural products were also initiated. For its part the Government formed the Admiralty Board of Invention and Research, the Munitions Invention Department, the Chemical Advisory Committee and others. Fellows of the Royal Society were key to both the Royal Society and Government initiatives. But who were the Fellows and why should they be of such strategic importance? Fellowship of the Royal Society is restricted, and requires individuals to be at the peak of their chosen scientific professions. All Fellows are experts in their chosen fields, which not only includes the traditional sciences, but also engineering and medicine. They are individuals whose scientific acumen, knowledge and skills are vital to solving seemingly intractable problems. It is no wonder that their expertise, opinions and help were sought during the dark days of the Great War. Remarkably, the exploits of the Fellows during the war are relatively unknown. Drawing from previously unpublished documents from the Royal Society archives deemed 'Secret' at the time, and wartime documents from the National Archives classified during the Great War as 'Subject to the Official Secrets Act', *Top Secret: British Boffins in WWI* brings a unique perspective on wartime inventions, research and developments from one of the darkest periods of 20th Century warfare. There are some remarkable examples of co-operation and effort often to tight deadlines using the utmost discretion. Some names may be familiar to you, some may not. All played their part, this is their story ...

I0894073

David Rogers is a scientist by training, obtaining a doctorate in chemistry before working for a Fellow of the Royal Society for his post-doctorate. He went on to spend many years in British industry working for a multi-national company in both research and manufacturing departments inventing, developing or helping to manufacture a range of products. He is a Fellow of the Royal Society of Chemistry, The Royal Photographic Society and of the British Institute of Professional Photography. He was a Visiting Professor in Business Psychology for three years and is now a Visiting Lecturer. He decided to transition to a career involving writing, consultancy and some teaching in 2004. Since that time, David has written or edited eight published books, mainly in the field of science/technology or wartime history. Married with two children, David has spent some of his spare time as a School Governor.

Top Secret

British Boffins in World War One

David Rogers

Helion & Company Limited

Helion & Company Limited
26 Willow Road
Solihull
West Midlands
B91 1UE
England
Tel. 0121 705 3393
Fax 0121 711 4075
Email: info@helion.co.uk
Website: www.helion.co.uk
Twitter: @helionbooks
Visit our blog http://blog.helion.co.uk/

Published by Helion & Company 2013

Designed and typeset by Farr out Publications, Wokingham, Berkshire
Cover designed by Euan Carter, Leicester (www.euancarter.com)
Printed by Lightning Source, Milton Keynes, Buckinghamshire

Front cover: Main image - Burlington House (Author's photo); central images, left to right - Sir Charles Frederick Arden-Close (© The Royal Society. Reproduced with permission), Sir George Beilby. (© The Royal Society. Reproduced with permission), Sir Richard Threlfall. (© Godfrey Argent Studio. Reproduced with permission).
Rear cover (left to right) - Professor Sir William Crookes (© The Royal Society. Reproduced with permission), Lord Rayleigh (© Godfrey Argent Studio. Reproduced with permission), Professor Hele-Shaw (© The Royal Society. Reproduced with permission).

ISBN 978 1 909384 21 7

British Library Cataloguing-in-Publication Data.
A catalogue record for this book is available from the British Library.

Contents

List of images

Acknowledgements

I spent three post-doctoral years working for a Fellow. Prior to taking up my appointment I thought three years as an undergraduate and three years for my doctorate taught me all I needed. How wrong I was!! I have never been so mentally stretched. Fellows are a breed of scientists and engineers at the top of their game. They attract the best talent (myself excluded), providing for many interesting conversations both in the laboratories and over drinks. Fellows also attract the best speakers, often other Fellows. The atmosphere surrounding these scientists is stimulating to say the least.

Yet there are other skills one can learn from Fellows, not least of which is time management. We all have 24 hours in any one day, it is interesting and enlightening to observe a Fellow at close quarters and watch how they spend their time. I am still grateful for the life skills I acquired along the way. Thank you Prof. (Professor Alan Roy Katritzky FRS). They always remain 'Prof' even when you reach maturity.

In writing about the Fellows and the Royal Society I have made some decisions in an attempt to help the reader. In all cases my decisions involved timing. Let me explain. A scientist or engineer may be awarded Fellowship at any stage of his or her career. Some have been elected whilst in their 30s, others later in life. I have chosen to ignore the specific date of election in this account. In other words all of the individuals mentioned below were at some stage elected Fellow of the Royal Society. It may be the case that the work I have documented took place before their election. My rationale for including all of these individuals is simple. It is the mental ability of the Fellows that sets them apart. This ability is not dependent on their election to Fellowship.

My second decision involved their form of address. The chapters are not chronological. Some chapters deal with subjects that were concurrent, others were separated by months or years. Some Fellows were knighted during the War. I took the decision to document the Fellows with their end of life title. This decision saved me addressing the same individual differently in different chapters. Additionally at least two Fellows inherited a peerage during the war. For example John William Strutt FRS inherited the title Lord Rayleigh I refer to this individual as Lord Rayleigh throughout to save confusion.

I offer sincere thanks to all of the Library Staff in the Royal Society. In particular Keith Moore, the Librarian, made some very useful comments early on in this project. Jo Hopkins, Picture Curator, helped with picture selection. These two Library staff are part of a larger team who all gave of their time. My thanks also extend to them.

Finally, my younger son James (a history undergraduate) and my wife helped in all sorts of ways. Thank you.

Introduction

At a meeting of the Royal Society on 12th November 1914, the Council decided to offer its services and that of its Fellows to aid Government work. Accordingly the Council appointed a War Committee the members of which informed the Admiralty, the War Office and the Board of Trade of their willingness to help the war effort. Within weeks separate committees for physics, chemistry and engineering were charged with addressing issues relating to wireless telegraphy, a quick and easy method of determining air density – a factor which has a great bearing on the rate of climb for machines detecting and catching submarines – a chemical propulsion method for torpedoes, the effects of explosions near to aircraft and the effects on humans of acceleration (preliminary studies for aircraft research). Other issues were presented by various Government Departments over time.

There was also the issue of supplying pharmacies with the relevant prescription drugs needed by our general practitioners and hospitals. Most pharmaceutical drugs at that time were obtained from German companies. The Royal Society enlisted the help of its Fellows and their contacts in Universities and other institutions. In all some 32 institutions offered to help produce pharmaceutical drugs, 3 were obliged to decline because their department staff and student numbers were severely depleted. Kew Gardens was also approached to help grow medicinal plants from which natural products could be extracted.

In addition to formal help, some Fellows were already active in industry. For example Sir Alfred Fernandez Yarrow FRS was an engineer who built many warships in his Clyde shipyard. Sir Henry Solomon Wellcome FRS was Managing Director of Burroughs Wellcome & Company and in that capacity provided much aid to the war effort. Of course post War he started his Wellcome Foundation, an organisation that is still active today. Even though he died in 1900, Lord Armstrong FRS cast a positive shadow on World War I for it was his company, known as Armstrong Whitworth & Co Ltd by the outbreak of War, which produced many armaments for the British and Allied armies.

Fellows with medical backgrounds were involved in many activities. For example the future Nobel Laureate Sir Alexander Fleming FRS, then a Captain in the RAMC, worked in a French laboratory investigating bacterial infection of wounds. Robert Newstead FRS investigated the importance of insects in warfare and in 1915 he was appointed by the War Office in charge of Entomological Commission to deal with 'insect prophylaxis' in France and Flanders. Frederick William Twort FRS worked on issues of dysentery prevention, Sir David Bruce FRS was the Director of the Trench Fever Committee, Sir Ronald Ross FRS became Consultant for Malaria to the War Office with the rank of Lieutenant-Colonel. Marcus Seymour Pembrey FRS was on a committee which recommended a reduction of the rations for trench-based soldiers, arguing that their relative inactivity in the trenches required fewer rations, see Figure 9.9!

Of course there were many who were active in the Military. John Alexander Sinton VC FRS is the only known Fellow to be awarded the Victoria Cross. Many others received medals.

These and other stories make fascinating reading.

1 Introduction, Administration and Infrastructure

The Royal Society is the oldest and the most prestigious learned scientific society in the world. It was founded on 28th November 1660, when a group of 12 scientists met at Gresham College following a lecture by Sir Christopher Wren. Granted its Royal Charter in 1662 by King Charles II, and with founding Fellows including John Wilkins, Robert Boyle, Sir Robert Moray, William, Viscount Brouncker and Wren himself, the Royal Society has elected to Fellowship or Foreign Membership the cream of world scientists for over 350 years. Sir Isaac Newton was a long time President, as was Sir Joseph Banks (a member of Captain James Cook's first great expedition to view the Transit of Venus and subsequent circumnavigation of the world in HMS *Endeavour*).

Most Nobel Laureates are Fellows or Foreign Members. Scientists in Britain and for that matter around the world aspire to be elected to its membership. The process of election to Fellowship is taxing as there is an upper limit of around 1,450. Accordingly only 40 or so scientists are elected annually. The Royal Society statutes do allow for Fellowship through other routes, notably the promotion of science through the media, or Royal Fellows. Prior to World War I the statutes also allowed election of Privy Councillors.[1] As one might imagine these routes to Fellowship are open to just a few individuals! For all practical purposes, Fellows are **the** world experts in their chosen fields, elected for their knowledge and expertise.

Initially meeting in small rooms, the Royal Society graduated through a series of buildings, starting with accommodation in Gresham College in London. By the outbreak of World War I, it had almost outgrown the rooms then occupied in Burlington House in London's Piccadilly.

Visitors to the modern accommodation of the Royal Society will be more familiar with the buildings in Carlton House Terrace, a most imposing building formerly comprising of the separate postal addresses of 6-9. From inside the building it takes an expert eye to realise that these were once separate addresses. Nevertheless, it was from Burlington House that Fellows and the Council of the Royal Society planned their war-work.

There were two distinct approaches adopted during World War I. The Fellows were active in both these initiatives, for they were separate and complementary. The first was the work of the Royal Society acting as a Corporate Body using

Figure 1.1. Burlington House. (Author's photograph)

Figure 1.2. Carlton House Terrace. (Author's photograph)

The President

Sir William Crookes [1913]; Sir Joseph John Thomson [1915]

Biological Sciences Secretary ('Sec. A')

responsible for overseeing the Society's scientific business

Sir John Rose Bradford [1908]; Sir William Bate Hardy [1915]

Physical Sciences Secretary ('Sec B')

responsible for overseeing the Society's scientific business

Sir Arthur Schuster [1912]; Sir James Hopwood Jeans [1919]

Foreign Secretary

responsible for overseeing the Society's international business

Dunkfield Henry Scott [1912]; Sir William Abbott Herdman [1916]

Treasurer

responsible for the accounts and administering the Society's finances

Sir Alfred Bray Kempe [1898]; Sir David Prain [1919]

Figure 1.3. World War I Royal Society Senior Council Members. (Author)

its resources and collective expertise.

Now, as during World War I, the President presides over the Board, which administers the Society and the 140 or so staff (2012 head count), and the Council which governs the scientific direction. The President is supported by four senior Council members (where the numbers in square brackets are the years of election), Figure 1.3.

These individuals and the rest of those Fellows elected to the 1914 Council, played a crucial role in determining the strategic wartime direction of the Royal Society acting as a Corporate Body. This activity was separate from any War involvement individual Fellows made. It led to the formation of wartime Sub-Committees, resulting in many hours of scientific endeavour at the highest level.

Secondly there were Government committees formed to investigate or develop specific technologies, populated to greater or lesser extents by Fellows. Although there were a few minor instances where the Royal Society recommendations were, for political or practical reasons set to one side, the vast majority of the time the output from the Royal Society War Committees was highly regarded. This includes submission of their reports to the Imperial War Cabinet, see for example Appendix I, item 17.

Sir William Crookes FRS, President at the outbreak of the War, chaired the meeting where the Royal Society became actively involved in the war effort. Sir William followed many notable scientists, some of his immediate predecessors are listed in Figure 1.4.

Name	Years as President
Sir Joseph John Thomson OM	1915-1920
Sir William Crookes OM	1913-1915
Sir Archibald Geikie OM KCB	1908-1913
Lord Rayleigh (John William Strutt) PC OM	1905-1908
Sir William Huggins OM KCB	1900-1905
Lord Lister (Joseph Lister) PC OM	1895-1900
Lord Kelvin (Sir William Thomson) PC OM	1890-1895

Figure 1.4. Presidents of the Royal Society 1890-1920[2]

Baron Kelvin of Largs FRS, Baron Lister of Lyme Regis FRS and Sir William Huggins FRS, all well known scientists of their day, indeed household names, sadly died in 1907, 1912 and 1910 respectively. Lord Rayleigh FRS, Sir William Crookes FRS and Sir Joseph John Thomson FRS were very active in their respective roles throughout the War.

At that Council meeting of the Royal Society (held on the 12th November 1914), a War Committee was established with three sectional Sub-Committees reporting to it. Initially there were committees for chemistry, engineering and physics. Later other committees were formed dealing with food, grain pests and the use of natural products.

Council resolved:

> ... that the following be appointed to organise assistance to the Government in conducting or suggesting scientific investigations in relation to the War ...

The committee had the power to add to their number and to appoint Sub-Committees with non-Fellow members. The War Committee initially comprised of:

Sir William Crookes PRS
Mr. William Duddell FRS
Sir Richard Glazebrook FRS
Sir Oliver Lodge FRS
Lord Rayleigh FRS
Sir Arthur Schuster FRS
Sir Alfred Ewing FRS
Admiral Sir Henry Jackson FRS
Sir William Ramsay FRS
Sir Edward Thorpe FRS

Council agreed that Secretaries of the Society write to the Admiralty, the War Office and the Board of Trade offering assistance to the Government.

Council also resolved:

> that the following Sub-Committees be appointed:
> ... For the investigation of telephony, wireless telegraphy, and general physics.
> Members were Sir Charles Boys FRS, Mr. S. Brown FRS, Mr. W. Duddell FRS, Sir Richard Glazebrook FRS, Sir Oliver Lodge FRS, Lord Rayleigh FRS, Sir

Figure 1.5. Professor Sir William Crookes. (© The Royal Society. Reproduced with permission)

Arthur Schuster FRS and Professor S. Thompson FRS

For the investigations into chemistry. Members were Dr. H. B. Baker FRS, Sir George Beilby FRS, Sir William H. Perkin FRS, Sir William Ramsay FRS and Sir Edward Thorpe FRS …

Council also resolved:

… that a circular letter be addressed to the Directors of Chemical Laboratories in the Universities and Colleges inviting the assistance of their workers, especially in the manufacture of drugs and other medicaments …

A week later on the 19th November 1914, the War Committee:

Resolved:

… That Lord Rayleigh FRS be appointed Chairman of the Physics Committee with Sir Richard Glazebrook FRS as Vice Chairman …

… that Dr. S.W.J. Smith FRS be appointed to the Physics Committee and asked to act as Secretary …

… that Sir William Ramsay FRS be appointed Chairman and Sir Edward Thorpe FRS Vice Chairman with Professor A.W. Crossley FRS as its' Secretary of the Chemistry Committee …

> … that the following be appointed to a Sub-Committee for the consideration of questions relating to engineering: Sir George Beilby FRS, Sir Charles Boys FRS, Sir Dugald Clerk FRS, Mr. W. Duddell FRS, Mr. H.R.A. Mallock FRS, Sir Joseph Petavel FRS, Professor E.H. Starling FRS and Sir Philip Watts FRS. Sir Dugald Clerk FRS was appointed Chairman of the Sub-Committee …

The following questions were submitted by the Admiralty as subjects for investigation, and are reproduced from the Royal Society War Committee Minute Book[3]. A separate copy can also be found in the National Archives[4].

Physics

- the detection of the direction from which Wireless Telegraphy Signals whose wave length exceeds 5,000 meters are coming – for use in ships. Both continuous and 'spark' waves to be considered
- the reception of Wireless Telegraphy signals sent by a system which constantly alters its wavelength
- the construction of a searchlight on the principle of the Beck Searchlight i.e., with the arc cooled by alcohol or other vapour
- a quick method of determining the density of air, suitable for air station use. This factor has a great bearing on the rate of climb of machines
- an investigation into the possibility of detecting the presence of submarine boats, and if possible submarine mines

Chemistry

- a method for making hydrogen filled airships invulnerable to incendiary attack

Engineering

- a device for catching submarines
- torpedo propulsion by chemical means
- the effect of a quantity of high explosive in proximity to aircraft, i.e., sound waves, pressure waves, velocity gusts
- to ascertain the variation in pressure at different distances from the centre of the explosion of each of several named explosives
- is anything known as to the amount of acceleration the human frame can stand, without injury?
- the movements of a submerged floating body in the neighbourhood of estuaries

It is worth reflecting on the impact lack of supplies from German factories made on Britain. Prior to the outbreak of World War I many pharmaceutical drugs, dyes and optical glass for lenses etc. were bought from German companies. War prevented the purchase of these materials, requiring them to be manufactured in Great Britain. Furthermore there were new technologies to understand and develop including wireless telegraphy, photography, aircraft, submarines, tanks etc. and the need for timely research to further develop or enhance them. The Fellows were instrumental in resolving many of these issues.

As the War developed other problems were put forward for consideration.

Then as now, the Royal Society lacks the capability to undertake fundamental research within its own buildings, it has always relied on Fellows using the facilities in their respective workplaces. Fortunately, as Director of the National Physical Laboratory (NPL) during the War, Sir Richard Glazebrook FRS was able to offer the NPL facilities. Of course there were costs associated with this war-work, some of which were paid by the Royal Society and some by the relevant government committee or department.

Such was their reputation that help offered by the Royal Society was gratefully accepted. For example, the Royal Society received a letter from the Health Insurance Commission, Buckingham Gate, dated 22nd December 1914 part of which reads[5]:

> … and I have to say that the Department will be very glad to invite the assistance of the Royal Society in connection with problems arising from time to time in regard to the supply of drugs and medical stores … (letter signed by John Anderson)

A letter from the Admiralty also expressed gratitude:

> … … .I further note with grateful thanks that the Royal Society propose to place a sum of money at the disposal of the Committee for the conduct of experiments … (signed Philip Dumas)

The need for secrecy was also discussed at that second meeting, i.e., 19th November 1914. The Council resolved:

> … that while there is no objection to the publication of the fact that the Royal Society is assisting the Government in regard to scientific questions arising out of the War, it is undesirable that either the existence or the composition of the various committees should be published …

This constraint was not a problem for the physics and engineering communities as much of their work was undertaken in Government establishments, the National Physical Laboratory or various research laboratories run by Fellows. The Sectional Chemical Committee had a problem of scale. Determining the methods of synthesis for the pharmaceutical drugs needed by the medical profession required more research establishments than were run by Fellows.

Indeed the minutes of the Sectional Chemical Committee held on Thursday 26th November and Wednesday 16th December 1914, recorded the following comments:

> ... 32 institutions offered to help produce drugs, 3 were obliged to decline because their department staff and student numbers were severely depleted ...
>
> ... Kew Gardens were also approached and asked to consider growing medicinal plants either in this country or in the Colonies ...
>
> ... The use of proprietary names for drugs is under consideration, and a conference will shortly be held of representatives of the Sectional Chemical Committee, the Pharmaceutical Society, the Wholesale Drug Trade, the British Medical Association, the General Medical Council, the Medical Departments of the Navy and the Army and Sir Robert Morant and Mr. Anderson as representing Government ...

In a meeting of the Sectional Physics Committee dated 4th January 1915, the minutes record agreement that the experiments should be carried out at the National Physical Laboratory. Two further meetings of this Sub-Committee were held following which the committee members commented:

> ... The subjects numbered 1-6 submitted by the Admiralty were discussed with the following results:
>
> Subject 1: it was agreed that the apparatus necessary to test a scheme prepared by Mr. W. Duddell FRS should be constructed, and that experiments with it should be carried out at the National Physical Laboratory
>
> Subject 2: it was agreed that, after consultation with the Admiralty, an attempt should be made to develop a satisfactory scheme at the National Physical Laboratory
>
> Subject 3: it was agreed that experiments should be carried out on the lines suggested by Sir Richard Glazebrook at the National Physical Laboratory
>
> Subject 4: a method of obtaining the necessary information has been suggested to the Admiralty by Sir Arthur Schuster FRS. It was agreed also to consult the Advisory Committee on Aeronautics
>
> Subject 5: the Sub-Committee is not yet in a position to make any definite recommendations
>
> Subject 6: it was agreed that it is improbable that any physical device for this purpose will compare favourably with chemical methods of renewing the air ...

Meanwhile, the minutes of the Sectional Engineering Committee dated 4th January 1915 record:

> ... Five meetings of the Committee have been held and the six questions have

been discussed

- question 1 has been considered and discussed and suggestions from the inventors have been examined
- question 2 has been considered and discussed and Sir Dugald Clerk FRS has investigated the matter and is now in communication with the Admiralty Officers with regard to trials to be made
- question 3 has been considered and discussed, but so far no agreement has been arrived at as to experiments to be made
- question 4 has been considered and discussed and Professor B. Hopkinson FRS has the matter in charge and is in communication with Mr. T. D'Eyncourt FRS
- question 5 has been considered and notes on the subject have been prepared by Professor E.H. Starling FRS and Lieutenant-Colonel Mervyn O'Gorman, which have been forwarded to the Admiralty
- question 6 has been considered and discussed, and experimental appliances are being prepared by the Admiralty in accordance with the designs of Sir Dugald Clerk FRS, Professor B. Hopkinson FRS and Sir Joseph Petavel FRS. They are in communications with the officials who are preparing the experiments

The Sub-Committee now consists of Sir George Beilby FRS, Sir Charles Boys FRS, Sir Dugald Clerk FRS, Mr. W. Duddell FRS, Professor Hopkinson FRS, Mr. A. Mallock FRS, Lieutenant-Colonel Mervyn O'Gorman, Sir Joseph Petavel FRS, Sir Arthur Schuster FRS, Professor E.H. Starling FRS, Sir Philip Watts FRS and Admiral Sir Henry Jackson FRS …

Lieutenant-Colonel Mervyn O'Gorman was, at that time, Superintendent of HM Aircraft Factory, Farnborough.

Over the next few months other questions were asked of the Royal Society Sectional Committees. For example, through Sir Henry Jackson FRS the Admiralty requested:

- as to mine sweeping

The Royal Aircraft Factory, through Lieutenant-Colonel Mervyn O'Gorman, requested:

- as to aeroplane bombs and darts

Whilst the War Office, through Colonel L.C. Jackson:

- as to appliances for listening in mines
- as to range-finders for aircraft

Whilst these and other questions were being investigated, there were personnel changes. For example the War Committee Minutes 9th June 1915 record Admiral Sir Henry Jackson FRS stepping down from the Sub-Committee as he had been promoted to First Sea Lord and did not have sufficient time to attend the meetings. Rear-Admiral Fremantle was appointed in his place for the Sectional Chemistry Committee, and the First Sea Lord was actioned to nominate an Admiralty representative for the other committees.

At that same meeting, the following resolution was passed:

> ….that a circular be sent to all Fellows of the society asking whether their services would be available for scientific work in connection with the War; or whether they can recommend any scientific men willing to give their services for the purpose …

By 24th June 1915, the Sectional War Sub-Committees were working efficiently with their counterparts in other organisations and Government Departments. Accordingly the Royal Society War Committee first created on the 5th November 1914 was discharged and the Council constituted itself a Committee for the purpose named in the original reference of the War Committee.

A Sectional Physiology Committee was constituted, as detailed in the War Committee minutes 24th June 1915, with the following membership:

Physiology: Sir William Bayliss FRS, Professor A.R. Cushny FRS, Sir Walter Fletcher FRS (Secretary), Dr. J.S. Haldane FRS, Sir Leonard Hill FRS and Sir Frederick Hopkins FRS, Professor F.G. Starling FRS (Chairman).

At this time the Sectional Physics Committee had the following membership:

Sir Charles Boys FRS, Mr. S.G. Brown FRS, Mr. W. Duddell FRS, Sir Richard Glazebrook FRS (Vice Chairman), Admiral Sir Henry Jackson FRS (pending a replacement), Sir Oliver Lodge FRS, Commander A.U. Moore (Admiralty), Lord Rayleigh FRS (Chairman), Dr. S.W.J. Smith FRS (Secretary), Sir Joseph J. Thomson FRS and Professor S.P. Thompson FRS.

For completeness the Sectional Chemical Committee comprised of:

Professor H.B. Baker FRS, Sir George Beilby FRS, Professor A. Crossley FRS, Sir Henry H. Dale FRS, Dr. H.J.H. Fenton FRS (Vice Chairman), Sir Martin Forster FRS, Professor P.F. Frankland FRS, Rear-Admiral S.R. Fremantle (Admiralty), Brig-General L.C. Jackson (War Office), Professor R. Meldola FRS (Chairman), Sir William H. Perkin FRS, Dr. J.C. Philip FRS (Assistant Secretary), Sir William Ramsay FRS, Professor A. Smithells FRS and Sir Jocelyn Thorpe FRS.

The Royal Society

War Committees

Chemistry	Engineering	Physics
drugs gas for airships etc.	submarine detection torpedoes aspects of flight aircraft handling etc.	wireless telegraphy searchlights etc.

Food	Grain Pests	Natural Products	Physiology
Diet including sugar, meat, bread, alcohol, fats etc.	safe food storage etc.	new sources of foodstuffs and increasing our resources etc.	effects of vapours on humans etc.

Reserved Occupations

Figure 1.6. The various Royal Society War Sub-Committees. (Author)

and the Sectional Engineering Committee:

Sir George Beilby FRS, Sir Charles Boys FRS, Sir Dugald Clerk FRS (Chairman), Mr. W. Duddell FRS, Sir James Alfred Ewing FRS, Baron Hankey FRS, Professor B. Hopkinson FRS (Secretary), Brig-General L.C. Jackson (War Office), Mr. H.R.A. Mallock FRS, Capt H. Norbury RN (Admiralty), Lieutenant-Colonel M. O'Gorman, Hon Sir Charles Parsons FRS, Sir Joseph Petavel FRS, Sir Philip Watts FRS and Admiral Sir Henry Jackson FRS.

Figure 1.6 shows the various committees and their areas of interest.

In addition to the War Sub-Committee work, the Royal Society was also approached to recommend Fellows to Government work. For example, in the War Committee Minutes of 15th July 1915, the following request was documented:

> ... The following letter was presented to the War committee. It originated from the War Office and is dated 3rd July 1915:
>
> I am commanded by the Army Council to inform you that the Council desire to extend further the investigations and researches concerning defence against poisonous and irritant gasses ... to this end the Council direct me to invite you to nominate two chemists and two physiologists to act as members of the Working Committee now conducting enquiries at the Royal Army Medical College and elsewhere, on such subjects as are referred to them or which they desire to initiate ....
>
> I am to add that the Army Council will be glad of an early reply ... (Signed

B.B. Culitt)

Professors P.F. Frankland FRS and Sir William Pope FRS as chemists and Professors A.R. Cushny FRS and Sir Leonard Hill FRS as physiologists were nominated and approved at the meeting.

During the same meeting the following suggestions were also discussed:

- that the Sectional Chemical Committee should be made public
- that members of the Committee should not be prohibited from disclosing at their discretion the fact of such membership
- that pending the establishment of an official badge, the Committee recommended that a Royal Society badge be distributed

Additionally the Sectional Physiology Committee asked that:

- members of the Committee should not be prohibited from disclosing their membership of the Committee

After much discussion the War Committee recommended that:

- a short article be sent to *Nature* indicating in general terms the help that the Royal Society was providing to the Government
- members of the Sectional War Committees should not be prohibited from disclosing their membership
- the matter of an official badge was referred to the Executive Committee for consideration

The issue of war-work badges and exemption from National Service will be covered later (see Chapter 5). Sadly Professor R. Meldola FRS died on 16th November 1915, recorded in the minutes of the meeting held on the 18th November 1915. It was resolved that Professor P.F. Frankland FRS be appointed to succeed him as Chairman of the Sectional Chemistry Committee.

Later, 6th December 1917 to be precise, the Royal Society formed two further committees connected with food. One was simply called the Food Committee, the other the Grain Pests Committee. The work of these two committees will be covered in Chapter 9 as their work was closely connected with the overall situation relating to agriculture. For example, the membership of the Grain Pests Committee reflected this in the appointment of Dr. Gertrude Dixon of the Wheat Supplies Commission.

Finally, on 24th January 1918, a Natural Products Committee was established with the following membership:

Dr. E.J. Allen FRS, Dr. G. Barger FRS, Professor B.T.P. Barker, Professor A. Brown FRS, Dr. A. C. Chapman FRS, Professor A.R. Cushny FRS, Sir John Farmer FRS (Chairman), Sir William Hardy FRS (Secretary Royal Society), Dr. T. Regan FRS, Mr. A. Wassall, with representatives from the Food Production Department, the Royal Commission on Wheat Supplies and the Ministry of Munitions.

At this stage in the War there was a need to consider all natural products as resources for food (humans and animals) and/or as raw materials for equipment, more of which in Chapter 2.

Of course many Fellows held posts which were directly linked with the war effort but not involving the various Royal Society committees and Sub-Committees. Some held Government posts or other positions of influence and importance.

Fellows in Government

Whilst not exhaustive, Figure 1.7 shows a list of Fellows who were elected to Parliament and sat as MPs during the War, or who were appointed to Government posts through, for example, the House of Lords. One must remember that some of these individuals were actually appointed to the Fellowship after the War, as explained in the preface.

Name	Wartime Position
Baldwin (Stanley) – 1st Earl Baldwin of Bewdley	MP for Bewdley Division of Worcestershire (1908-37) Financial Secretary to the Treasury (1917-1921)[6]
Balfour (Arthur James) – 1st Earl of Balfour	Privy Councillor (1885) Leader of the House of Commons (1895-1906) Prime Minister (1902-1905) First Lord of the Admiralty (1915-1916) Foreign Secretary (1916-1919)[7]
Cavendish (Victor Christian William) – 9th Duke of Devonshire	Civil Lord of the Admiralty (1915-1916) Governor-General of Canada (1916 onwards)[8]
Chamberlain (Arthur Neville)	Member of the Central Control Board (Liquor Traffic) (1915) Lord Mayor of Birmingham (1915-1916) Director-General of National Service (1916-1917)[9]
Churchill (Sir Winston Leonard Spencer)	First Lord of the Admiralty (1911-1915) Chancellor of the Duchy of Lancaster (1915) Minister of Munitions (1917)[10]
Curzon (George Nathaniel) – 1st Marquess Curzon of Kedleston	Leader of the House of Lords (1916-1924) Lord President of the Council and member of the War Cabinet (1916-1919) Lord Privy Seal (1915-1916) Secretary of State for Foreign Affairs (1919-1924)[11]

D'Abernon (Edgar Vincent) – Viscount	Chairman of the Dominions' Royal Trade Commission (1912-1917) Chairman of the Central Control Board for Liquour Traffic (1915-1920)[12]
Fisher (Herbert Albert Laurens)	Member of the Royal Commission on the Public Services of India (1912-1915) Member of the Royal Committee on alleged German Outrages (1915) President of the Board of Education (1916-1922)[13]
Hankey (Lieutenant-Colonel Sir M.P.A.)	Secretary to the Imperial War Cabinet (1916) Imperial War Cabinet (1917-1918) Secretary, Committee Imperial Defence (1912-1938)[14]
Lindsay (David) – 27th Earl of Crawford and 10th Earl of Balcarres	MP for Chorley (1895-1913) Lord Privy Seal (July 1916-1918) President of the Board of Agriculture and Fisheries (1916) Chancellor of the Duchy of Lancaster (1919-1921)[15]
Long (The Right Hon W.)	President of the Local Government Board (1915-1916) Secretary of State for the Colonies (1916-18)[16]
MacDonald (James Ramsay)	MP Leicester (1906-1918)[17]
Moulton (John Fletcher) – Baron Moulton	Member of the committee on Chemical Products (1914) Member of the Committee on High Explosives (1914) Director General of Explosives, Ministry of Munitions (1914 onwards)[18]
Smuts (Jan Christian)	Minister of Defence in the House of Assembly (Pretoria) (1910-1920) South African Representative on the Imperial War Cabinet (1917-1918)[19]

Figure 1.7. Royal Society Fellows in Government

Some of the individuals in Figure 1.7, were also members of the Imperial War Cabinet. Of course this membership varied from time to time following promotions etc. A composite list of active members is shown below and combines the membership from two cabinet meetings from the 12th January 1917 and 9th February 1917.[20]

The Right Hon David Lloyd George Prime Minister
Admiral Sir J.R. Jellicoe First Sea Lord of the Admiralty
Commodore L. Halsey Fourth Sea Lord
General Sir W.R. Robertson Chief of the Imperial General Staff
Lieutenant-General Sir C.F.N. MacReady Adjutant General to the Armed Forces
Major-General C.E. Callwell
Major-General Sir E. Campbell Geddes
Major-General Sir G.M.W. MacDonogh Director of Military Intelligence, War Office
Mr. Neville Chamberlain FRS Director-General of National Service
Mr. U.F. Wintour Permanent Secretary, Minister of Food
Sir A. Lee Director-General Food Production Department
Sir Arthur Thring Parliamentary Counsel
Sir R.H. Rew Permanent Secretary, Ministry of Food
The Right Hon A. Chamberlain FRS Secretary of State for India
The Right Hon A. Bonar Law MP Chancellor of the Exchequer
The Right Hon A. Henderson MP
The Right Hon A.J. Balfour FRS Secretary of State for the Foreign Office
The Right Hon C. Addison Minister of Munitions
The Right Hon H.A.L. Fisher FRS President of the Board of Education
The Right Hon H.E. Duke Chief Secretary for Ireland
The Right Hon J. Hodge MP Minister of Labour
The Right Hon Lord Hardinge of Penshurst
The Right Hon Sir Edward Carson First Lord of the Admiralty
The Right Hon Sir J. Maclay Shipping Controller
The Right Hon The Earl Curzon of Kedleston FRS
The Right Hon the Earl of Derby Secretary of State for War
The Right Hon the Lord Rhondda President of the Local Government Board
The Right Hon The Lord Robert Cecil MP Minister of Blockade
The Right Hon the Viscount Milner
The Right Hon W. Long FRS Secretary of State for the Colonies
Lieutenant-Colonel Sir M.P.A. Hankey FRS Secretary
Major C.L. Storr Assistant Secretary
Mr. G.M. Young Assistant Secretary
Mr. T. Jones Assistant Secretary

In attendance for specific minutes:
Lord D'Abernon FRS Central Board of Control
Lord Devonport Ministry of Food
Sir Albert Stanley President of the Board of Trade
Sir George Cave Home Office

In addition to Members of Parliament and/or members of Government, Fellows also worked in a variety of government-sponsored occupations, for example:

Sir Alfred Daniel Hall FRS – Commissioner for the Development Fund established by Lloyd George[21]

Sir Thomas Little Heath FRS – Assistant Secretary of the Treasury[22]

Sir Thomas Ranken Lyle FRS – Scientific Advisor to the Naval Board 1914-1918[23]

Sir Basil Mott FRS – Engineer worked in France on defence schemes and on various Government Committees[24]

Sir Harry Work Melville FRS – Scientific Adviser to the Chief Superintendent of Chemical Defence, Ministry of Supply[25]

Some of the current, and future, Nobel Laureates held somewhat more prosaic posts, for example, Walter Nernst drove a car across Europe. Figure 1.8 outlines some Laureates activities.

Nobel Laureate	Subject and Year	Wartime activity
Aston (Francis William)	Chemistry 1922	Served as Technical Assistant at the Royal Aircraft Establishment at Farnborough and crashed in an experimental aeroplane in 1914. He worked on aeroplane dope and fabric, and invented a special type of neon tube for short flashes.[26]
Barkla (Charles Glover)	Physics 1917	Accepted the Chair in Natural Philosophy in the University of Edinburgh in 1913, held until his death in 1944.[27]
Bragg (Sir William Henry)	Physics 1915	Founding scientist of the Admiralty Board of Invention and Research (BIR) and later Resident Director of Research Admiralty Experimental Station (1916-1917), Scientific Member Anti-Submarine Division Admiralty (1918).[28]
Buchner (Eduard)	Chemistry 1907	Major in a field hospital at Folkschani in Rumania. Wounded on 3rd August 1917 and died of these wounds in Munich eleven days later.[29]
Butenandt (Adolf)	Chemistry 1939	Helped in field hospitals 1917-1918.[30]

Nobel Laureate	Subject and Year	Wartime activity
Churchill (Sir Winston Leonard Spencer)	Literature 1953	First Lord of the Admiralty (1911-1915) Chancellor of the Duchy of Lancaster (1915) Minister of Munitions (1917).[31]
Dale (Sir Henry Hallett)	Physiology or Medicine 1936	Director of the Department of Biochemistry and Pharmacology at the National Institute for Medical Research in London in 1914.[32]
Einstein (Albert)	Physics 1921	Appointed Director of the Kaiser Wilhelm Physical Institute and Professor in the University of Berlin (1914).[33] He became a German citizen in 1914 and remained in Berlin until 1933.
Fleming (Sir Alexander)	Physiology or Medicine 1945	Captain in the RAMC working at the wartime laboratory for medical research at the casino in Boulogne.[34]
Hahn (Otto)	Chemistry 1944	Awarded the Iron Cross Class II for his part in the Autumn Offensive (1915). Took part in the fraternization which occurred between German and British troops in Christmas Eve and Christmas Day.[35]
Harden (Sir Arthur)	Chemistry 1929	Studied vitamins whilst running the Lister Institute (the Director was away at War).[36]
Haworth (Sir Walter Norman)	Chemistry 1937	Academic in the University of St Andrews working on the production of fine chemicals and drugs.[37]
Hevesy (George de)	Chemistry 1943	Was instructed to supervise and accelerate the coining of War medals which were produced in the Carpathian Hungarian State Foundry.[38]
Heyrovsky (Jaroslav)	Chemistry 1959	Posted to a military hospital for service and remained there as dispensing chemist and roentgenologist until the end of the War.[39]
Hill (Archibald Vivian)	Physiology or Medicine 1922	Captain and Brevet-Major, and as Director of the Anti-Aircraft Experimental Section, Munitions Inventions Department Secretary of the Royal Society.[40]

Nobel Laureate	Subject and Year	Wartime activity
Hopkins (Sir Frederick Gowland)	Physiology or Medicine 1929	Professor of Biochemistry at Cambridge University from 1914.[41]
Landsteiner (Karl)	Physiology or Medicine 1930	Prosector in the Wilhelminaspital in Vienna (1908-1919. Professor of Pathological Anatomy in the University of Vienna (1911).[42]
Meyerhof (Otto Fritz)	Physiology or Medicine 1922	When Professor Höber assumed the Directorship of the Institute of Physiology, Meyerhof was appointed Assistant (1915). In 1918 he became Assistant Professor.[43]
Millikan (Robert A.)	Physics 1923	Professor at Ryerson Laboratory at the University of Chicago from 1910.[44]
Nernst (Walther Hermann)	Chemistry 1920	Army driver during the German push through Belgium into France, also involved in the German introduction of gas warfare, and for this reason he was placed on the list of those to be extradited in 1919.[45]
Perrin (Jean Baptiste)	Physics 1926	Officer in the engineer corps during which he devised a method and constructed an apparatus for determining the direction of the sound from an aeroplane.[46]
Ramsay (Sir William)	Chemistry 1904	Formally retired in 1913.[47]
Rayleigh (Lord John William Strutt)	Physics 1904	Served for six years as President of a Government Committee on Explosives, and from 1896 to 1919 he was Scientific Adviser to Trinity House.[48]
Richardson (Sir Owen Willans)	Physics 1928	Appointed Wheatstone Professor of Physics at King's College London in 1914.[49]
Robinson (Sir Robert)	Chemistry 1947	Professor of Chemistry in the University of Liverpool working on pharmaceutical drugs, also forged close relations with British Dyes Ltd, a company formed with government money in 1915 to take over the dye-making plant of Read Holliday & Co. at Huddersfield.[50]

Nobel Laureate	Subject and Year	Wartime activity
Rutherford (Lord Ernest)	Chemistry 1908	Founder member of the Admiralty BIR and on the Submarine Sub-Committee.[51]
Sherrington (Sir Charles Scott)	Physiology or Medicine 1932	Chairman of the Industrial Fatigue Board (throughout the War), he worked for a time in a shell factory at Birmingham, and the daily shift of 13 hours, with a Sunday shift of 9 hours.[52]
Soddy (Frederick)	Chemistry 1921	Professor of Chemistry at the University of Aberdeen from 1914 where he made pharmaceutical chemicals, also worked for the Marine Sub-Committee of the BIR where he worked on steam raising by addition of water to strong or anhydrous caustic soda.[53]
Thomson (Sir Joseph John)	Physics 1906	Member of the Advisory Committee of the Admiralty BIR.[54]
Urey (Harold Clayton)	Chemistry 1934	Shortly after his graduation in 1917, research chemist to the Barrett Chemical Company in Philadelphia to help make War material.[55]
Willstätter (Richard Martin)	Chemistry 1915	Professor of Chemistry at the University of Munich from 1915.[56]
Wilson (Charles Thomson Rees)	Physics 1927	Appointed Observer in Meteorological Physics at the Solar Physics Observatory (1913), Reader in Electrical Meteorology (1918).[57]

Figure 1.8. Nobel Laureate WWI Wartime activities

Of course there are many Fellows. Some worthy of mention here worked in positions of responsibility outside of Government and made unique contributions in different ways, Figure 1.9.

Fellow	Post
Anderson (John) – Viscount Waverley	Worked at the National Health Insurance Commission in 1914, two additional responsibilities were the provision of pharmaceutical drugs (undertaken through the Royal Society) and the redistribution (on a voluntary basis) of General Practitioners as some areas of the country were sparsely populated and some overly so.[58]

Fellow	Post
Arden-Close (Sir Charles Frederick)	As Director-General of the Ordnance Survey of the United Kingdom responsible for drawing and printing the many maps required by the armed forces, particularly large-scale trench maps.[59]
Beilby (Sir George Thomas)	Chairman and first Director of Fuel Research Board (1917).[60]
Bourne (Sir Alfred Gibbs)	Director of the Indian Institute of Science at Bangalore.[61]
Cripps (Sir Richard Stafford)	Medically unfit for the Army, he went to France as a Red Cross lorry driver. He was recalled to work in the Explosives Department of the Ministry of Munitions, and was Assistant of the Government factory at Queensferry.[62]
D'Eyncourt (Sir Eustace)	Director of Naval Construction from 1912 and oversaw the construction of 21 capital ships, 53 cruisers, 133 submarines of eleven different classes during his term of office.[63]
Egerton (Sir Alfred Charles Glyn)	Sir Eric Geddes, First Lord of the Admiralty, appointed Egerton and others to examine the activities of the Admiralty Board of Invention and Research and make recommendations.[64]
Evershed (John)	Director of the Kodaikanal Observatory in India (1911-1923).[65]
Field (Sir Arthur Mostyn)	Admiralty representative on the Board of the Port of London Authority (from 1909) Commissioner under the Pilotage Act of 1913 Nautical Assessor to the House of Lords.[66]
Hjort (Johan)	At the invitation of the Canadian Government Hjort conducted a series of fishery investigations in the Gulf of St Lawrence.[67]
Milne (Edward Arthur)	Defective eyesight excluded him from active military duties. Joined the Anti-Aircraft Experimental Section of the Munitions Inventions Department. Commissioned as a Lieutenant RNVR in 1917, in order to ensure against his being conscripted and transferred to much less useful work.[68]
Moulton – Lord Justice Fletcher	Director General of Explosives Supply.[69]

Fellow	Post
Paterson (Sir Clifford Copland)	Served on the Home Office Committee on the Lighting of Factories and Workshops. Member and later Chairman of the Board of Trade Committee on Ships' Navigation Lights.[70]
Price (Thomas Slater)	Initially involved the preparation of various pharmaceutical drugs. Commissioned as Lieutenant in the RNVR (1916) and sent to the Royal Naval Experimental Station at Stratford for secret war-work for which he was promoted to the rank of Lieutenant-Commander.[71]
Stapledon (Sir Reginald George)	Seconded Director of the Official Seed Testing Station within the Food Production Department.[72]
Vincent (Edgar) – Viscount D'Abernon	Chairman of the Central Control Board Liquor Traffic.[73]
Yule (George Udny)	Seconded from Cambridge (1915) to statistician for the Director of Army Contracts, and then to the Ministry of Food where he eventually became Director of Requirements.[74]

Figure 1.9. Fellows in senior positions during World War I

To single out just one Fellow from Figure 1.9 would be unjust as all of these Fellows, and indeed many others worked tirelessly throughout the War. Perhaps the work of Sir Charles Frederick Arden-Close FRS might illustrate the value of their work, figure 1.10. As Director-General of the Ordnance Survey, Sir Charles and his department had to provide up to the minute information on the trenches. The maps that Department produced are staggering in their quality. A selection are available for study in the National Archives.[75]

The detail is staggering considering that the information needed to continually update these maps was obtained from a War zone. Furthermore each map is about the size of a modern Ordnance Survey map and to comparable scale. Each map needed updating regularly as the trenches were continually expanded, some bombed out and perhaps others abandoned as the battle front moved. A remarkable achievement!

A few Fellows also found themselves working in positions connected with the weather. Perhaps more than any other wartime period, the wind played an important factor in lighter than air dirigibles, as well as in trench warfare and (very) light aircraft. Sir Henry George Lyons FRS was a serving Captain but relieved of his military duties in 1915 to work in the Meteorological Office providing information to Vice Admiral Commanding Operations in the Dardanelles.[76] Sir William Napier Shaw FRS was a Scientific Advisor to the

Figure 1.10. Sir Charles Frederick Arden-Close. (© The Royal Society. Reproduced with permission)

Government and Chairman of the Meteorological Committee.[77]

Secret Patents

As we shall see later, the Government Committees were just as active in promoting scientific work and invention as the Royal Society War Sub-Committees. Doubtless, every scientist was keen to develop their ideas and in so doing make a fundamental breakthrough in their allocated fields. Within the Department of Munitions Inventions was a group of individuals whose job it was to protect those inventions likely to be of use after the War. To that end a system was implemented of documenting 'secret patents' whose content was deemed SECRET during the War but later released into the national system. Figure 1.11 shows just a sample of these secret patents. Note that some of them were written by Fellows.

Title	Authors	Patent Number	Date filed
Improvements in the synthetic production of ammonia	Henry Edward Fane Goold-Adams and Harold Cecil Greenwood	2742	24/2/17
Improvements relating to heat interchange between fluid media or between a fluid medium and an external body	Henry Edward Fane Goold-Adams and Harold Cecil Greenwood	2743	24/2/17
Improvement method of purifying and/or drying gases	Henry Edward Fane Goold-Adams	2744	24/2/17
An improved method of and apparatus for mixing compressed gases in definite proportions	Henry Edward Fane Goold-Adams and Harold Cecil Greenwood	2745	24/2/17
An improved method of and apparatus for detecting water vapour or either of the gaseous components	Henry Edward Fane Goold-Adams, William Robert Bousfield FRS and George William Todd	14,030/17	28/9/17
Improvements in the removal of sulphur and sulphur containing bodies from gases	Eric Keightley Rideal FRS and Hugh Stott Taylor FRS	3702/18	2/3/18
Improvements in the purification of hydrogen	Eric Keightley Rideal FRS and Hugh Stott Taylor FRS	4532/18	14/3/18
Improvements in or relating to the synthetic production of ammonia	Harold Cecil Greenwood	5630	2/4/18
Improvements in the construction of catalyst furnaces for use in the synthesis of ammonia or in similar gaseous reactions or operations	Harold Cecil Greenwood and William Ronald Tate	8584	23/5/18

Figure 1.11. A partial list of secret patents[78]

Colonel Henry Edward Fane Goold-Adams was the Comptroller of Munitions Inventions and in that capacity appeared on several secret patents.

Not all wartime inventions were written up as secret. Sidney George Brown

FRS was a prolific inventor, patenting more than 1,000 of his inventions. His single point microphone relay was used by the fledgling Royal Flying Corps for signalling between aircraft and ground batteries. Another of his inventions was used in the Royal Navy by widening the range of wireless communications between shore stations and ships. Early recognition followed from his inventions. He was appointed by the Council of the Royal Society to serve as a scientific adviser to the Admiralty Ordnance Council, a member of the Board of Awards to Inventors and a scientific advisor to Lord Fisher's Investigating Council.[79]

Unfortunately, not all secret patents had successful outcomes, for at least one led to a flurry of activity from MI5.[80] Some correspondence survives between Major Anson of MI5 stationed in the War Office in SW1 and Major W.H.D. Clark OBE who was Assistant Comptroller in Munitions Inventions based in Princes Street:

S.F. 53/11/1/MI5 G2 (EA) MI5
War Office
London SW1

Confidential
23rd October 1918
Dear Major Clark,

Regarding my interview with you on the 11th instant concerning the possible leakage of details of inventions relating to arms, ammunition and instruments of warfare through the indiscreet talk of inventors.

You will remember requesting me to represent the matter officially to your department and suggesting that the communication should be based on the following:-

'Information as to the trial of inventions, knowledge of which comes into the possession of inventors either through their personal attendance at official trials, or because of information supplied by the authorities conducting trials, must be regarded as being highly confidential and not communicable by the inventor to any persons other than those immediately concerned in the initiation or production of the inventions, all of whom must be held equally responsible for its secrecy.'

I have consulted our legal branch and there seems no doubt that leakage of such imparted official information is already covered under the Official Secrets Act, but as inventors may, in many cases, not realise their responsibility it would seem a good idea to call their attention to it by embodying a note on the subject in your 'Form No 1'.

The point which at present does not appear to be covered is that arising out of the indiscreet conversation of the inventor, during the period between the date of submission of the invention to the Government and the date of its acceptance, concerning details of his invention which were not acquired from Official sources, and so are not covered by the Official Secrets Act.

Under Regulation 18B (a) D.R.R. there is power conferred upon the Controller General … ….

Signed
Major Anson
MI5

Major Clark replied on the 9th December 1918:

Dear Anson,

I am sorry that under stress of work arising out of reconstruction and other matters incidental to the cessation of hostilities, I have up to the present failed to send you the note I promised on the different phases arising in the life history of inventions and ideas and the remedies that have been, or could be, devised for the purpose of ensuring, during a state of War, that knowledge of such inventions should not come into possession of the enemy.

Roughly speaking certain well-defined phases may exist in the life-history of an invention; these are given in column A of the attached statement and the remedies to ensure non-publication to the enemy in Column B.

I think I have covered … ..

Yours truly
Clark

Note: Part of the document referred to in the letter is reproduced below, Figure 1.12, for completeness and also to show the criteria under which the system operated.

Column A	Column B
(1) The original conception and early development of the invention by a single individual prior to its communication to any other person (2) The phase in which the inventor shares the knowledge of the invention with other individuals, either for the purpose of obtaining advice or experimental or workshop assistance	I have great difficulty in suggesting any means by which official control can be exercised in these circumstances. The conditions do not come within the Official Secrets Act inasmuch as there is the pre-supposition that no communication to an official has been made. It would certainly be difficult to establish by Statutory Provisions any control under the conditions (1) and (2) which did not unduly interfere to obtain assistance in the prosecution of an invention which might be of great value to one of the Services or even national importance; moreover, such statutory provision would be very difficult of execution
(3) When the inventor approaches the Munitions Inventions Department or similar Government organisation under seal of secrecy for the purpose of bringing any invention likely to be of use in the Service to the notice of the appropriate authority	Secrecy has been maintained under the normal working conditions of the Munitions Inventions Department, the rights of inventors in regard to subsequent patenting being preserved by D.R.R. 8 C.C.
(4) When the inventor takes out a British Patent which may by either: (a) a secret patent (b) an ordinary patent in respect of which particulars of the invention are, in accordance with ordinary statute law, published as soon as the necessary stages at the Patent Office are passed	(a) From its very nature there is no disclosure of information regarding inventions which are the subject of this class of patent. (b) Under D.R.R. 18B. The acceptance of any specification likely to be of service to the enemy has been delayed and consequently the complete specification has not been printed and published by the Patent Office. Under the same regulation (18B) the Controller has power to prohibit the publication in any way of the invention in respect of which the patent is sought. The machinery for this purpose has worked satisfactorily and could be reintroduced in the future if and when occasion required it owing to the incidence of renewed hostilities or the outbreak of another War

Figure 1.12. The administration of ideas leading to secret patents

The above example is presented here to demonstrate the system used by the

Government War

Committees

Board of Invention and Research

Section 1 - aeronautics
Section 2 - submarines
Section 3 - naval construction
Section 4 - anti-aircraft devices
Section 5 - ordnance and gases

Department of Munitions Inventions

inventions assessment
height and range finders
ground and works section
patents and rewards

includes

Chemical Inventions Committee
Nitrogen Committee

Other Committees

Chemical Advisory
Ordnance
etc.

Figure 1.13. Some of the World War I Government War Committees. (Author)

Fellows when they applied for secret patents during World War I. The author does not intend to imply that any Fellow was in any way negligent or made inappropriate comments. This system was administered by the Department of Munitions and Inventions. There were many Government departments and committees set up during World War I, Figure 1.13 shows some of them.

Fellows working in these departments and committees acted as individuals and were not sponsored by the Royal Society in their activities unlike the Royal Society War Committee and Sub-Committees. However, one might be forgiven for thinking that some of these committees were indeed sponsored as many of these committees had significant representation from the Fellowship – see Chapter 3 for more details.

2 The Royal Society War Sub-Committees

One might be forgiven in assuming that the Royal Society was only involved in technical support for various Government Departments. It wasn't. There were vital administrative functions that also needed resolution. For example, procedures were needed for a range of situations including:

- ensuring workers thought essential for work in research laboratories were not called to active service
- ensuring those already enlisted were utilised to their full potential – particularly those individuals with research skills

Additionally, the National Physical Laboratory (NPL), which was funded through the Royal Society at the start of the War, was transferred to the Treasury during the War requiring, resolution of pension rights, salary reviews etc. A procedure was also needed for appointing the Director (Sir Richard Tetley Glazebrook FRS was Director from 1899-1919). Of course Sir Richard was himself on various Royal Society and Admiralty Committees and most of the Sectional Physics Committee work was undertaken at the NPL. Negotiations must have taxed those tasked with the transfer.

Accordingly the Royal Society found itself working with the Reserved Occupations Committee, the War Badges Department and the Department of Scientific and Industrial Research in addition to the scientific contributions to various Committees and Departments.

Chemistry

How circumstances change! The initial list of activities involving chemistry the Royal Society War Committee were asked to resolve were:

- a method for making hydrogen-filled airships invulnerable to incendiary attack
- a device for taking air from the sea for submarines

This list of activities changed dramatically over the course of the War. There were also several changes in the personnel of the Committee. Professors R. Meldola FRS and Sir William Ramsay FRS died with Professor P. Frankland FRS elected replacement Chairman. Admiral Fremantle FRS was promoted and, lacking the time to attend the meetings, resigned being replaced by

Commander J.A. Duncan. Further, Professors F.G. Donnan FRS and Sir William Pope FRS along with Dr. A. Scott FRS were added to the Committee.

Over a number of years the activities of the Committee included the following:

(a) **Pharmaceutical drug production.** Undertaken at the request of, and in co-operation with, the National Health Insurance Commission, this activity was designed to maintain supplies of key pharmaceutical drugs previously supplied to Britain by German companies. The National Health Insurance Commission funded the cost of the chemicals, gas, light, water and damage to apparatus, however labour costs were not covered and seen as voluntary. Incidentally the National Health Insurance Commission also proposed the creation of reserve medical personnel for use in epidemics etc., which also ensured there were sufficient medical personnel to administer the drugs. Drugs and intermediates synthesised in this way included:

- butyl chloral hydrate. About 5kg of this substance was prepared at Glasgow University by Dr. Desch.
- diethylaminoethanol – an intermediate in the preparation of Novocain. About 160kg of the ethanol was produced with a surplus of about 40kg of diethylamine (another intermediate).
- orthoform Neu. About 6kg of the drug produced.
- sugars and allied substances. These were arabinose (nearly 1kg) dulcitol, inulin (nearly 4kg), levulose (4kg) and maltose.
- β-eucaine. About 75kg of hydrochloride and 17.5kg of lactate were sent to the National Health Insurance Commission.

In addition to these pharmaceutical drugs, other chemicals were analysed or prepared for a variety of purposes. For example:

- Professor Sir Robert Robinson FRS also worked on atropine.[1]
- Professor A. Smithells FRS worked on indigo dye.[2]
- Dr. H. King FRS worked on the large scale preparation of salicylic acid, and developed a satisfactory process for the preparation of aspirin.[3]
- Dr. J. B. Cohen FRS worked on the antiseptic action of substances allied to Acriflavine an antiseptic.[4]
- there was also some general work by a number of chemists on alternative sources of decolourising charcoal as a replacement to Eponite

Figure 2.1 lists the various academic institutes and schools involved in wartime drug production. Note the number of Fellows involved with this activity!

Institute	Lead Scientist
Aberdeen University	Professor Soddy FRS
Aberystwyth University College	Professor Findlay
Armstrong College, Newcastle-on-Tyne	Mr. S.H. Collins
Bangor University College	Professor Orton FRS
Bedford College	Professor Crompton FRS
Birkbeck Institute	Dr. Senter
Birmingham Municipal Technical School	Dr. Price FRS
Birmingham University	Professor Frankland FRS
Blackburn Municipal Technical School	Sir Robert Pickard FRS
Cambridge University	Dr. Fenton FRS
Cheltenham Ladies College	Dr. Taylor
Cooper Laboratory	Mr. Nuttall
Dundee University College	Professor McKenzie FRS
East Ham Technical Institute	Dr. Dunstan FRS
East London College	Dr. Pope
Edinburgh University	Professor Walker
Glasgow Royal Technical College	Professor Henderson
Glasgow University	Dr. Patterson
Guy's Hospital	Dr. Lowry FRS
Hackney Technical Institute	Dr. P.R. Kirk
Heriot Watt College	Dr. Boon
Holloway College	Professor Moore
Huddersfield Technical College	Dr. Bruce
Imperial College of Science and Technology	Professor Thorpe FRS and G. Kon FRS
Leeds University	Professor Cohen FRS
Liverpool University	Professor Baly/ Sir Robert Robinson FRS
Manchester Municipal School of Technology	Dr. Knecht
Manchester University	Professor Lapworth
Nottingham University College	Professor Kipping FRS
Oxford University	Sir William H. Perkin FRS and Dr. Chattaway FRS
Paddington Technical Institute	Mr. A.G. Cook
Pharmaceutical Society	Professor Greenish
Queen's University, Belfast	Dr. Macbeth

Institute	Lead Scientist
Reading University College	Dr. Everest
Rugby School	Mr. E.R. Thomas
Sheffield University	Professor Wynne FRS
St Andrews University	Professor J.C. Irvine FRS and Sir Walter Haworth FRS
St Mary's Hospital	Dr. P. Haas
University College	Dr. Smiles FRS
University College, London	Professor Collie FRS
Various London Polytechnics	organised by Dr. Keane
Whitchurch War Hospital	Dr. Stanford

Figure 2.1. Wartime Institutes involved in drug production

Surprisingly, Cheltenham Ladies College, not readily associated with academic research in this way, was actively involved. The first activity undertaken by these institutes was to work out what formula was being used by the previous supplier, secondly a robust method of synthesis needed to be determined. In some cases these were well known or in the chemical literature, in other cases the relevant workers needed to start by analysing the available samples.

Various chemical companies offered their support, or provided the scaled up materials. They included (a reference is provided where exact details of their involvement is known):

- Boake Roberts and Co. – the separation of methyl alcohol and acetone[5]
- Boots Ltd
- British Dyes Ltd, a company formed with government money in 1915 to take over the dye-making plant of Read Holliday & Co. at Huddersfield[6]
- Burroughs Wellcome and Co.
- Cooper Laboratory for Economic Research – a sensitising dye which would replace pinacyanol[7]
- Holliday and Co. – β-eucaine and Novocain
- Moss Distillery Co. – following a letter from the Ministry of Munitions – involved Professor Fernbach
- Strange and Graham
- The Kerfoot factory – the manufacture of Novocain
- The Reynard Chemical Co. – production of Phenacetin

(b) **Exemption of Chemists from Military Service** – the Committee undertook to secure War Service Badges for the various chemists working on drug production. About 150 were issued. The Sectional Chemical Committee also sent Colonel Crossley, Sir Martin Forster FRS and Professor P. Frankland FRS to a Board of Trade Conference on this matter. One outcome from this conference was that 'Analytical, Consulting and Research Chemists' were added to the Schedule of Reserved Occupations – see Chapter 5 for further details.

(c) **1851 Scholars and War Bursars** – the Commissioners of the 1851 Exhibition offered their Scholars for approved war-work shortly after the formation of the Sectional Chemical Committee. Accordingly six holders of 1851 Exhibitions came under the supervision of the Committee, and a further six special War Bursaries were awarded by the Commissioners. The bursar then carried out work assigned him by the Committee. They were:[8]

1851 Exhibitioners (reappointed 1915):

Recommended:

- English, S. – to continue working at the Cassel Cyanide Co.
- Garner, W.E. – to continue war-work at University College
- Reilly, J. – to continue working as Chemist at new Admiralty Explosive Works
- Ross, J.D.M. – to undertake war-work investigations under Professor Baker FRS
- Scarborough, H.A. – to continue working in factory of Messrs. Chance and Hunt
- Stephen, H. – to continue war-work at Manchester University

Recommended for award of special War Bursary, on the understanding that the bursar carries out the work proposed by the Sectional Chemical Committee:

- Cantelo, R.C. – to report himself to Lord Moulton FRS for employment in – some of the Government factories
- Gibson, W. – to carry on war-work at the University of Leeds
- Robertson, G. – to continue war-work at St. Andrews University
- Royle, F.A. – to continue war-work at Manchester University
- Silvester, W.A. – to continue synthetic drug work at Sheffield University, – thereafter proceeding to Cambridge University
- Warneford, F.H.S. – to go to Sheffield University to take up synthetic drug work, – thereafter proceeding to Cambridge University

The Commissioners have approved of this selection and their offer of a War Bursary has been accepted in all six cases.

There were no immediate plans to recall previous 1851 Exhibition scholars who were on active service.

(d) **Tar Testing Work** – the analysis of tar for toluene content was an additional task needing resourcing. This required establishing a number of test centres throughout the country working on behalf of the Sectional Chemical Committee in conjunction with the Department of Explosive Supplies. The lead chemists for these centres were: Professor Bedson (Newcastle), Professor Cobb (Leeds), Professor Francis (Bristol), Professor Frankland FRS (Birmingham), Professor Gray (Glasgow), Professor Kirkaldy (London) and Professor Lapworth FRS (Manchester). This activity resulted in 16,000 samples being analysed over a 2½ year period.

(e) **Supplies of photographic chemicals and paper** – Sir William Pope FRS instigated a special research program at his laboratory in Cambridge University financially supported by the Department of Scientific and Industrial Research.

(f) **Consultancy for various organisations**. For example their opinions were sought by:
- the Air Department of the Admiralty and the Royal Aircraft Factory, Farnborough with various questions related to aircraft dope[9] (these questions were handed over to Dr. H.J.H. Fenton FRS)
- the Ministry of Food concerning a method for the production of saccharine
- etc.

Some references for additional help were vague to say the least! For example:

> ... Item 2 d. Regarding secret document S8468 (Admiralty) Rear Admiral Fremantle had been consulted. He requested that certain experiments should be continued and a full report of the Special Sub-Committee should be forwarded to the Admiralty when these had been concluded ... [10]

The following were all discussed at the same meeting.[11]

> ... Item 4. Admiralty secret document (S8468) was referred for action to a small committee consisting of Sir William Ramsay FRS, Professors Crossley FRS and Thorpe FRS, who already had this matter in hand
>
> Item 10. The secretary reported that a letter had been received from Sir Richard Glazebrook FRS in reference to the probable need for help in the chemical testing of munitions material. In the meantime the necessary work was

to be carried out at the National Physical Laboratory, but at a later stage it might be desirable to have additional centres. A reply had been sent expressing the readiness of the Sectional Chemical Committee to co-operate if necessary

Item 12. The Secretary of the Royal Society reported receipt of a letter from the War Office asking for the names of two chemists to act as members of a working Committee which is conducting enquiries at the Royal Army Medical College. It was agreed to recommend the Executive Committee to appoint Professor P. Frankland FRS and Sir William Pope FRS as the two representatives of the Royal Society …

And from the meeting on 29th July 1915[12]

… Item 6. A letter was read from W.J. Anderson stating that Messrs T Morson and Sons had now undertaken the manufacture of chloral formamide

Item 12 …… that the Special Chemicals Company was able to cope with the supply of dimethylglyoxime …

Interestingly, it has proved impossible to trace document S8468 through the Royal Society or the National Archives. There is a report which may be related in the miscellaneous reports of the Admiralty, reproduced in Chapter 7.

We may never know if the cryptic comment in the Royal Society minutes refers to the work outlined in Chapter 7, however there is no other report in the BIR data kept by the National Archives relating to chemistry that cannot be accounted for. Note Professor Frankland FRS and Sir William Pope FRS are once again involved!

Indeed Sir William, (with Mr. C.S. Gibson), is also credited with determining the synthesis of mustard gas which was manufactured by Levinstein Ltd and used in the War.[13] Superficially at least, mustard gas seems like an innocuous chemical, Figure 2.2, easy to produce with no obvious toxicity issues – at least to the lay person. Deployed in the field of war, however, it produced devastating results.

As if these issues were not enough, help was also needed in aircraft component design.[14]

Item 3 – matters arising out of the minutes:

… a) considered Dr. Fenton's FRS preliminary report on aircraft dope (a copy

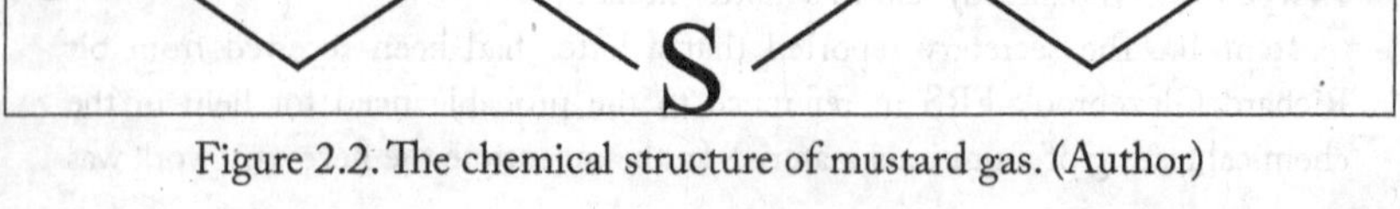

Figure 2.2. The chemical structure of mustard gas. (Author)

of which had already been sent by Dr. Fenton FRS to the Air Department of the Admiralty), and Professor Donnan FRS and Dr. Fenton's FRS report on their visit to the Royal Aircraft Factory.

Agreed:

- that Professor Donnan FRS and Dr. Fenton FRS should continue to investigate the problems in connection with aircraft dope brought to the notice of the Committee by the Air Department of the Admiralty and by the Royal Aircraft Factory
- that it was desirable to co-ordinate the work being carried out in connection with these problems by different persons for different Government Departments, and that the Air Department of the Admiralty be invited to take the initiative in this matter
- that, in dealing with applications for work, applicants should be informed what this Committee takes for granted that all out-of-pocket expenses (that is travelling expenses, cost of apparatus and materials, and such assistance as this Committee deems necessary) incurred at the instance of the Committee will be repaid
- that steps should be taken in the proper quarter to encourage the production of cellulose acetate in this country[15]
- that, as regards benzyl alcohol, the plant at the Royal Aircraft Factory should be extended and, if this were impossible, that steps should be taken to have it made by manufacturing firms
- that Lieutenant-Colonel O'Gorman be asked to supply the Committee with a definite statement as to his requirements for benzyl alcohol, and with a report on the tests so far carried out at the Royal Aircraft Factory in connection with the standardisation of cellulose acetate
- that Lieutenant-Colonel O'Gorman should be informed that, in the opinion of the Committee, the chemical staff of the Royal Aircraft Factory required strengthening and that, if he so desired, the Committee would be prepared to make representations to this effect in the proper quarter

There were many balls in the air!!!
Later in the year:[16]

Item 5:

a) that the conference of drug workers had been duly held on 22nd March, and had been attended by representatives of practically all the institutions co-operating with the Committee, and that the suggestions emanating from the Conference had been embodied in a detailed report already submitted to the Drugs Sub-Committee and considered by them

b) that the conference had suggested that the Committee should reconsider the question of insuring the drug workers against accident …

Item 7:

... reported that, in accordance with a suggestion emanating from the Drug Conference, the Drugs Sub-Committee were contemplating the preparation of lists of chemicals, with the idea of tabulating the manufacturing sources in this country from which these chemicals could be obtained ...

Item 8:

... that applications for information regarding the preparation of synthetic drugs had been received from Messrs. Burroughs Wellcome & Co, the Cooper Laboratory. Messrs Boots and Messrs Strange and Graham ...

The issue of photographic products and their components formed part of the discussion towards the end of the year, with the promise of much needed funding![17]

Item 6: Research on sensitising dyes

Reported:

... that a letter had been received from the Secretary of the Royal Society, empowering the Sectional Chemical Committee to undertake the general supervision of the grant of £700 made by the Advisory Research Council for research on sensitising dyes ...

Agreed:

... after discussion, that, either directly or through the Secretary of the Royal Society, these proposals with regard to the researchers and their allowances should be put before the Advisory Research Council, together with the request that the conditions under which the grant had been made be modified in two respects, namely:

1. that the sum of £700 should be available for the purpose of research over a period of two years instead of one
2. that a proportion of the grant should be available for defraying the cost of apparatus and materials

Of course some of those chemists who were able, also took advantage of the system of filing secret patents mentioned in Chapter 1. A letter was filed in the Admiralty Board of Invention and Research for Invention No. C.P. Secret Patent 2825/1915.[18]

Treasury

19th May 1915.

Sir,

Mr. W. Duddell's, Sir Richard Glazebrook's & Mr. F.E. Smith's Invention No. C.P. Secret Patent 2825/1915

In further reference to your letter of the 8th instant I beg to enclose the engrossment of the Assignment of this Invention for execution by Mr. Smith and yourself in the presence of a witness in accordance with the pencil direction on the document.

Will you be so good as to forward it to me as soon as this has been done. It will be observed that the engrossment has already been executed by Mr. Duddell.

I am,

Sir,

Engineering

Whilst there were many engineers involved in the wartime effort, Sir Dugald Clerk, awarded a KBE in 1917, stands out for the sheer volume of wartime correspondence he produced. As Chairman of the War Engineering Committee of the Royal Society one might expect a degree of correspondence, however by any standards Sir Dugald was the most prolific of the Sub-Committee Chairmen.

Arguably the reason may simply be the number of inventors who supplied their ideas to the Royal Society for consideration, and hopefully their adoption. Royal Society archives hold many such ideas submitted by members of the public to their War Engineering Committee. There were some common themes relating to range-finding. The mathematics and practicalities of determining the range of stationary objects from gun emplacements was well known. The issue which exercised the minds of the engineering inventors related to the determination of the distances between two moving objects, i.e. aircraft.

For example, an idea was submitted to the War Engineering Committee concerning 'Improvements in Range-finders' by Sir John Ambrose Fleming FRS of University College Gower Street in March 1915. Sir John started his letter:

> ... My invention consists in an appliance which can be added to any ordinary telescope having an erecting eyepiece with a convex lens ... magnifying a real image formed by the object glass can be converted into a range-finder to discover the distance of any object of approximately known dimensions for military purposes or in hunting or other reasons ...

Professor Louis submitted an idea which was ultimately rejected. In a letter from Sir Richard Glazebrook FRS to William Ernest Dalby FRS[19]

> ...Louis' idea was similar to others that had been submitted, with some of the other ideas being 'distinctly simpler' and more likely to be successful ...

Figure 2.3 Sir Dugald Clerk. (© The Royal Society. Reproduced with permission)

As with most inventions the timing is just as crucial as the idea.

Sir Charles Vernon Boys FRS wrote an undated letter to the War Engineering Committee on the subject of munitions for aerial attack which begins:

> … I think it likely that a useful form of attack on Zeppelins by aircraft could be made by means of Thermite, the idea being that where for safety the aeroplane has to be at a considerable height above the Zeppelin for the sake of better security the power of aiming and hitting by a bomb will be correspondingly less and I propose that if the aeroplane were flying in such a direction as to cross the length of the Zeppelin a stream of Thermite ions at 3,000°C or so would be far more likely in some proportion of its length to meet the body of the airship …

The reply from Murray F. Seuter dated 16th December 1914 is as follows:

> … we have in the air service a Thermite bomb of about 20 lbs (of the petrol bomb type casting). It was first introduced by Major Turner of Woolwich Arsenal last August, and not proceeded with … A fortnight ago the matter was discussed, and it was decided to carry out further trials with this bomb, which have proved satisfactory within certain limits, inasmuch as that, except as an incendiary,

> Thermite (weight for weight) is not nearly as valuable as T.N.T. ... The scheme of flying over a Zeppelin and dropping a bomb is not considered as efficient as an incendiary bullet.. .I think a 'Thermite rocket' might easily be evolved, and Major Turner had under consideration a scheme for placing a burster in a Thermite bomb so that the burning mass is scattered in all directions (like the old 'carcass shell') ...

Mr. F. E. Brandt, of Connaught Street, Hyde Park, submitted an idea of an invention for an aerial torpedo. Following some short correspondence a meeting was arranged for 19th July 1915 at 12 o'clock between Brandt and Sir Dugald Clerk. Not only was Sir Dugald receiving and generating large amounts of correspondence he was also heavily involved in meetings with inventors.

Further examples of inventions involved the installation of a fan for dispelling gas in the trenches, another concerned the production of high temperatures at a distant point by the projection of radiant heat.

Of course all ideas were evaluated to greater or lesser extents. The problem for this War committee in particular was that there may have been some facet of a seemingly inappropriate idea which contributed to solving a major issue. The watchword here was patiently sifting through all ideas and calling in relevant experts for their opinions on an 'as and when' basis. Whilst these invaluable ideas submitted by the public, there were the list of 'questions' needing solution posed by various government agencies.

Progress for work suggested by government departments were often referred to as the six 'questions' as a shorthand means of describing the tasks in hand. This reporting method continued outside of the formal minutes into individual reports. The engineering requests outlined in Chapter 1 thus became:

Question 1 – a device for catching submarines

Question 2 – torpedo propulsion by chemical means

Question 3 – the effect of a quantity of high explosive in proximity to aircraft, i.e., sound waves, pressure waves, velocity gust

Question 4 – to ascertain the variation in pressure at different distances from the centre of the explosion of each of several named explosives

Question 5 – is anything known as to the amount of acceleration the human frame can stand, without injury?

Question 6 – the movements of a submerged floating body in the neighbourhood of estuaries

The Engineering Sub-Committee met on numerous occasions, some of the minutes of their meetings are filed at the National Archives, for example:[20]

> CONFIDENTIAL
> Royal Society War Committee.

Interim Report of Engineering Sub-Committee.

The Engineering Sub-Committee was appointed by the War Committee on November 19th, 1914, and six questions were referred to it for discussion and action.

Five Meetings of the Committee have been held and the six questions have been fully discussed.

Question No. 1 has been considered and discussed and suggestions from inventors have been examined.

Question No. 2 has been considered and discussed, and Sir Dugald Clerk FRS has investigated the matter and is now in communication with the Admiralty officers with regard to trials to be made.

Question No. 3 has been considered and discussed, and Professor B. Hopkinson FRS has the matter in charge and is in communication with Sir Eustace Tennyson D'Eyncourt FRS.

Question No. 5 has been considered and discussed, and Notes on the subject have been prepared by Professor E. Starling FRS and Lieutenant-Colonel Mervyn O'Gorman, which have been forwarded to the Admiralty.

Question No. 6 has been considered and discussed, and experimental appliances are being prepared by the Admiralty in accordance with the designs of Sir Dugald Clerk FRS, Professor B. Hopkinson FRS, and Professor Sir Joseph Petavel FRS. They are in communication with the officials who are preparing the experiments.

The Sub-Committee now consists of the following: Sir George Beilby FRS, Sir Charles Boys FRS, Sir Dugald Clerk FRS, Mr. W. Duddell FRS, Professor Hopkinson FRS, Mr. A. Mallock FRS, Lieutenant-Colonel Mervyn O'Gorman, Sir Joseph Petavel FRS, Sir Arthur Schuster FRS, Professor E.H. Starling FRS, Sir Philip Watts FRS, and Admiral Sir Henry Jackson FRS.

Professor Hopkinson has been appointed by the War Committee to be a Member and Secretary of the Sub-Committee, and Lieutenant-Colonel Mervyn O'Gorman, Superintendent of H.M. Aircraft Factory, to be a Member of the Sub-Committee.

DUGALD CLERK
Chairman.

There are a few documents filed in the Royal Society covering question 4 which are interesting and detail the variations in pressure at different distances from the centre of the explosion of each of several named explosives.[21]

Natural products

Figure 1.6 mentioned the formation of a Royal Society Committee whose remit was to re-examine the use of available natural produce. The Natural

Figure 2.4 Sir John Farmer. (© The Royal Society. Reproduced with permission)

Products (War) Committee was formed in 1918, the first meeting being on the 19th February at Burlington House. Those present at this meeting, Sir John Farmer FRS (in the chair) figure 2.4, Dr. E.J. Allen FRS, Dr. G. Barger FRS, Professor Adrian Brown FRS, Dr. A. Chaston Chapman FRS, Sir William Hardy FRS Sec. R.S. and Mr. Arthur Vassal resolved:

> ... that a Committee to be called the Natural Products Committee be appointed to consider the use of natural animal and vegetable products for the purpose of adding to the Food supply or otherwise increasing the resources of the country. That the Committee have powers to report their proceedings to the Government Departments likely to be interested, and to announce the formation the Committee in the of public press in such a way as to encourage useful suggestions from outside ... and that the Committee consist of:
>
> Dr. E.J. Allen FRS, Dr. G. Barger FRS, Professor B.T.P. Barker, Professor A. Brown FRS, Dr. A. Chaston Chapman FRS, Professor A.R. Cushny FRS, Sir John Farmer FRS, Sir William Hardy FRS Secretary Royal Society, Dr. T. Regan FRS, Mr. A. Vassall, with representatives from: The Food Production Department (Sir Rowland Biffen FRS); The Royal Commission on Wheat Supplies (Dr. Gertrude Dixon); The Ministry of Munitions (Colonel Sir Frederic Nathan).

Unlike the launch of earlier Royal Society Committees, this one agreed to a public announcement of its formation, and indeed actively canvassed public input.

The initial focus of the Committee investigations were:

Horse Chestnuts: these were being used in the manufacture of acetone. Sir John Farmer FRS mentioned some experiments to remove the bitter taste so that they could be used as cattle fodder, whilst Professor A.B. Brown FRS informed the Committee of the potential use for the production of baker's yeast. All Committee members were aware that acetone production was paramount and that no additional supplies of horse chestnuts would be forthcoming (acetone was used in the manufacture of explosives). There was a discussion of the residues left from acetone production however.

Acorns: the Committee decided to consult with the War Agricultural Committees of the County Councils. Fellows needed more information concerning the use of acorns for pig feeding. There were also some experiments made at the Admiralty factory, Wareham, on the suitability of acorns for the production of acetone.

Bracken fern as a source of starch: Mr. Vassall agreed to make enquiries.

Production of Fat and Proteins by rapidly growing fungi: The results of some yeast experiments were reported by Professor A. Brown FRS which indicated the difficulty of separating the fat. Another series of experiments, which were successful but on an unknown species, were reported by Dr. A. Chaston Chapman FRS.

Artificial Tea & Coffee: suggestions of using young hawthorn leaves and buds as a tea replacement and parsnips as a coffee substitute were presented.

Other items raised at the meeting included:

- baker's yeast from potatoes
- extraction of oil and starch from lumber refuse
- plankton as a source of fat
- the possibility of utilising bulbs
- the use of heather
- the utilisation of straw

A further meeting on the 17th June 1918 continued to explore the various options outlined above. Where possible, updates were provided for each topic.

The Committee were aware of an offer from the Marmite Food Extract Company which was willing to erect a processing plant providing quantities of 20 tons of pressed yeast per week were being collected.

New agenda items discussed during the meeting included:

- cereal substitutes
- dog-fish, the large stocks of dog-fish constitute a reserve of food
- Irish moss
- rabbits' paunches (offal), the paunch is valuable food readily eaten by dogs, pigs and poultry
- sea-weeds, although Dulse (Rhodymenia palmate) and Irish moss (Chondrus crispus) were already in the food chain their uptake was slight. Also other sea-weeds should be considered
- slaughter-house offal, particularly blood which could be utilised as fully as possible as a nitrogenous adjunct to fodder.

The final item on the agenda stated:

> … the Committee understand that the collection of sea-birds' eggs has been arranged for …

Perhaps the issue here is that someone had owned up to using sea birds eggs!!

Of course when this committee was established the duration of the War was unknown. Little did the committee members realise how short-lived their activity was going to be. Accordingly, there are no more Committee minutes recorded in the Royal Society archives.[22]

Physics

Chapter 1 outlined the formation of the Physics Committee and mentioned the agreement that most of the work for this committee would take place in the National Physical Laboratory (NPL). Perhaps it is worth recording here how busy the NPL was at the start of the War.[23]

STRICTLY CONFIDENTIAL
THE NATIONAL PHYSICAL LABORATORY
Experiments carried out or in progress in consequence of the War
12th November 1914.
For the Admiralty:
Design of Periscopes
Investigations as to the suitability of certain optical glasses
Tests on sundry methods of protecting ships from mines, etc.
Enquiry as to means of obtaining pure potash
For the War Office:
Construction of special apparatus for wireless telegraphy
Tests and examination of special gauges and instruments
The Aeronautics Division of the Laboratory is also very fully occupied with

investigations relating to various problems.
For the Board of Trade Committee:
Examination of the glass use for miners' lamps, etc.
General:
Examination and analysis of glasses used for chemical apparatus, lamp chimneys, thermometers, and other special purposes
Investigation of materials suitable for and method of manufacture of cylinders for use in acetylene signal lamps
Enquiry as to materials for base metal thermocouples
Examination of new optical glasses
Means of detecting the flash from smokeless powder
In addition to these, tests of the usual character on optical & electrical apparatus for the Navy are being made, though much apparatus is being taken into service without the usual tests being insisted on ...

The Royal Society work was in addition to the above. A report of the Physics Sub-Committee dated January 4th, 1915, i.e., just after the above minutes from the NPL outlines the additional work the NPL needing resourcing.[24]

CONFIDENTIAL
Royal Society War Committee.
Interim Report of Physics Sub-Committee.
Two Meetings of the Sub-Committee have been held. The Subjects numbered 1 to 6 (Physics) submitted by the Admiralty were discussed with the following results:-
Subject 1 – It was agreed that the apparatus necessary to test a scheme prepared by Sir William Duddell FRS should be constructed, and that experiments with it should be carried out at the National Physical Laboratory.
Subject 2 – It was agreed that, after consultation with the Admiralty, an attempt should be made to develop a satisfactory scheme at the National Physical Laboratory on lines considered by the Sub-Committee.
Subject 3 – It was agreed that experiments should be carried out on the lines suggested by Sir Richard Glazebrook FRS at the National Physical Laboratory.
Subject 4 – A method of obtaining the necessary information has been suggested to the Admiralty by Sir Arthur Schuster FRS. It was agreed also to consult the Advisory Committee on Aeronautics.
Subject 5 – The Sub-Committee is not yet in a position to make any definite recommendations.
Subject 6 – It was agreed that it is improbable that any physical device for this purpose will compare favourably with chemical methods of renewing the air.

By the 28th January 1915 the Royal Society Physics Committee reported on work undertaken at the NPL on their behalf. It covered (see note 24):

- variable wave signals
- induction balance
- direction of long waves
- the Beck Lamp

In the same minutes, Sir Richard Glazebrook FRS read two letters from:

- the War Office, which wanted a method of detecting the approach of aircraft by means of a kind of trumpet
- the Admiralty, which wanted to know the feasibility of detecting submarines of a boat with two windows in her bottom, closed by thick glass

Inevitably some physics experiments needed to be carried out at sea, or at least beyond the grounds of the NPL. The letter below is part of the ongoing dialogue that existed between the National Physical Laboratory and Dover Fortress.[25]

Head Quarters, Dover Fortress,
The Castle, Dover.
30th December 1914.
Dear Sir,

I enclose a report on a proposed Sound Indicator which would be, in a more perfect state, of the greatest assistance to the large number of anti-aircraft detachments now watching for hostile visitors. I have seen the instrument in use and its value is even now indisputable. The difficulty is to minimise the loud sea-shell noise caused in a high wind.

I should be very glad if you could give this matter some attention in view of the very great value that such an adjunct would possess, and I feel sure that your experts would very soon overcome the difficulties experienced here and produce a form of indicator which would do what is required.

Yours faithfully,
F.H. Crampton
Brigadier General,
Commanding Dover Fortress

It did not take the scientists at the NPL long before they too were filing secret patents. The following exchange of letters illustrates one of the first of them.[26]

The Envelopes of all letters to this Department relating to Admiralty legal business should be addressed:
The Treasury Solicitor, (*A.*)
Treasury Chambers,

Whitehall, TREASURY,
London, S.W.
10th May 1915.
Sir,
Mr. W. Duddell's, Sir Richard Glazebrook's & Mr. F.E. Smith's Invention No.C.P. Secret Patent 2825/1915.

I am obliged by the receipt of your letter of the 8th instant enclosing the draft Assignment of the invention approved by Mr. Smith and yourself.

The document shall now be engrossed for execution.

I am,
Sir,
Your obedient Servant,
(signed)
Sir Richard Glazebrook, CB, FRS,
National Physical Laboratories,
Teddington,
Middlesex.

Considering all that was going on at the time the Admiralty reply was extremely fast.

The Treasury Solicitor, (*A.*)
Treasury Chambers,
Whitehall, TREASURY,
London, S.W.
19th May 1915.
Sir,
Mr. W. Duddell's, Sir Richard Glazebrook's & Mr. F.E. Smith's Invention No.C.P. Secret Patent 2825/1915.

In further reference to your letter of the 8th instant I beg to enclose the engrossment of the assignment of this invention for execution by Mr. Smith and yourself in the presence of a witness in accordance with the pencil directions on the document.

Will you be so good as to forward it to me as soon as this has been done.

It will be observed that the engrossment has already been executed by Mr. Duddell.

I am,
Sir,
Your obedient Servant,
(signed)
Sir Richard Glazebrook, CB, FRS,
National Physical Laboratories,

Teddington,
Middlesex.

For completeness, the following is the first page of the draft secret patent.[27]

DRAFT PROVISIONAL
IMPROVEMENTS IN APPARATUS FOR
DETERMINING THE DIRECTION OF WIRELESS SIGNALS
We (handwritten) W Duddell Esq of 56 Victoria St
Sir Richard Glazebrook CB Director of the National Physical Laboratory & F E Smith Esq Principal Assistant with NPL do hereby declare that the nature of this invention to be as follows:-

It is sometimes desirable to be able to locate the directions from which wireless signals are being received when one does not know the position of the transmitting station. For instance, it is essential to be able to find the position of a ship in distress at sea, and there are many other cases where the possibility of being able to locate the position of an unknown transmitting station would be of considerable value.

Several methods have already been proposed, and some are in practical use. The general principle of these methods consists in employing two or more aerials at a certain distance apart, connected to a common receiving apparatus. In general, for the long wave lengths it is necessary to place the aerials far apart, and to use aerials of considerable size. Each of the aerials employed in these methods acts in the same way as the ordinary wireless aerials, and their combined action enables the direction to be determined. If the aerials are similar, and symmetrical, the currents induced in the individual aerials are practically identical in strength, but ... [and so forth]

A further patent was granted to David Wright Smith of Glasgow who concerned himself with sound direction.[28]

Smith's Patent Localizable Sound-Signal and Receiving Apparatus.
This special Fog-Signal is supplementary to the ordinary whistle and is intended to be sounded immediately after it, on the approach of another vessel.

The direction of another vessel sounding the signal in fog can be at once located to a single degree. At the second or third blast the course of the other vessel can be deduced from the difference, if any, in the bearing, and the presence or absence of a dangerous position will thus be early determined.

The signal consists of a loud hissing sound, and the sound producer is shown at Fig. 1 overleaf. It is actuated by an ordinary stop-valve and lever and is fitted to a branch from the steam pipe supplying the whistle.

One striking advantage which this signal possesses is, that it will be hardly, if at all, returnable by an aerial echo; so that, if heard, it may be taken to be proceeding direct from the source.

Two forms of receiver are shown. Fig. 2 is suitable for a bridge where the rail is covered with a wind screen. Fig. 3 is adapted for the top of a deck house. The concave reflector shown can be readily unshipped and stowed away when not in use, the pedestal with the indicating-plate being a permanent deck fitting.

On a whistle being heard, the direction of which is required, the officer, having the ear pieces in his ears, grasps the handle, releasing the spring clip from the grooves on the underside of the brass indicating-plate, and swings the reflector rapidly through a few points of the compass, covering the direction from which the whistle is supposed to proceed. If the other vessel sounds the supplementary signal, the hissing sound will be heard through a small arc, and the clip will be released at the position of maximum intensity.

As the ear pieces block out the sound of the signal, except what comes through the ear tubes, the signal is not heard at all, unless the apparatus is pointing approximately in the direction of the sound source, and this fact makes a mistake as to direction impossible.

A moderate rolling or pitching will not interfere with the use of the instrument; but in small vessels it may occasionally be necessary to unship the reflector and hold it in the hands.

The work at the National Physical Laboratory was relentless, yet the unit was transferred from the Royal Society to the Department of Scientific and Industrial Research during 1918. There are many documents concerning this transfer as there were many people whose employment terms and conditions and indeed their pensions needed addressing. For example:[29]

Department of Scientific and Industrial Research
15, Great George Street
Westminster
London S.W. 1
16th March 1918
Sir,
I am directed by the Committee of the Privy Council for Scientific and Industrial Research to submit for the consideration of the Lords Commissioners of His Majesty's Treasury, the following statement:

1. Of the liabilities of the Royal Society in respect of certain retiring allowances of past and present members of the staff of the National Physical Laboratory and
2. Of the proposals of the Royal Society for dealing with these liabilities on the transfer of the Laboratory to this Department on April 1st 1918

The Committee of Council have been furnished with an extract from the

Minutes of the Council of the Royal Society of November 2nd 1899 (copy attached) from which it will be seen that the terms of appointment of the present Director entitles him to a pension of £500 per annum on retirement, that he became eligible for this pension on the completion of 15 years' service on January 1st 1915, and that he will normally retire on attaining the age of 65, which he will do in the course of about two years from now.

To meet the liability for the Director's retiring Allowance, the Royal Society have made investments in consols of £400 per annum since January 1st 1900, the interest accruing thereon having been reinvested for the same purpose. These Investments are shown in the accounts of the 'Pension Fund' including in the Accounts of the National Physical Laboratory as at the 30th September 1917 and to call attention to the statement on pages 24 and 25 to the marked entries on pages 2, 3, 5 and 6. The Committee of Council are informed that since these Accounts were …

The relevant Royal Society Council meeting minutes are also interesting:

Extract from the Council Minutes of the Royal Society of November 2, 1899
11. The Officers reported that, having on July 21 consulted the members of Council by letter as to whether the various resolutions of Council provisionally appointing the General Board, the Executive Committee and the Director of the National Physical Laboratory should be acted upon, the Executive Committee and the Director.

The terms of appointment of the Director are as follows:

1. That the salary of the Director be fixed at £1,300 a year, with the promise of re-consideration at the end of three years, and with provision for a pension of £500 per annum at the age of sixty, or at such a later time as may bring his total length of service, as Director, up to fifteen years
2. That sixty five be fixed as the age for the compulsory retirement of the Director
3. That his appointment be terminable by six months' notice on either side
4. That he be allowed forty-eight working days' vacation per annum
5. That special consent of the Executive Committee should be given before the Director is allowed to undertake work not connected with the Laboratory
6. That the Director shall not be debarred from serving on the Council, or on the Committees of the Royal Society

The Council have also offered to make the Director an allowance of £150 for the expenses of removal to within a convenient distance of the Laboratory.

The Director shall enter upon his duties on January 1st 1900.

The action of the Officers and the terms of appointment were approved.

It seems unusual that these sorts of detailed issues were being discussed and undertaken during a war!

Physiology

The Royal Society Sectional Committee on Physiology was established on 24th June 1915 with its first meeting also on that day. Although there may have been committee minutes during 1916 and 1917, the first interim report is dated 23rd January 1918.[30]

Perhaps the first paragraph of this report is worth reproducing here:

> …The Committee was appointed on June 24, 1915, and their first meeting was held upon that day. From that time to the present the Committee have had under consideration a great variety of physiological questions brought before them on the grounds of nation urgency in time of War.
>
> The work of the Committee has constantly aimed at securing the best theoretical and practical consideration of these problems, and the best economy of the time and work of scientific men. With this in view they have co-operated closely with other bodies officially engaged in the same or cognate problems, with a view to avoiding overlapping and repetition.
>
> Two main objects have engaged the largest part of the time of the Committee from the beginning:
>
> 1. the physiological problems of food supply confronting
>   (a) the enemy populations
>   (b) the United Kingdom
> 2. the physiological and bio-chemical problems of gas warfare both on the offensive and defensive sides …

Committee membership as of 20th August 1917 comprised of:[31] A.R. Cushny FRS (Chairman), Sir Walter Fletcher FRS (Secretary), Sir Joseph Barcroft FRS, J.S. Haldane FRS, Sir Leonard Hill FRS, Sir Frederick Hopkins FRS, Sir William Hardy FRS, Fleet-Surgeon Munday, Major Raper R.A.M.C., Sir Charles Sherrington FRS, Professor E.H. Starling FRS, Professor A.D. Waller FRS with additional members H.D. Dakin FRS and J.S. Edkins. Two additional people were invited to all meetings until further notice. They were F. Shufflebottom and Captain A.E. Boycott FRS (WO Experimental Ground, Porton).

Most of the Fellows on this Committee had medical degrees. The inclusion of F. Shufflebottom and Captain A.E. Boycott FRS reflected some of the work of the Committee which was done in Porton Down.

Filed in the National Archives, and formally assigned to the Director General of the Trench Warfare Department, is a document titled: Poisonous

Gases and vapours and their physiological effects

This report drawn up for the Physiology War Committee of the Royal Society, September 1915 and revised March 1916.[32] It was written as background information for those Fellows on the Sectional Committee on Physiology who were involved in the problems of gas warfare.

The details of the gas warfare experiments will add no value here. The work of this committee with respect to food supply is detailed in Chapter 9.

3 Government Invention and Research Committees

Figure 1.13 in Chapter 1 outlined some of the major government committees and departments of World War I. There was a concerted effort to minimise, if not prevent, duplication between the various activities. Arguably the most extensive – at least from the point of view of Fellows of the Royal Society – was the Admiralty Board of Invention and Research (BIR). This comment refers not to the importance of the work, just the sheer scale of the activities.

The Admiralty Board of Invention and Research

The President of the BIR was Lord Fisher. His launch meeting was attended by some of the best scientists and engineers the Royal Society could field.[1] Below is a copy of the meeting minutes and in Appendix II the full complement of scientists and engineers (as at 21st September 1917).

TOP SECRET
This paper is the property of HM Government and is subject to the provisions of the Official Secrets Act Thursday, 29th July, 1915
The first GENERAL MEETING of the
BOARD OF INVENTION AND RESEARCH
was held this day at Victory House,
Cockspur Street, S.W.

Central Committee	Panel	Attending
Lord Fisher	Professor H.B Baker FRS	Vice-Admiral Bacon
Sir Joseph Thomson FRS	Sir William Bragg FRS	Mr. W. J. Berry
Sir Charles Parsons FRS	Sir Henry Carpenter FRS	Sir Frederick Black
Sir George Beilby FRS	Sir William Crookes FRS	Marquis of Bristol
	Mr. W. Duddell FRS	Duke of Buccleuch

Central Committee	Panel	Attending
	Professor P. Frankland FRS	Sir Trevor Dawson
	Professor B.Hopkinson FRS	Sir Eustace D'Eyncourt FRS
	Sir Oliver Lodge FRS	Marquis of Grantham
	Sir William Pope FRS	Commodore Hall
	Lord Rutherford FRS	Mr. A. W. Jones
	Mr. G.G. Stoney FRS	Commander Masterman
	Lord Rayleigh FRS	Mr. Saxton Noble
		Sir Henry Orsm
		Rear-Admiral Singer
		Commodore Sueter
		Sir Richard Threlfall FRS
		Commander Usborne
Secretary:	Captain Crease	
Ass. Secretary:	Sir R. Paget	
Ass. Secretary:	Mr. Hoste	
Ass. Secretary:	Engineer Lieutenant-Commander Hawkes	
Ass. Secretary:	Lieutenant Perrin	
Ass. Secretary:	Mr. Phillips	

The President of the Board (Lord Fisher), in opening the proceedings, said he proposed to take as his text certain words communicated to him by Mr. Balfour:

...The question of turning the scientific and inventive powers of the county to their best use is one of great importance. There are two quite separate ends to be kept in view: the first is to sift inventions; the second is to promote them ...

Now, some erratic genius might send in a proposition which, though 99 percent of it were worthless, contained some little germ of value. The proposal was to take up the idea that seemed to be of value, without of necessity further consulting the individual who advanced it, though his share in the matter would be recognised by his name being associated with the invention. Up to the present this had been beyond the power of the Admiralty Departments, already overburdened as they were with work. Now, however, this Board would take up such ideas, and indeed would be better qualified than any Department to take a survey of the scientific and experimental resources of the country and to apportion the business of investigation amongst those best able to carry it out.

The second duty of the Board would be to promote invention. They would not as a Board be asked to invent. Individual members of it might have valuable ideas, and the discussion of these by the Board might lead to valuable results. The most important part of their business would be, with the help of the Departments concerned, to formulate practical demands for new devices. Such devices, if put forward with the great weight of authority attaching to this Board (which it might be mentioned would act in harmony with the War Committees of the Royal Society) would disarm opposition from any quarter.

Vague expressions of desire were of little or no use. No purpose, for example, would be served by informing the scientific world that the Admiralty would very much like to be furnished with a sure and easy method of destroying submarines – such a statement would be perfectly true and perfectly futile. But there were many problems of a scope much narrower and more precise which this Board might 'farm out' for theoretical consideration and practical experiment to the various learned bodies with whom they would be in touch. In determining what these were, the Board would take what initiative they pleased. This was a most important point and one which had Mr. Balfour's cordial support – the Board would not be 'facile dupes' or 'servile copyists': the Board would initiate. It was not Mr. Balfour's desire in any way to discourage initiative on the part of the technical Departments of the Admiralty, or to prevent them pursuing their own investigations in their own way; but they might be trusted to give all assistance to the Board, and it was equally certain that they would find the work of the Board extraordinarily helpful themselves. Such had been his (Lord Fisher's) experience as Chairman of the Royal Commission on Oil Fields and Engines, in connection with which the cordial co-operation of the Department concerned with the Commission had led to the happiest and most satisfactory results. It was his intention, as President of this Board, to communicate in the same way as formerly with the various Departments, as necessary, inviting their co-operation; and this course had Mr. Balfour's full approval.

The foregoing, Lord Fisher explained, completed his test, except that he might add that Mr. Balfour, though attaching no very great value to public sentiment in such a subject, believed that the establishment of a Board such as this had done much to satisfy a public demand.

He would like now to offer, on behalf of each to the other, grateful thanks for being present. All associated with the work of the Board were present, many in order to attend having put aside urgent and important private business. He suggested giving an outline of the procedure proposed to be followed by the Board. An idea existed in certain quarters that the Board would proceed too hastily; but in War the great secret was to 'hustle'. Celerity was the key of War, and War was the object of this Board. Rashness in War was very often Prudence, and Prudence was criminal. Similarly, in War it is the man who knows when to disobey orders who goes up; in Peace it is the man who obeys orders who goes to the top; but any fool could obey orders, only 'Nelsons' can disobey orders, as in the classic case of the Battle of Cape St. Vincent. No one of those present could know what the 'careful' man cost his country in this War. What was wanted was Imagination – big Conceptions and quick Decisions.

As regards the precise procedure of the Board, nothing has as yet been definitely settled, but the following proposal seemed worthy of consideration and adoption. In the first place, there was a Central Committee of Four; then came the Panel of distinguished scientists in their various branches (the 'Grand Jury'); and then intimately associated with the work would be small Sub-Committees, consisting of two or three Members and a Secretary, and dealing with:

1. Airships
2. Aeroplanes
3. Seaplanes
4. Protection against torpedo and mine
5. Submarine development
6. Propelling machinery
7. Internal combustion engine
8. Submarine offence
9. Submarine defence
10. Naval artillery
11. Mines
12. Noxious gases in shell

Quite apart from the foregoing, there were eight Secretaries who scrutinised the numerous communications and sorted them out to be dealt with by the respective Sub-Committees. The Sub-Committees would look into the various suggestions, and say whether in their opinion, they should be proceeded with or not. Nothing would be regarded as trash. The Board, in conjunction with the members of the Panel interested in the particular subject, would then decide as to the action to be taken in developing the invention or suggestion, and by whom it should be done.

The great aim was to foster imagination. We must get ahead of our enemy. We must not be content to be 10 or 50 percent better, but immeasurably superior.

The next General Meeting will be held at noon on August 13th, and all of those present were particularly desired to forward before that date any suggestions they might wish to make in regard to the organisation and work of the Board.

In conclusion, Lord Fisher said that on finding himself in so distinguished a company, he thought of Montaigne:

I have culled a garland of Flowers; mine only is the string that binds them ....

Sir George Beilby FRS, Figure 3.1, was an interesting scientist. Not only was he father-in-law to Frederick Soddy FRS, a future Chemistry Nobel Laureate (1921 – see Figures 1.8 and 2.1 for more details of Soddy's work), his election citation reads[2]:

Figure 3.1. Sir George Beilby. (© The Royal Society. Reproduced with permission)

> ...Ex-President, Society of Chemical Industry. Scientific Director of Chemical Works in Great Britain, Germany and America. Inventor of Processes for the manufacture of cyanides, ammonia, fuel gas and paraffin oils, which have had an important influence on these industries. Is recognised as an authority on the industrial use of fuel ...

Clearly a man in the right place at the right time.

Distribution of work

Such a large undertaking required a good organisation. Six sections were created for which a lead contact was appointed, Figure 3.2.[3]

> N.B. – This is a preliminary distribution, and will be amended as experience suggests.
> 26th July 1915

These Admiralty personnel were the respective point contacts for the work undertaken in the six 'sections' – they must have been kept busy. By way of example some of the papers published by the Airships Sub-Committee, Section

Board of Invention and Research distribution of work

Mr Hoste	Section I. Airships, aeroplanes, air bombs and aeronautics generally (see section IV)
Sir Richard Paget	Section II. Submarines and mines (construction and employment of), offensive and defensive measures, torpedoes, torpedo nets etc.
Eng. Lieut. Commander Hawkes	Section III. Naval construction and engineering, internal combustion engines, oil fuel, armour etc.
Lieut. Perrin	Section IV. Anti-aircraft devices of all kinds
Commander Bridge	Section V. Naval questions, ordnance, ammunition, explosives, noxious gases and miscellaneous

Figure 3.2. BIR distribution of work. (Author)

1, are listed below, illustrating the volume of research and paperwork generated by just one Sub-Committee of one section![14] Note the large number of papers submitted by Fellows, particularly those of Lord Rayleigh FRS, Figure 3.3.

- Correspondence and reports relating to the supply of helium gas for naval airships – Sir Richard Threlfall FRS
- Removal of PH_3 from hydrogen (from silicol) – A.W. Wheelwright and P Phelps
- Use of Liquid Hydrogen on airships – Lord Rayleigh FRS
- Interim report to the Committee on airships, BIR – Sir Richard Threlfall FRS
- Report of Sub-Committee for aeroplanes on night flying of aeroplanes – T.H. Hoste
- Airships Sub-Committee – manufacture of hydrogen – Alfred Wilson and Sir Richard Threlfall FRS
- A note on the general illumination of a belt or region for the detection of enemy aircraft – F.W. Lanchester FRS
- Detection of holes in fabric of an airship – Lord Rayleigh FRS
- Researches on a hydrogen indicator – Sir Richard Threlfall FRS
- Letters and reports relating to the production of hydrogen from oil by means of the generator system called The Rincker and Wolter process – C.B. Tully
- The condensation of water from the exhaust gases of a petrol motor –

Figure 3.3. Lord Rayleigh. (© Godfrey Argent Studio. Reproduced with permission)

Sir Richard Threlfall FRS

- Lithium hydride – its sources, manufacture and use as a means of generating hydrogen – Sir Richard Threlfall FRS
- Report of research on purification of hydrogen – E.C. Rossiter
- Preliminary report on the Silicol Process for the production of hydrogen – Lord Rayleigh FRS
- Report on natural gas wells of Kansas etc. – Professor Boulton
- Note on electrically heated garment for airship pilots – Lord Rayleigh FRS
- Investigations concerning aircraft dope – preliminary report by Dr. H.J.H. Fenton FRS and a paper by Commander Randall R.N.A.S.
- A short interim report on recent work on the detection of aircraft by sound – Lieutenant V.C. Richmond R.N.V.R.
- Report on the helium content of the natural gas wells of Ontario, Canada – Sir John McLennan FRS of the University of Toronto
- Reports on wing curves – Squadron Commander Seddon RNAS and Lieutenant Manning R.N.V.R.
- Note on the heating effect to be obtained from the exhaust of an airship, used to raise the inside temperature of the ship – Lord Rayleigh FRS

- Final report on the helium sources in Canada – Sir John McLennan FRS
- Spectroscopic examination of metal samples from Zeppelin L 15 carried out under the supervision of Professor A. Fowler FRS (Imperial College)
- Investigation concerning aircraft dope interim report – Dr. H.J.H. Fenton FRS
- Reports on the practical problems and difficulties associated with flying by night with a note by Flight Commander Sippé DSO RN by Mr. F.W. Lanchester FRS and Squadron Commander Babington DSO RN
- Report to BIR on the question of night flying etc. – Squadron Commander Babington DSO RN
- Report on further model experiments on the temperature attainable from the exhaust gases in airships applied to heat the envelope – Lord Rayleigh FRS
- Second report on experiments for obtaining a high lift curve for seaplane wings – Wing Commander Seddon RNAS
- Preliminary note to the Aeroplane Committee of the Board of Invention and Research concerning fire control ranging and spotting by aircraft in naval actions – Mr. F.W. Lanchester FRS
- Report on a research on aeroplane dopes – Dr. H.J.H. Fenton FRS
- Report on the separation of hydrogen and oxygen by diffusion – Professor Dixon
- Report on a proposed new method of comparing aerofoils – Wing Commander JW Seddon assisted by Squadron Commander J Travers and Flight Sub-Lieutenant E.S. Goodwin. Mathematical argument by Mr. Arthur Berry MA

It would add no value to document all of the reports from all Sub-Committees and sections. Perhaps it might be informative to document just a few parts of some of the more unusual investigations. A meeting, chaired by the Duke of Buccleuch of one of the Section II Sub-Committee's help on the 9th January 1917, had a somewhat unusual subject. To highlight the interesting item all of the other agenda item titles have been included, showing the range of the meeting.[5]

> SECRET.
>
> This paper is the property of H.M. Government and is subject to the provisions of the Official Secrets Act.
>
> BOARD OF INVENTION AND RESEARCH.
>
> Victory House, Cockspur Street, S.W.
>
> Memorandum of Meeting of Sub-Committee, Section II., held on Tuesday,

January 9th, 1917.
PART I.
Present:
The Duke of Buccleuch (in the Chair)
Mr. Berry
Professor Sir William Bragg FRS
Mr. W. Duddell FRS
Captain Dumas
Commodore Hall
Lieutenant-Commander Hichens
Mr. Merz
Lord Rutherford FRS
Commander Salmond
Sir Richard Threlfall FRS
The Secretary: Lieutenant James and Mr. Hilliar
Lieutenant-Commander Hichens conveyed the regret of Captain Dreyer that he was unable to be present.

Towed Listening Apparatus
Experiments with Seals and Sea-Lions
The Secretary reported that through Dr. Allen the Board was in correspondence with 'Captain' Woodward, the trainer of performing seals, who was carrying out a program of experiments on the power of these animals to hear sounds in water. It had been established that they could hear quite weak sounds, such as the tinkle of the kind of bell that is put on a dog's collar, at speeds of up to 9 knots, and that they could tell the direction. Tests were about to be made to compare the listening ability of the seals with that of a hydrophone. The subject was of interest in connexion with the problem of listening at speed, and Dr. Allen was studying the structure of the animals' ears. Apart from that, there was some hope that they might be trained actually to track submarines, if the distractions of the open sea could be overcome. As to this, experiment was now being made on the effect of muzzling the animals, and some success had already been obtained. Seals were available in very large numbers, and were said to be easier to train than any other animal.

The Secretary added that Lieutenant Brock had reported that he found he could hear quite well when swimming under water, and that his own movements did not appear to cause any noise.

Captain Parson's Sound-Proof helmet
Diaphragms
Fessenden Sound-Signalling Apparatus
Sound spectrum of Ships
Noises made by Electric Motors
Non-Contact-Firing Mines ...

The potential use of seals and sea-lions was no idle curiosity. The initial experiments were undertaken two days before the above meeting by Captain J. Woodward. This individual was not a real Captain but a sea-lion trainer using the title as part of his onstage persona. Nevertheless, his experiments, reproduced below and also available in the same folder at the National Archives, detail some of the experiments he undertook.

SECRET
This paper is the property of H.M. Government and is subject to the provisions of the Official Secrets Act.
B.I.R. 2228/17. – BOARD OF INVENTION AND RESEARCH,
VICTORY HOUSE,
COCKSPUR STREET, S.W.
BEHAVIOUR OF SEA-LIONS TOWARDS SUBAQUEOUS SOUNDS

Experiments carried out on 7th January 1917 in Glasgow by Captain J. Woodward and A. B. Wood.

The sea-lions employed in the experiments to be described were two highly-trained animals which were capable of performing tricks of considerable difficulty. Attempts had previously been made by Captain Woodward to familiarise the animals with under-water sounds.

Muzzled Sea-lion in Bath with Live Trout – Attempts to lure it away from the Live Fish by ringing a large bell under Water

A large bell was supported at the deep end of a bath 56 feet long and 3 to 6 feet in depth. Immediately the animal entered the bath an exciting chase began, the attention of the sea-lion being very definitely concentrated on the live trout. At this stage ringing of the bell had little or no effect on its behaviour, but as the animal began to realise the futility of chasing the trout it gradually became more attentive to the bell signals. Even in the short space of an hour or so during which these observations were made it became fairly clear that the animal could be trained to ignore the live fish which gave no satisfaction to its appetite and concentrate its attention mainly on the bell signals, a response to which resulted in an unfailing supply of dead fish.

The above experiments were the first of that type. Earlier experiments had been made with the bell attraction only, no live fish being present. Naturally, one could not expect perfection on the first occasion, but the results give considerable promise of success. Observations are to be continued regularly by Captain Woodward and his assistants, and records of progress kept.

Comparative Hearing Tests of a Sea-lion and a Watch-type Hydrophone.

These experiments were carried out in an open-air bath at Alexandra Park, Glasgow. The bath, concrete …

Echoing the words of Lord Fisher at the BIR launch meeting of exploring every potential idea, further work was undertaken concerning seals and sea-lions. These formal scientific experiments were undertaken by E.J. Allen FRS. The long report covers many topics. For brevity only the titles are documented here, Figure 3.4. The full paper with the others in this sequence is stored in the National Archives.

SECRET

This paper is the property of H.M. Government and is subject to the provisions of the Official Secrets Act.

B.I.R. 30051/17.BOARD OF INVENTION AND RESEARCH,

VICTORY HOUSE,

COCKSPUR STREET, S.W.

Report upon Experiments on the Hearing Powers of Sea-Lions under Water, and on the possibility of Training these Animals as Submarine Trackers

By E.J. Allen, D.Sc., F.R.S., Director of the Marine Biological Laboratory, Plymouth.

(Received 23rd July 1917.)

CONTENTS PAGE

Figure 3.4. Sea-lion experiments

The titles illustrate that this potential idea was thoroughly investigated, demonstrating the commitment to follow through on each and every idea.

Figure 3.5 shows the number of inventions dealt with by the BIR from 5th July 1915 to 30th June 1917 reproduced here to show the many ideas and inventions for which research was undertaken.[6]

Section	**1915 total**	**1/1/16-30/6/16**	**1/7/16-31/12/16**	**1916 total**	**1/7/17-30/6/17**	**Grand Total**
Section I	1,119	525	447	972	956	3,047
Section II	2,420	1,058	1,251	2,309	9,926	14,655
Section III	2,674	1,099	1,777	2,876	8,135	13,685
Section IV	1,401	456	452	908	173	2,482
Section V	2,798	1,215	1,183	2,398	1,539	6,735
Section VI	445	239	139	378	---	
Total	10,857	4,592	5,249	9,841	20,729	41,127

Figure 3.5. Total number of BIR inventions receiving work mid 1915-mid 1917

The figures in the actual document differ in two sub-totals to those numbers reported above. The final grand total however, does match the source document. I hope that my additions using a modern spreadsheet have not led me astray!

Chapter 1 introduced the Imperial War Cabinet Minutes for 13th December 1917, which are reproduced as Appendix I. These Minutes are also relevant to this discussion. Items 21and 22 relate to submarines – a new instrument of War at the time. Arguably no discussion of the BIR would be complete without mentioning the work on submarine detection undertaken at Hawkcraig, a secret Government establishment in Scotland.

Hawkcraig Point played host to a Government experimental station during the early years of World War I. Those who have read through the reports from Hawkcraig, as it became known, will doubtless be drawn to two names, Lord Rutherford FRS and Sir William Bragg FRS, Figure 3.6. Both ran the scientific department with Lord Rutherford passing his duties to Sir William during the War. Of course both of these eminent scientists have already been mentioned in Chapter 1, Figure 1.8 as both physicists were awarded the Nobel Prize (in 1908 and 1915 respectively). A visit to Hawkcraig in 1915 was documented thus:

SECRET
This paper is the property of HM Government and is subject to the Provisions of the Official Secrets Act.
BIR 10071/16

Figure 3.6. Sir W.H. Bragg. (© The Royal Society. Reproduced with permission)

Report by the Duke of Buccleuch, Lord Rutherford FRS and Sir R. Paget on visits to the Experimental Station under Commander Ryan RN, Granton on September 15, 16 and 21 1915.[7]

On September 15th two of us, viz. Lord Rutherford and Sir R Paget, visited the Hydrophone Station at Hawks Craig Point, and listened to the sounds produced in the different hydrophones by six different ships viz a torpedo boat, two different 'drifters' separately, a 30-ton steam yacht and a paddle steamer. Unfortunately the submarines were all absent on active service.

Six out of eight experimental hydrophones were in excellent working order, though they had been in position for several months; one was temporarily inoperative. It was of an old type which had not been provided with a tapping device to free the carbon granules in case of 'packing'.

The 'natural' sounds – in the absence of moving vessels in the neighbourhood – were very slight and did not compare in intensity with those produced by the two torpedo boat destroyers at a distance of 4 or 5 miles.

The sounds of the different types of boats mentioned were clearly and easily distinguishable at ranges between 1 and 2 miles on the case of the smaller vessels, and at 3 or 4 miles in the case of the torpedo boat and the torpedo boat destroyer ... Commander Ryan informed us that a submarine, submerged, gave a quite distinctive sound of intensity even greater than that due to a torpedo boat destroyer at the same distance ...

Later in the same month Lord Rutherford FRS published a report, extracts of which appear as Appendix III.[8] A further report in the same series, by Dr. W. Duddell FRS, on submarine sound signalling, appears as Appendix IV. These two reports have been included as exemplars of the work undertaken on submarine detection and signalling.

Whilst there are many scientists who worked with Rutherford during this period, Albert Beaumont Wood, known as A.B. Wood, stands out. Wood joined the BIR in October 1915 and worked on the detection of underwater sound most of his professional life. At various times he was Chief Scientist of H. M. Mining School, Deputy Director of Physical Research for the Royal Scientific Civil Service and Deputy Superintendent of H. M. Signal School. Two further scientists known for their contribution to submarine detection were Paul Langevin and Robert William Boyle. The latter (Canadian) physicist designed a form of quartz transducer in 1917, which was known as an ASDIC (A(nti-)S(ubmarine) D(etection) I(nvestigation) C(ommittee)) which in turn led to the SONAR (so(und) na(vigation and) r(anging)).[9]

Not all work of the BIR was done by scientists. Some very skilled craftspeople and engineers supplied all manner of equipment. An optics department was directed to develop optical instruments and the design of new types of instruments including periscopes and telescopic sights. They also produced some optical tables for the Ministry of Munitions.[10]

Department of Munitions Inventions

Unlike some of the War committees, the formation of the Department of Munitions Inventions was announced in *The Times*, prior to which the following terms of reference were agreed:[11]

... To enumerate the various bodies now dealing with War Inventions, i.e. -

- Naval Inventions Board
- Inventions for Land Warfare hitherto under the Admiralty
- Inventions Department of the War Office
- Inventions Committee of the Front
- Trench Warfare Department of the Ministry of Munitions
- Ordnance Board
- etc. etc.

The first step towards co-ordination has been taken by the Admiralty handing over to the War Office the care of inventions for land warfare with a view to their being eventually transferred to the Ministry of Munitions; and by the agreement between the War Office and the Ministry of Munitions to transfer to the latter all matters relating to Army inventions within the scope of the Ministry of Munitions.

We understand that when this transfer is made the Minister of Munitions intends to set up a Munitions Inventions Branch to deal with the matter, with a Panel of scientific advisers. This Branch will receive the stream of proposals from Inventors. It will in the first place, ascertain the past history, if any, of each project from the War Office archives. It will then proceed with the aid, if necessary, of its expert consultants to a preliminary ...

An extract from *The Times* appears in the same folder within the National Archives (MUN5/118) dated 12th August 1915.

SCIENCE AND MUNITIONS.
NEW INVENTIONS BRANCH FORMED.
The following official statement was issued last night:-

The Minister of Munitions has constituted a Munitions Inventions Branch of the Ministry, and has appointed as comptroller Mr. E. W. Moir, M.Inst.C.E. and M.Am.Soc.C.E.

The branch, which for the present is located in Armament Buildings, Whitehall Place, will have the duty of considering projects for inventions relating to munitions for warfare on land or matters appertaining to thereto.

The Comptroller and staff of the branch will be assisted in their work of examination, and, if thought necessary, in the investigation and development of any projects that may be considered worthy of being developed, by a Panel of honorary scientific and other experts.

The following gentlemen have accepted Mr. Lloyd George's invitation to act on this Panel: Colonel Goold Adams, Sir Horace Darwin FRS, Macdougal Duckham, W. Duddell FRS, Sebastian Z. de Ferranti FRS, Professor Sir Richard Glazebrook FRS, Sir Robert Hadfield FRS, Professor J.S. Haldane FRS, Colonel N.B. Heffernan FRS, Sir Alexander Kennedy FRS, F.W. Lanchester FRS, Professor A.P. Laurie, M.A., D.Sc., Professor Vivian Lewes M.A., Michael Longridge, W.H. Maw, M.I.C.E., Sir Hiram Maxim, Captain Moore RN, Sir Henry Norman MP, F.G. Ogilvie C.B., Major-General G.K. Scott-Moncreiff, Wilfrid Stokes, Sir James Swinburne FRS, Sir Joseph John Thomson FRS, A.J. Wilson KC, C.J. Wilson

All communications should be addressed to the Comptroller at the above address.

Mr. Lloyd George, in his statement on munitions in the House of Commons on July 28, announced that he had just completed arrangements to constitute an Inventions Board of the Ministry of Munitions, and that he hoped it would do for inventions for land warfare what Lord Fisher's Board was doing for naval warfare. The War Office was handing over the whole question of Army inventions to the

Minister of Munitions. Mr. Lloyd George stated then that he had appointed Mr. E. W. Moir to take charge of the new branch …

A staff questionnaire addressed to the Department of Munitions Inventions (known as MID, the Department was sometimes known as the Munitions Invention Department) still survives. The model answers for which are:[12]

D1. What have been the functions of your Department in the Ministry?

Reply

The chief functions of the Department of Munitions Inventions have been to receive ideas, proposals and inventions likely to be of service in carrying on land and aerial warfare from whatever source they might emanate, whether relating to war material, or to manufacturing devices and processes intended to promote the manufacture of such material; to examine and consider, and to provide funds for developing, experimenting with and completing, such inventions as are thought to be of promise, with a view to their being brought into service; to reject such proposals as are not considered of sufficient novelty or practical utility to justify further action being taken with them; and to initiate research in furtherance of the above objects.

This and other work is undertaken by the following sections of the Department:

Advisory Panel

This is an honorary body of scientific, technical and military men from which Committees are drawn who advise the Comptroller with regard to inventions and ideas placed before the Department.

Technical Examination Section

This Section consists of a Staff of Technical Examiners and Assistant Examiners, who are constantly employed in the investigation of inventions.

Drawing Office and Workshop

A Drawing Office and Workshop have been set up in the Department for the purpose of giving assistance to inventors.

Anti-Aircraft Experimental Section

This section was formed for the development of Height and Range-finders, and to undertake experimental and research work in connection with the ballistics of High-Angle Fire against Aircraft. It has also performed the duty of training officers, N.C.O.s and men in the use of various new instruments.

Experimental Ground and Works Section

This section undertakes experimental and research work and the general conduct of trials in connection with inventions submitted to the Department.

Chemical and Physical Research Section

This section was brought into being by an extension of the activities of the Nitrogen Products Committee. It is concerned with processes for the fixation of atmospheric nitrogen, more particularly the synthetic ammonia and the ammonia oxidation processes.

Patents, Rewards and Royalties Section

This section deals with all questions relating to Patents, Rewards and Royalties in respect of War Office, Air Board and Ministry of Munitions Supplies, Processes, Tools, Machinery, etc ...

The various Committees of the MID had significant Fellow representation, viz.

Chemical[13]	**Ordnance and Ammunition**[14]	**Instruments**[12]
Professor A.P. Laurie	Col Goold Adams	Sir Richard Glazebrook FRS
Mr. C.O. Bannister	Sir Horace Darwin FRS	Major L. Darwin
Mr. W.R. Bousfield FRS	Mr. McD Duckham	Sir Horace Darwin FRS
Dr. C.C. Carpenter	Sir Richard Glazebrook FRS	Mr. W. Duddell FRS
Sir A. Duckham	Sir Robert Hadfield FRS	Mr. S.Z. de Ferranti FRS
Dr. R.C. Farmer	Col N.B. Heffernan	Professor A. Gray FRS
Co-opted	Sir Alexander Kennedy FRS	Sir Alexander Kennedy FRS
Mr. D.L. Chapman FRS	Mr. M. Longridge	Sir Henry Norman
Dr. J.A. Harker FRS	Sir Hiram Maxim	Major F.G. Ogilvie
Dr. J.S. Haldane FRS	Mr. W. Stokes	Sir James Swinburne FRS

Dr. E.C. Jee	Comm C.D.C. Bridge	Sir Joseph Thomson FRS
Mr. M.C. Lamb	Col Matherson (BIR)	Mr. A.J. Walter
Dr. A. Scott FRS	Lord Edward Grosvenor (BIR) – both committees	
Dr. A.T. Masterman	Mr. Alfred Dobrée	
Major T.G. Tulloch		
Mr. C.J Wilson		

The work of the MID Committees was just as varied as that of the Committees of the Board of Invention and Research. For example, there was a report on 'Range-finders, Anti Aircraft Guns and Sighting' written by Major Colley, dated 9th December 1915.[15] Written for the Comptroller of the MID this report begins:

> … I have enquired fully into the above and have had various opportunities lately of inspecting various forms now in use in the Services. Apart from any reports you may receive from time to time from the Sub-Committee upon this question, I have the honour to submit to you my personal observations as you requested …

The report then details all of the range-finders currently in use and formed the basis for examining new technologies commensurate with the new instruments of War, for example developing range-finders for aircraft. Of course at that time aircraft were constructed from timber. The MID were also involved in a survey of sawn timber (see reference in footnote 13).

> Private and Confidential   Board of Trade
> Pitwood and Timber Department
> 6 Whitehall Gardens
> November 29th 1916
> Sir,
>
> I am directed by the Board of Trade to inform you that, under Section 1 of the Articles of Commerce (Returns etc.) Act 1914, a census is now being taken of all the sawn timber in the United Kingdom and that return forms for this purpose are now being issued.
>
> In order that the Board may be in a position to check the accuracy of the figures which will be given them, I am to ask you to be good enough to supply in the space provided below and at the back hereof, particulars of the stocks in the Harbours or Docks under your control on November 30th 1916, stating the owner's name where possible.

I am to request that this form shall be returned in the enclosed envelope not later than 11th December 1916 and to state that any information which you are able to provide shall be treated as confidential.

I am, Sir,
Your obedient Servant
R.S. Troup …

R.S. Troup FRS held the post of War Controller of Timber Supplies within the MID and was closely associated with this work, more of which in Chapter 8.[16]

There was also the opportunity for secret patents for work emanating from the MID.[17]

… I wish to apply for patents covering the mechanical devices described in the enclosed documents.

I understand that I have to apply through my C.O. (C.M.D.) for permission to take out these patents, I should be obliged if you could forward to me the necessary form or forms.

As regards the patents themselves, as these devices will only be of military value, it is presumed that the necessary action regarding the preparation of specifications etc. will be undertaken by you. It is suggested that the patents should be secret.

(signed) Sir H.C.L. Holden Major RA …

Sir Henry Capel Lofft Holden FRS had an interesting career. His address in the Royal Society Past Fellows database is listed as Royal Arsenal, Woolwich for 1894 with honours of a CB (1911) and KCB (1916)[18]. Sir Henry was elected a Fellow on 13th June 1895. His citation, recorded in his Certificate of a Candidate for Election, stated:

…In India from 1877-1884, he carried out a number of experiments in telephony and telegraphy for the Indian Government. Since 1885 he has been in charge of the Department for the proofs of Naval and Land Service Ordnance, and Gunpowder, and for experimental work connected therewith, and has invented and constructed many pieces of apparatus connected with the science of artillery, as well as with electrical and scientific research. Amongst those which have been publicly exhibited are his devices in connection with the chronograph, for measuring the velocity of projectiles; an extremely accurate and sensitive hydrometer for measuring the variations of the density of the acids in the electrolyte accumulator cells …

His application for a secret patent involved a range-finder, known as Major

Holden's Anti-Aircraft Director Apparatus. A letter dated October 21st 1918 records the construction of his apparatus by E.R. Watts and Son, so the idea was developed having passed the patent stage. However, his idea came too late in the War and was withdrawn from active pursuit by the Department of Munitions Inventions in March 1919.[19]

> Reference to Major Holden's Anti-Aircraft
> Director Apparatus
> In view of the general situation it is desired to close this matter as far as this Department is concerned. It is therefore proposed that Messrs. E.R. Watts and Son shall be paid their expenses up to March 31st, 1919 by this Department after which date this Department will cease to have further responsibility in the matter. It is understood that you are already dealing with the V.C. and the Vickers Instruments, and it is therefore suggested after the above date that further action, if any, should be taken by you in respect of Major Holden's apparatus. I should be glad to receive your concurrence in this course ...
> MID
> 10.3.19

In addition to the work mentioned above, Fellows were also involved in the Chemical Inventions Committee.

Chemical Inventions Committee

The following document outlines those involved and the purpose of the Committee.[20]

> Munitions Inventions Panel
> Chemical Inventions Committee
> On May 3rd, 1916, a meeting of the Sub-Committee appointed the previous day to consider further steps to be taken with regard to a memorandum submitted by the Faraday Society concerning the synthetic preparation of nitrogen products took place at which the following were present:
> Colonel Goold-Adams, Comptroller
> Professor Laurie, Chairman
> Dr. Farmer
> Mr. Dickinson, Secretary
> Mr. French, Examiner
> Sir Robert Hadfield FRS, President of the Faraday Society
> Professor A.K. Huntington, Vice President of the Faraday Society
> Dr. J.A. Harker FRS, Faraday Society
> Professor Laurie, on the Comptroller's invitation, took the Chair. He gave

> a brief outline of the position re nitrogen products so far as it was known to the Committee up to the time of receiving the proposals of the Faraday Society, which was in fact that sufficient information was not available to enable any effective steps to be taken in the matter. The memorandum submitted by the Society appeared, however, to change the position, and it was a question whether the Committee, the Ministry as a whole, or some independent body should take up the experimental work. The Comptroller reminded the meeting that he had authority to incur expenditure for experimental work without special reference to the Minister.
>
> Professor Huntington gave a brief resumé of the views which had led up to the Faraday Society preparing the memorandum. The Committee appointed to draw up a report consisted of himself, Dr. J.A. Harker, Mr. W.R. Cooper, Dr. F. Mollwo Perkin and Mr. J. Knox, author of a work on 'the fixation of atmospheric nitrogen'. To these had been added Dr. Greenwood, a 1851 Exhibitioner and former assistant to Dr. F. Haber at Karlsruhe who had really been the one to make the latter's process a practical success. Dr. R. de Rossignol, a British subject born in Jersey who had still later knowledge of Haber's process, was interned in Germany. The Faraday Society Committee had inside information from a very large number of gentlemen including Dr. R. Messel FRS, Mr. Murray-Morrison, Managing Director of the British Aluminium Co., a technical advisor to the Russian Government and others ...

By the third meeting, held on Friday 12th May, Lord Moulton FRS, Dr. G.T. Lander and Dr. T.M. Lowry FRS had joined the Committee.

The Faraday Society was founded in 1903 for the study of physical chemistry. It merged with several organisations which led to the formation of the Royal Society of Chemistry. The Faraday Society was interested in nitrogen products, particularly the synthesis of ammonia, because some explosives are nitrogen based and fertilisers can be generated from ammonia. As the blockades became more effective, and ever more land in Britain turned over to growing food, fertilizers were of strategic importance. As with the Royal Society the Faraday Society did not have the physical space in which to undertake the necessary experiments needed to deal with these concerns. Accordingly, members of the MID supporting the Nitrogen Products Committee (a Sub-Committee of the Chemical Inventions Committee) met with a few members of the Royal Institution (RI). The RI did, and indeed still does, have laboratory space with an impressive list of eminent scientists who have spent time there.

The following were present at the Conference held on May 23rd 1916.

Department of Munitions Inventions	Royal Institution
Colonel Goold-Adams, (Comptroller)	Dr. Horace Brown FRS
Professor A.K. Huntingdon	The Hon R. Clere Parsons
Dr. J.A Harker FRS	Sir William Phipson Beale
Lieutenant H.C. Greenwood RNVR	Sir Joseph J. Thomson FRS
Dr. E.B. Ludlam	Colonel G.H. Hills Hon. Sec.
Mr. H.W. Dickinson, Secretary of the Panel	Sir James Dewar FRS (in part)
Mr. R.T.G. French, Examiner	

Sir William Beale chaired the meeting. After a full discussion it was decided that the Royal Institution was not an ideal location for the nitrogen work. A subsequent meeting then took place, on June 5th 1916 at King's College London. Those present were:

Department of Munitions Inventions	King's College
Colonel Goold-Adams, (Comptroller)	Professor R.M. Burrows, (Principal)
Dr. J.A. Harker FRS	The Hon R.C. Parsons
Mr. H.W. Dickinson, Secretary of the Panel	
	Sir Herbert Jackson FRS
Mr. R.T.G. French, Examiner	Sir Owen Richardson FRS
	Mr. W. Smith, Secretary

Professor A.K. Huntingdon was also present.

Sir Owen Richardson FRS was Wheatstone Professor of Physics at King's College and was later awarded the 1928 Physics Nobel Prize.[21]

The Hon R.C. Parsons was in the chair. The King's College staff had the following issues needing answers:

1. the exact nature of the investigations, i.e., whether it could be carried out in underground laboratories such as those at Kings College
2. whether the research was for Government or for industrial purposes
3. whether the processes proposed were the subject of patents and if so whom the patents belonged
4. whether the experiments were likely to be dangerous
5. what machinery was required
6. who was to make the experiments, the College staff or the staff of the MID
7. the probable length of the investigation

The meeting was a success in that King's College agreed to host the work once the agreement was 'embodied in a letter'. University College, London also agreed to lend some space for this activity. Accordingly, research at the University College facility was to work on the Haber process under the supervision of Lieutenant Greenwood, with some electro-chemistry equipment shipped down from Lord Rutherford's laboratory in Manchester. Dr. Ludlam was tasked with supervising the work at King's College. With facilities in place, and a firm plan for the research, the Committee met several times to review progress. Minutes of the meeting held on October 2nd 1916 documented the following Committee members:

Colonel H.E.F. Goold-Adams, Acting Comptroller
G.S. Albright
C. Carpenter
Professor J.N. Collie FRS
W.R. Cooper, representing the Physical Society
Lt. Colonel A. Crossley FRS, representing the Chemical Society
Sir James J. Dobbie FRS, representing the Board of Agriculture and Fisheries
Professor F.G. Donnan FRS
A. McD Duckham, Deputy Comptroller
R.C. Farmer
F. Gossling, representing the Board of Trade
J.A. Harker FRS
Professor A.K. Huntington, representing the Faraday Society
Lord Moulton FRS
Sir Edward Russell FRS
Lord Rayleigh FRS
Sir John F.C. Snell, representing the Institution of Electrical Engineers
R.T.G. French, Secretary to the Committee
H.W. Dickinson, Secretary to the Munitions Inventions Panel

The Committee decided to form targeted Sub-Committees, i.e.,:[22]

The Power Sub-Committee terms of reference were:

- to collect the necessary information and advise upon the question of power in its bearings upon the different processes for the fixation of nitrogen applicable to the United Kingdom and the Empire
- to advise as to what steps could be taken to conserve and increase the national resources in by-products derivable from fuel and to limit their wastage by the introduction of improved methods of combustion
- to consider the bearing upon the cost of power of the various methods of carbonisation and of complete gasification of fuel, having regard to the products derivable therefrom

The Experiments Sub-Committee terms of reference were:

- to carry out experimental work on such processes as the Committee decided shall be investigated and to advice as to staff, accommodation, apparatus etc. necessary to carry out the work

The Processes Sub-Committee terms of reference were:

- to collate information on the various methods, synthetic and otherwise, for nitrogen fixation, and in consultation with the Power Committee to advise as to which processes are best adapted for use in 1) the United Kingdom and 2) the British Empire
- to ascertain how best to meet the requirements of the country in a number of substances obtainable as by-products of nitrogen fixation processes, eg argon and helium

The Economics Sub-Committee terms of reference were:

- to obtain data as to:
  - ◊ pre-war production and consumption including exports and imports of the different products; also their pre-war and War manufacturing costs and selling prices
  - ◊ how far these have been increased or modified by the War
  - ◊ how far these modifications are likely to persist under post-war conditions
  - ◊ how far a reduction in price of nitrogen products would influence the consumption of fertilisers
- to obtain from the proper authority data as to what extent 1) the United Kingdom and 2) the British Empire should be rendered independent of external supplies of nitrogen products as a security against a shortage in time of War, and to advise as to the scale on which manufacturing operations should be conducted in 1) the United Kingdom and 2) the Empire, to that end
- to indicate how far and in what manner plant excess of post-war peace requirements, put down to the above end, could best be utilised

Chemical Advisory Committee

There are two bound minute books in the National Archives relating to chemistry. The first are minutes of the General Chemical Sub-Committee,[23] dated June 29th 1915. They are hand written with the following attendees:

Professor H.B. Baker FRS, Sir George Beilby FRS, Professor A.W. Crossley FRS, Sir Boverton Redwood and Sir Thomas Thorpe FRS.

Unfortunately, there are no terms of reference for this Committee, the Minutes simply starting with:

The following documents were considered (June 29th Minutes):

F.W.3A/13.M.71	Mr. J.B. Williams' suggestion re use of acetylene for offensive trench warfare.	Rejected
F.W.3A/13.M.72	Mr. R.C. Cooper's suggestion re use of pyridine for offensive warfare.	Rejected
F.W.3A/13.M.73	Lt. Allen's suggestion re use of ammonia.	Rejected
F.W.3A/13.M.115	Mr. Stephenson's suggestion re use of hollow bamboo poles.	Rejected
B.M.174	Dr. Shakespeare's suggestion re a chlorine detector.	Referred to Sir Richard Glazebrook FRS and Professor B. Hopkinson FRS
B.M.364	Mr. MacNaught's suggestion re use of carbon disulphide vapour as protection from bromine fumes.	Rejected
B.M.362	Mr. S. Hodder's suggestion re use of carbon disulphide for offensive purposes.	Rejected
B.M.363	Dr. A. Tarquin's letter.	Further information requested

The minutes of the meeting held on August 7th with the same attendees had three guests, General Jackson, Colonel Foulkes and Mr. Roger. The position of chemical warfare was discussed thus:

> … Colonel Foulkes stated that he was only in charge of gas operations and had nothing to do with chemical grenades. He regards their use with favour, and they may play an important part, for example in turning the enemy out of craters caused by mines.
>
> The chemical grenades will be used by the infantry, and at present there is no one among the officers in charge with the expert knowledge of the chemistry and physiology of the proposed grenades. It is stated that schools of instruction are to be formed. If this is so the Committee are of the opinion that the officers in charge of the schools should be sent home to gain information and experience.
>
> The various types of grenades were discussed with Colonel Foulkes, who had formed a good opinion of the efficiency of S.K. (a tear gas developed at Imperial College in South Kensington – see Chapter 7, figure 7.4) in trenches.
>
> The Chief of Staff desires that the production of all types of effective grenades should continue …..

The last Minutes of the General Chemical Sub-Committee are dated 7th

August, only a few months after the first Minutes. The second Minute book of interest from the National Archives relates to the work of the Chemical Advisory Committee Minutes, the first Minutes for which are for the 15th August.

It **is** speculation, however the General Chemical Sub-Committee may have been renamed as the Chemical Advisory Committee (CAC). The meeting of the CAC of the 15th August involved General Jackson, Professor H.B. Baker FRS, Sir George Beilby FRS, Colonel Crossley FRS, Sir Boverton Redwood and Sir Thomas Thorpe FRS. This attendees list is almost identical to that of the General Chemical Sub-Committee Members mentioned above. Furthermore the minutes suggest that the agenda items were very similar – at least initially. Over time the CAC changes its focus adding various other members. By the 18th May 1917 the CAC Members had grown in number and the agenda radically changed.

CAC Members for the initial meeting on the 15th August 1916 and 18th May 1917 are shown below:[24]

Meeting on the 15th August 1916	Meeting on the 18th May 1917
Colonel Crossley	Colonel Crossley
General Jackson	Lieutenant Fortuna
Professor Baker	Dr. Scott possibly Alexander Scott dob 28/12/1853
Sir Thomas Thorpe FRS	General Jackson
Sir Boverton Redwood	Mr. Barcroft
Sir George Beilby FRS	Professor Baker
	Professor Cadman
	Sir Thomas Thorpe FRS
	Sir Richard Threlfall FRS
	Sir Boverton Redwood
	Sir George Beilby FRS
	Dr. Young (Secretary)

Two other Members of this expanded Committee are definitely Fellows. Unfortunately without first name initials it is difficult to confirm the other members of the Committee. The expanded numbers for this committee suggests that there was plenty of work needing completion.

The first few minute items for the meeting of 18th May 1917 detail the function of this Committee, viz:

1. the committee considered:

(a) intelligence report, Naval and Military supplies, 114314, (Mins.XIII, 11, 4, e). It was stated that experiments with potassium cyanide have been made near Berlin, that a very powerful gas was tried near Verdun and that large quantities of a strongly corroding substance used in October and November

1916 in the attack on Tschara.

Noted.

(b) C.L. Report 2010 d/8/5/17 on protection afforded by SBR against a mixture of diphosgene and chloropicrin.

Note: General Thuillier agreed that the protection appears to be satisfactory.

(c) Intelligence Report, Military Supplies, 114031 (Mins XIII, 3,3,c) relating to new hand grenades (incendiary and asphyxiating), the latter being stated to be so large as to necessitate rolling on the ground.

Noted.

(d) T.W. B.M.8212/A. 'New V.N. plant at Beckton' (Mins IX, 159, 5, b). Sir George Beilby FRS reported that Lieut. Coates' statement of the yield of A.C. on sodium cyanide is satisfactory. Since the product is stable and of good quality, and the apparatus at Stratford appears to be operated with safety to the workers. It appears to be desirable that the proper course is to erect the new plant on the lines of the Stratford plant embodying all the improvements which can be suggested by the staff at Stratford.

The Committee concurred in Sir George Beilby's report, but it was decided to defer action upon it until Mr. Adam of the Gas, Light and Coke Co has been seen by the Sub-Committee consisting of Professors Baker and Cadman and Dr. Scott and the whole position explained to him.

(e) The carrying out of field trials with cyanogen. The Secretary explained that it had been agreed at the last joint meeting of the Anti-Gas and Chemical Advisory Committee to carry out such ...

The remit for this Committee is unknown. It is difficult to imagine that this Committee could obtain intelligence reports without some help from a senior source. One might also speculate on the readership of these Minutes ....

Assuming – and it is a BIG assumption – that the General Chemical Committee was renamed, some likely Fellows attending the Chemical Advisory Committee are:[25]

Dr. Alexander Scott FRS – Distinguished by having paid great attention to the exact determination of atomic weights and of combining proportions by volume. Author, in conjunction with Professor Dewar, of papers on the Vapour Densities of Potassium and Sodium; on the Atomic Weights of Manganese, Oxygen, and Silver; and on the Molecular Weights of Substituted Ammonias

Sir Joseph Barcroft FRS – Fellow of King's College, Cambridge. Lecturer in Physiology. Distinguished as a Physiologist. Author of the following papers:- 'The Gaseous Metabolism of the Submaxillary Gland' (Journ Physiol, 1900 and 1901); 'A Method of Estimating the Oxygen and Carbonic Acid in Small Quantities of Blood' (with J. S. Haldane, ibid, vol xxviii, 1902); 'The Estimation of Urea in Blood' (ibid, vol xxix, 1903)

Professor Herbert Brereton Baker FRS – Senior science master at Dulwich College. Distinguished for his researches on the influence of moisture on chemical change. He has shown that dry carbon and phosphorus will not inflame when heated in dry oxygen; that dry ammonia and hydrogen chloride when mixed do not unite, and that dry ammonium chloride and calomel respectively vaporise without dissociation

Baron Cadman of Silverdale FRS – Chairman of Anglo-Iranian Oil Company and the Iraq Petroleum company. Member of Advisory Council of Department of Scientific and Industrial Research, and of various technical Committees on behalf of Government …

If not these four gentlemen, then who?

Item B.M. 174 of the Chemical Advisory Committee mentioned above, shows an entry for a chlorine detector which was referred to Sir Richard Glazebrook FRS and Professor B. Hopkinson FRS. The Physics Sub-Committee Minute Book[26] documents such referrals. For example, the meeting held on July 21st 1915, with just Sir Richard and Professor Hopkinson in attendance, discussed the following:

1. further information awaited in accordance with letter already sent of July 19th to Captain A. Rousseau (B.M. 345)
2. unless it is decided to use hydrofluoric acid the device is not required (B.M. 285)
3. it is understood that the method of designing an armoured car for going through barbed wire entanglements and carrying various offensive devices is under consideration. These papers should be handed to Mr. Vincent (B.M.372)
4. Rejected. It does not appear that this machine has any advantages over existing machines of similar type (84/H/5253)
5. Rejected (B.M.323)
6. it does not appear to come within the purview of the Trench War Committee. Suggest it might be passed on to the Anti-Aircraft Corps (Ref Mr. J. Stephenson)
7. Rejected (B.M.443)
8. …

Sir Richard Glazebrook FRS was heavily involved in the Royal Society Physics War Committee as well as being Director of the National Physical Laboratory.

Physiology Committee

The National Archives information concerning the Physiology Committee within the Department of Munitions Inventions has many papers on the effects of gas attacks. In one series of papers there are even the names of some of the victims. It would add no value here to document those unfortunate individuals, nor indeed the chronic effects of gas attacks. What is missing from the papers contained with the National Archives folder MUN 4/6911 are minutes from any of the meetings. Indeed the names of committee members are also absent. It is therefore not possible to definitively document involvement of the Fellows, however it is possible to mention a few who were involved because their papers survive at the National Archives. Furthermore, there is a reference to some Fellows in Obituary Notices held at the Royal Society.

Ernest Henry Starling FRS was at one time Head of the Anti-Gas Department and was succeeded by Henry Stanley Raper FRS. Also within that Department were Harold Ward Dudley FRS and Sir Charles Arthur Lovatt Evans FRS. Raper's Royal Society Obituary Notice comments: [27]

> ... at the invitation of Starling he then joined the Anti-Gas Department, and there Raper met many of those who were to be his life-long friends, including Ernest Henry Starling FRS, Harold Ward Dudley FRS and Sir Charles Arthur Lovatt Evans FRS. Raper joined them in the researches which the Chemical Warfare Department was then undertaking; the problems, indeed, were many and various ... Raper succeeded Starling as Head of the Anti-Gas Department and was awarded the CBE in 1918 in great measure for his services in this field ...

The Obituary Notice does not provide the full details of names of the Fellows, they have been added following further investigation. For example Dudley's Obituary Notice comments:[28]

> ... he obtained a commission in the army and was detailed for special work on the protection against the new chemicals of War ... ... he also undertook part in an advisory mission to the United States (early 1918) to the new anti-gas organisation of the US Army and also its mechanisms of supply ...

Professor E.H. Starling FRS appears in Chapter 1 as he was Chairman of the Royal Society Physiology (War) Committee. As Chairman, Starling would doubtless have read two papers, copies of which are housed in the National Archives (MUN 4/6911):

- the pathology and treatment of the effects of pulmonary irritant gases – June 20th 1917
- notes on the pathology and treatment of the effects of pulmonary

irritant and corrosive gases – June 20th 1917

Figure 3.7 documents some of the papers of Fellows:

Name(s)	Title
Francis Arthur Bainbridge FRS and Sir Henry Hallett Dale OM FRS	Observations on poisoning by gas (phosgene) with special reference to the effect on the coagulation of the blood
Sir William Maddock Bayliss FRS	The effect of bleeding on the results of inhalation of chlorine gas
J. S. Haldane FRS	Investigations of chronic cases of gas poisoning
Henry Stanley Raper FRS	Information required on the action of toxic substances now in use or capable of being used in gas warfare

Figure 3.7. Some Physiology Committee papers from the National Archives[29]

A comment in John William Trevan's (FRS) Biographical Memoir mentions his work with F.A. Bainbridge, suggesting another Fellow involved in gas warfare.[30]

> ... from 1914 he was a demonstrator in physiology and casualty physician. He worked with FA Bainbridge later FRS and Langdon Brown. In 1917 he joined the army as a Captain and pathologist in the RAMC spending 18months in Cairo and Salonika ...

Of course Sir Henry Hallett Dale OM FRS is mentioned in earlier Chapters. Sir Henry went on to receive a Nobel Prize in Physiology (1936) and Presidency of the Royal Society (1940-45).

4 In uniform / Seconded / National Service

There were countless millions of people who lived through World War I each doing what they could to help the war effort. The Fellows were equally busy. Some were in senior leadership positions where their drive and unique abilities were assets to be fostered. For example:

Sir Richard Threlfall FRS was a Panel Member and involved with Section I and II of the Board of Invention and Research, see Appendix II. He was also active in the Chemical Advisory Committee, see Chapter 2, and as the Director of the Air Department.[1]

Born in Hollowforth, Woodplumpton, (near Preston) Lancashire, on 14th August 1861, Sir Richard was at one time Professor of Experimental Physics, University of Sydney, New South Wales. He was awarded KBE in 1917 and GBE 1927.

Professor Arthur Stewart Eve FRS was a Private in the McGill Provisional Battalion at the outbreak of War. He raised and trained the 3rd and 4th University Companies, and following a series of promotions, was placed Second in Command of the 148th Battalion affiliated with the McGill Contingent COTC and as a Major joining the Canadian Expeditionary Forces. Following the departure of Sir William Bragg from the Admiralty Experimental Station at Harwich (Bragg became an advisor to the Admiralty), Eve became Director of the Harwich facility.[2]

Sir David Bruce FRS was born on the 29th May 1855 in Melbourne, Australia and later became Surgeon-Major, Army Medical staff. Prior to World War I, Sir David made important contributions to the causes of Malta Fever and established the link between the Tsetse Fly and an endemic disease of horses in Zululand. Throughout World War I, Sir David was Commandant of the Royal Army Medical College (actually holding the post from 1914 to 1919). He was also Director of the Trench Fever Committee.[3]

Sir Vito Volterra FRS was born on 03 May 1860 in Ancona, Italy. He nearly died aged three months when his town was besieged and a bomb destroyed his cradle. His father died when Sir Vito was two. Nevertheless Sir Vito started reading books about calculus when aged fourteen, and was later appointed Professor of Pure and Applied Mathematics at the University of Rome, and elected Royal Society Foreign Member on 30th June 1910. He enlisted in

Figure 4.1 Sir Richard Threlfall. (© Godfrey Argent Studio. Reproduced with permission)

Figure 4.2. Sir Henry Holden. (© The Royal Society. Reproduced with permission)

the army aged 55, and transferred to the Air Force helping to perfect a new type of airship. He also designed a system of firing from an airship, something thought impossible at the time. His efforts were recognised by the Mention in Dispatches and a decoration of the War Cross. Sir Vito established the Italian Office for War Inventions (from 1917) and became its first Chairman. Sir Vito died in Rome on the 11th October 1940.[4]

Sir Henry Capel Lofft Holden FRS, Figure 4.2, was mentioned and something of his career documented in Chapter 3 during a discussion of range-finders. Sir Henry retired in 1912 but became Assistant Director and subsequently Director of Mechanical Transport during the War. He was made a K.C.B. in 1916 and retired (for the second time!) as Brigadier-General in 1918.[5]

Herbrand Arthur Russell FRS was the 11th Duke of Bedford and Colonel commanding 3rd Battalion Bedfordshire Regiment.[6]

This is but a small sample of the many Fellows involved in some senior position during World War I. There is one individual who is unique, even amongst such elite company. As far as can be determined he is the only Fellow awarded the Victoria Cross (1916). Captain John Alexander Sinton VC FRS deserves a special mention (he retired from the army as an Honorary Brigadier).

Figure 4.3 J.A. Sinton VC FRS. (© The Royal Society. Reproduced with permission)

Brigadier Sinton VC FRS

The following citation was printed in the *London Gazette*:[7]

> His Majesty the KING has been graciously pleased to award the Victoria Cross to the undermentioned Officer and Man: —
>
> Capt. John Alexander Sinton, M.B., Ind. Med. Serv. For most conspicuous bravery and devotion to duty. Although shot through both arms and through the side, he refused to go to the hospital, and remained, as long as daylight lasted, attending to his duties under very heavy fire. In three previous actions Capt. Sinton displayed the utmost bravery.

This was not the only occasion Captain Sinton appeared in the Gazette. He also received the the Russian Order of St. George, 4th Class[8], and a military division OBE.[9] Arguably, the awards and honours of such a singular individual are worth recording here, just to demonstrate his breadth and depth of knowledge and experiences.[10] [11] A list of his 200 or so research papers appears in his Royal Society Biographical Memoir.

Academic qualifications

Degrees: M.B, B.Ch., B.A.O. Queen's College Belfast (University of Ireland) where he took a First Class Honours in Medicine, Second Class Honours (first place) with Exhibition in Surgery and a First Class Honours with Exhibition in Midwifery and Gynaecology; D.T.M. Liverpool School of Tropical Medicine (1911); Riddell Demonstrator in Pathology, Queen's University. At this time he was also Honorary Pathologist to the Benn Ulster Eye, Throat and Ear Hospital and Clinical Pathologist to the Mater Infirmorum Hospital, Belfast.

Honorary Degrees: Hon MD Queen's University Belfast 1917; DSc (QUB); MB BCh BAO (RUI); DPH Cantab and Belfast; DPH Liverpool.

Fellow of the Royal Society 21st March 1946.

Arnott Memorial Medallist, Irish Medical Schools' and Graduates Assoc 1917

Chalmers Memorial Medallist, Royal Society of Tropical Medicine and Hygiene 1928

Bisset-Hawkins Medallist Royal College of Physicians London 1944

Robert Campbell Memorial Orator and Medallist, Ulster Medical Society 1946

Mary Kingsley Medallist, Liverpool School of Tropical Medicine 1949

Anti-Gambia Memorial Medal from the Egyptian Government 1950.

Army Life

Sinton joined the Indian Medical Service (taking first place in the entrance examination) but was seconded for a year as a research exhibitioner (a scheme for post-graduate study administered through Queen's University) during which he studied protozoology.

Sinton's first appointment in India was as a Regimental Medical Officer to the 31st Duke of Connaught's Own Lancers stationed at Kohat (North West Frontier Province). Promoted to Captain he was posted to the Indian Expeditionary Force D in Mesopotamia. Sinton served in:

- the European War 1914-1918
- Transcaspia 1918-1919
- Waziristan 1919-1920
- Mahsud 1920
- Retired 1938
- Re-employed War 1939-1945

Mentioned in Dispatches four times

VC (1916); Russian Order of St George 4th Class (1917); OBE, military (1921)

Civilian Life

- President of the North Ireland Branch of the British Legion 1946-1953
- Member of the Council of the North Ireland Branch of the British Legion 1949-1952

- Vice President of the North Ireland Branch of the British Legion from 1952
- Honorary Member of the National Malaria Society USA 1930
- President of the Malaria Commission of the League of Nations 1937-1946
- Vice President of the Malaria Commission of the League of Nations 1945-1947
- Member of the Malaria Commission of the Medical Research Council
- Honorary Fellow National Society of India and other Mosquito-borne diseases
- Honorary Consultant Malariologist, War Office
- Director Malaria Survey of India
- Honorary Member of the Queen's University Service Club from 1946
- Member of Senate Queen's University 1948
- Pro-Chancellor Queen's University Belfast 1952
- President of Queen's University Association 1953-1954
- Honorary Member of the Ulster Medical Society 1920
- Honorary Member of the Royal Society of St. George 1946
- Governor of the Royal Academical Institute, Belfast 1946-1950
- Old Instonians Association Vice President 1946-1952, President 1952-1953
- President of the Co Tyrone Branch of the Forces Help Society (formerly Sailors', Soldiers' and Airmen's Help Society) 1946-1952
- High Sheriff for Tyrone N Ireland 1953
- Deputy Lieutenant Tyrone N. Ireland 1954
- Magistrate (JP) for Co. Tyrone from 1947
- Represented North Ireland at the 11th Conference of the British Empire Service League at London in 1951
- Honorary Fellow Ulster Medical Society
- Manson Fellow London School of Hygiene and Tropical Medicine

Note: The Victoria Cross was instituted in 1856 by Her Majesty Queen Victoria as a means of rewarding acts of valour and devotion to the country in the face of the enemy. It is the highest award for acts of valour and devotion.[12]

The Russian Order of St George 4th Class was discontinued in 1917 and only recently re-instated. It is the highest military decoration of the Russian Federation, instituted on 26th November 1769 by the Empress Catherine the Great. The *London Gazette* entry for Sinton's award reads:[13]

> The following formed part of the Russian Decorations awarded in July, 1916, to the British Forces for distinguished services rendered during the course of the campaign:

His Majesty the King has given unrestricted permission in all cases to wear the Decorations and medals in question.

General Headquarters, Indian Expeditionary Force ' D' 22nd December, 1916. The Order of St. George, 4th Class.

Captain John Alexander Sinton, V.C., Indian Medical Service.

Although Brigadier Sinton is a unique Fellow in his award of a Victoria Cross, other Fellows also received awards from grateful nations. The Military Cross was awarded to several, Figure 4.4. The British Army website describes the award thus:[14]

> ... Awarded to all ranks of the RN, RM, Army, and RAF in recognition of exemplary gallantry during active operations against the enemy on land ...

The Croix de Guerre avec Palme is described in the *Encyclopaedia Britannica* as:

> ... French military decoration created in 1915 and 1939 to reward feats of bravery, either by individuals or groups, in the course of the two World Wars. This medal may be conferred on any member of the armed forces, on French citizens and foreigners who have been mentioned in army dispatches, and, in special cases, on military units and towns ....

Figure 4.4 lists some of the Fellows awarded these medals.

Name	**Medal/Mentioned in Dispatches**
Banting (Sir Frederick Grant)	Saw service in England and in France and received the Military Cross for exceptional bravery while attending the wounded under fire. Wounded at Cambrai and for a time thought he would lose his right arm.[15]
Deslandres (Henri Alexandre)	Won the Croix de Guerre 1914-18, was a Commander of the Légion d'Honneur.[16]
Elliot (Walter)	Joined the Royal Scots Greys, a cavalry regiment, as a medical officer. Served in France and was awarded the Military Cross and Bar.[17]
Gleb (Anrep)	Twice wounded and awarded St. George Cross. The company in which he served as a doctor had been almost completely surrounded and he led his company by day and night through swamps and forests to safety. When the revolution broke out in 1917 he joined the White Russians.[18]

Name	Medal/Mentioned in Dispatches
Kellaway (Charles)	Went with the Australian Forces to the Western Front, and there in 1917 while serving as Regimental MO with the 13th Australian Infantry Battalion, his action won him the award of a Military Cross.[19]
Lees (George Martin)	Attended the Royal Military Academy, Woolwich in preparation for taking part in the First World War, then in progress. From Woolwich he was commissioned in the Royal Artillery in which he served in France. He soon transferred to the Royal Flying Corps and won the MC.[20]
Pilgrim (Guy Ellock)	2nd Lieutenant in the 125th Napier's Rifles received some medals for service in Mesopotamia and Persia.[21]
Woollard (Herbert Henry)	Took an active part in the War attaining the rank of Lieutenant-Colonel in the Australian Army Medical Service. He was also Mentioned in Dispatches and awarded the Croix de Guerre avec Palme.[22]

Figure 4.4. Some of the Fellows decorated for outstanding acts of bravery

Of course there were many acts of bravery for which no medal was awarded. Arguably some Fellows in the Royal Army Medical Corps (RAMC) worked close to the fighting in all theatres of war. Indeed Figure 1.8 in Chapter 1 records the death of the Chemistry Nobel Laureate Eduard Buchner following a wound whilst working in a field hospital. Figure 4.5 below records some of those working in uniform for RAMC units. One name in this list stands out, that of Alexander Fleming. Sir Alexander Fleming as he later became, was awarded the Physiology or Medicine Nobel Prize in 1945 largely for his work on the clinical effects of penicillin. The roots of his later success can be traced to his treatment of wounds in World War I.

Name	RAMC
Bradford (Sir John Rose)	Accepted the chance to join the Expeditionary Force in France as a Consulting Surgeon. As Colonel, later Major General ... he understood the military aspect of the various medical problems.[23]
Cannon (Walter Bradford)	Member of the Harvard Hospital Unit attached to the British Army.[24]

Name	RAMC
Cathcart (Edward Provan)	Transferred (1915) to the RAMC for anti-gas duties, later becoming Deputy Director Anti-Gas Services, Home Forces. 1917 transferred to the personal staff of the Director-General Army Medical Services with the rank of Lieutenant-Colonel for special work in connection with feeding the army.[25]
Douglas (Stewart Rankin)	Appointed to the Staff of the Medical Research Committee as Chief Assistant to Sir Almroth Wright … he then joined the RAMC and soon became involved in special research. October 1914 he described a new method of preparing an excellent medium in which to grow cultures by digesting cooked meat with trypsin. His medium proved to be a great success. It was still in use when the Obituary Notice was written.[26]
Fleming (Sir Alexander)	Wright was called upon to set up a laboratory in France for the study of wound infections, and he took Fleming with him – with the rank of Captain, RAMC. That first wartime laboratory for medical research was established at the Casino in Boulogne (since destroyed during World War II).[27]
Gordon (Mervyn Henry)	Original member (1909) of the Army Pathological Advisory Committee, and after his service in the 1914-18 War remained Consulting Bacteriologist to the Army.[28]
Gye (William Ewart)	Became a temporary Lieutenant, RAMC, early in 1915 and later promoted to Captain. Because he spotted and confirmed the diagnosis of a case of cerebro-spinal meningitis he was promptly given the post of hospital pathologist. He served in France and Italy, was at one time in charge of a field laboratory, and was Mentioned in Dispatches.[29]
McDougall (William)	Following a spell in the French Army driving an ambulance, McDougall was absorbed into the RAMC and put in charge of nervous patients 'I was put in a position where I could select from this vast stream whatever cases seemed most susceptible to treatment. And soon I was head of a hospital section full of 'shell-shock' cases'.[30]

Name	RAMC
Myers (Charles Samuel)	Over 40 when commissioned in the RAMC, eventually appointed Consultant Psychologist to the British Armies in France and his work had a profound influence on the psychological treatment of what was then called 'shell shock'.[31]
Parsons (Sir Leonard Gregory)	1916 found Parsons serving with the RAMC in Salonika as Officer in Charge of the Medical Division of the Birmingham Territorial Hospital. Later he was appointed Consulting Physician to the Serbian Army, and in 1917 he received the Order of St Sava.[32]
Ross (Sir Ronald)	Sent to Alexandria to investigate dysentery prevailing in the Dardanelles. He became Consultant for Malaria to the War Office and in 1917 was sent to Salonika on a malaria survey … In 1918 he became Temporary Colonel in the RAMC and demobilised the same year.[33]
Salaman (Redcliffe Nathan)	Joined the RAMC as Lieutenant (March 1915) and later promoted to Captain, served in England till 1917, when he went as Medical Officer to the Jewish Regiment, 39th Royal Fusiliers, and served in Egypt and Palestine. He was Mentioned in Dispatches.[34]
Twort (Frederick William)	At the outbreak of War he tried to interest the War Department in ideas he had been developing on dysentery. They failed to accept his scheme, but in 1915, they interrupted his work by asking him to take charge of a base laboratory at Salonika. Again his proposal to deal with dysentery, which he suspected was likely to occur, was refused. When the outbreak of dysentery duly broke out, Twort was inundated with routine and could no longer pursue his research … . he was allowed to resign his commission and returning to England he wrote up his dysentery work with special reference to mistakes of the Medical Advisory Committee.[35]
White (Philip Bruce)	The opportunity came with an appointment as a civilian pathologist, attached to the RAMC at Tidworth Military Hospital and District Laboratory. Here from 1916-1919 with untrained and often only casual help he dealt with pathological specimens at the rate of eight to nine thousand per year.[36]
Wright (Sir Almroth Edward)	Went to Boulogne with Sir Alexander Fleming and set up a research laboratory in the Boulogne Casino which was then a large hospital.[37]

Figure 4.5. RAMC Fellows

Figure 4.6. Bushy House. (Author's photograph)

Some Fellows were already well established as research workers by the outbreak of War. Those Fellows over the normal recruiting age were often to be found in Reserved Occupations, more details will be provided in Chapter 5. Many Fellows seconded or who simply volunteered whose research acumen came to the fore during the War. In these cases the Fellows were posted to restricted Government establishments or other institutes.

Mention has already been made of the National Physical Laboratory (NPL), and some of the work of its first Director Sir Richard Glazebrook FRS, see Chapters 1 and 2. Arguably this establishment typified the use of a large, isolated country house set in grounds the access to which could be closely monitored. Visitors and workers to the establishment could be vetted and the work undertaken in the utmost secrecy. The first building occupied by the NPL was Bushy House. Built by Edward Progar during the reign of King Charles II, Bushy House was returned to the Crown in 1896, and thought an ideal building for the NPL by its Executive Committee, Figure 4.6.

Although still maintained by the NPL it is no longer used as a research establishment – far more modern and purpose-built NPL buildings are nearby.

Set on the edge of the Royal Park, which can be seen from the front lawn, and from where the picture was taken, this building was the scene of many research projects.[38] For example, Sir John Edward Lennard-Jones FRS, was seconded to NPL for War research. In fact some of the work for the 'bouncing bomb' was also undertaken here in World War II.

A small selection of Fellows seconded to War research facilities is provided below, Figure 4.7.

Name	Research organisation
Bengough (Guy Dunstan)	Captain and Adjutant to the Royal Garrison Artillery 1915-1916, seconded for research work at the request of the Admiralty (1916).[39]
Cook (Gilbert)	Commissioned in the Royal Garrison Artillery and posted to a coastal defence battery on the Humber. Transferred to artillery headquarters and became responsible for much of the technical work of the organisation and in particular for the development and experimental work in connection with range-finding equipment ... Early in 1917 invited to join the technical branch of the Mining and Mine Sweeping Service of HMS Vernon with a commission in the RNVR.[40]
Kon (George)	Was in the Tyrol in August 1914, managing to drive across the Brenner before the declaration of War. Returning to England by a circuitous route he joined the team at Imperial College engaged on the preparation of essential drugs ... was naturalised in 1916 and joined the army as a Lieutenant in the Anti-Gas Department .... he was Mentioned in Dispatches and left the army at the end of the War with the rank of Captain.[41]
Lennard-Jones (Sir John Edward)	Obtained his wings in 1917 and saw service in France; he also took part in some investigations on aerodynamics with Messsrs Boulton and Paul and at the National Physical Laboratory.[42]
Townsend (Sir John Sealy Edward)	Took up wireless research for the Royal Naval Air Service with the rank of Major on the special list (RNVR). He worked for several years at Woolwich where he developed, for example, small robustly constructed and accurately calibrated wavemeters.[43]

Figure 4.7. Some Fellows seconded to research establishments.

Potentially there were many problems in conducting wide-ranging research in diverse locations, each deemed secret. Duplication of effort and waste of resources spring to mind. In an attempt to avoid these and other issues, a meeting was held at 11:30 on July 13th 1915.[44] A letter was sent to interested parties, a blank for which is stored in the National Archives:

... by direction of the Prime Minister a meeting will be held for the purpose of considering the co-ordination of the various committees dealing with inventions at 2 Whitehall Gardens at 11:30 July 13th. Your presence is requested … .

This is dated July 12th 1915 leaving little time to rearrange diaries. It may also indicate the urgent need for a co-ordinated effort. Unfortunately the author of the note, and those invited to attend the meeting are unknown. There may have been a great many people at that meeting. A handwritten document in the National Archives, stored with the above blank letter in folder MUN 5/118, records those institutes engaged on scientific work just for the Ministry of Munitions.

Institutions engaged upon Scientific & Research Work, directly or indirectly for the Ministry of Munitions

I. Inventions Department

1. Imber Court Experimental Ground – Thames Ditton (miscellaneous research not connected with guns, bombs or grenades)
2. Claremont Park Experimental Ground – Esher (bombs, grenades, rifles, fuses, guns etc.)
3. Sub-Station at Chattenden – Chatham (boring, mining, excavating)
4. Anti-Aircraft Experimental Section – Whale Island (Portsmouth Harbour) (anti-aircraft apparatus, height, finders, etc. – working in close relations with computing staff at Headquarters)
5. Anti-Aircraft Experimental Sub-Station at Gosport (training of personnel for sound-locating instruments)
6. Anti-Aircraft Experimental Sub-Station at Rochford (sound-locating instruments)
7. Chemical Research Station (fixation of atmospheric nitrogen – production of pure hydrogen – working in connection with University College, London)
8. Chemical Waste Products Committee (utilisation of waste chemical products – working in connection with Institute of Chemistry in London)
9. Building Materials Committee (utilisation of waste materials for building purposes – working in connection with Department of Scientific & Industrial Research)
10. Tube Composition Committee. (time fuses for A.A. gunnery)

II. Chemical Warfare Department

1. 1. R.E. Experimental Station Porton (chemistry, physiology, field trials of chemical missiles)
2. W.D. Experimental Ground, Wembley (explosives, pyrotechnics, chemical fillings, etc. field trials of bombs, signals flares)
3. Anti-Gas Department, University College (chemical fillings – anti-gas appliances – respirators)

III. Aircraft Production Department

1. Royal Aircraft Establishment, Farnborough (light alloys, brass, varnish, aeroplane construction)
2. Aircraft Inspection Department Laboratory, Inver Street (miscellaneous research on design & construction of aircraft)
3. Air Ministry Laboratory, South Kensington (research & testing of aeroplanes)

IV. Trench Warfare Department

1. Experimental Ground, Porton
2. Experimental Ground, Richmond Park (both – design & improvement of trench mortars & ammunition – grenades, armour etc.)

V. Mechanical Warfare Department

1. Experimental department, Dollis Hill (tank design – anti-tank methods)

VI. Other Institutions maintained for Research in connection with Ministry of Munitions

- Research Department, Woolwich Arsenal (chemistry, metallurgy, and ballistics for Design & Explosives Supply Departments)
- Chiswick Laboratory (Chemical research for Explosives Supply Department)

VII. Institutions utilised for Research in connection with Ministry of Munitions

- National Physical Laboratories, Teddington (gauges, metallurgy)
- Institute of Chemistry, Russell Square (glass, optical munitions)
- Guy's Hospital (effects of TNT on workers)
- King's Hospital, London (glass for optical munitions)
- Cambridge University (gas & anti-gas research)
- Sheffield University (cupro-nickel, glass for optical munitions)
- Birmingham University (cupro-nickel)
- British Engineering Standards Association.(problems re internal combustion engines)
- Birmingham Technical School (light alloys for aircraft construction)
- Royal School of Mines, South Kensington (breakages in steel for aircraft construction)
- Royal Navy College, Greenwich (fatigue of metals employed in aircraft construction)
- Sir John Cass Institute/St Bartholomew's Hospital (X-ray glass & tubes)
- Imperial College of Science and Technology (glassware for chemical warfare)
- Imperial Institute, South Kensington (potash)
- Botanical Department, Royal College of Science (formally independent now

part of Imperial College) (glue for aircraft construction)

- Lister Institute (physiological research)
- Technical College, Finsbury (chemical warfare research)
- Meteorological Office, South Kensington (metrology for aircraft navigation)

These institutes were connected with the Department of Munitions Inventions. Many other establishments were involved in inventions and research. It would have made for an interesting meeting and must have involved some of the Fellows.

Not all Fellows, or indeed scientists, were fortunate to work in research in the UK. Some, however, were posted to facilities in the United Kingdom, Figure 4.8, and others abroad, Figure 4.9.

Name	UK posting
Copeman (Sydney Arthur Monckton)	Advanced military hygiene, serving as Divisional Sanitary Officer, 1st Division of the Territorial Force, receiving the Territorial Decoration. During the War of 1914-18 with the rank of Colonel, he was in charge of the Hygiene Department of the Royal Army Medical College.[45]
Cuthbertson (Clive)	Joined Corps of Instructors on Musketry as a Staff Sergeant (1914), then with the 22nd Division 67th Brigade. 1915 onwards worked in the Foreign Office, Contraband Department.[46]
Filon (Louis Napoleon George)	Later appointed to the technical staff of the Admiralty Air Service.[47]
Greenwood (Major)	Though still attached to the staff of the Lister Institute until 1919, Greenwood took service as an RAMC officer (1915-16) in the Sanitary Service, from which he was seconded for statistical work to the Health and Welfare section of the Ministry of Munitions as its first senior Statistical Officer.[48]
Kaye (George William Clarkson)	Captain in the London Electrical Engineers (Territorials) in charge of searchlights in Shoeburyness, Thames Haven, Minster and Gravesend.[49]
Lyons (Sir Henry George)	Major in a special unit of the Royal Engineers as Commandant in London specialising in Metrology.[50]

Name	UK posting
Mallock (Henry Reginald Arnulph)	Civilian member of the Ordnance Committee he wrestled with many of the problems of ballistics. As a member of the Aeronautical Research Committee he gave the James Forrest lecture. Also engaged with many problems for the Admiralty.[51]
Morgan (Walter Thomas James)	Because of his chemical experience he was posted to HMS President, a shore-based research and manufacturing station in East London making toxic agents, smokescreen floats and other chemicals and equipment for the Navy.[52]
Richardson (Lewis Fry)	Meteorological Office (1913-1916), Superintendent of Eskdalemuir Observatory (1916-1919) in the Friends' Ambulance Unit in a motor convoy (SSA13) attached to the French Infantry Division.[53]

Figure 4.8. Some Fellows posted in the UK

The vast majority of able-bodied men were sent abroad to fight in the various theatres of war, and the Fellows were no exception.

Name	Posted abroad
Agar (Wilfred Eade)	In June 1915 the 52nd Division was ordered to Gallipoli and Agar was appointed Adjutant to the Divisional Base Depot, to be stationed at Alexandria. After about a year in Alexandria he had a severe attack of enteric and was sent home in a hospital ship … eventually declared unfit for further service the authorities decided that he would be more use in his old post to which he returned in April 1918.[54]
Farmer (Ernest Harold)	Volunteered for active service, and in 1915 was gazetted to the Loyal North Lancashire Regiment, serving with them until he was demobilised in 1919. In 1917 he was severely wounded and spent the next two years in hospital while surgeons struggled to save his right arm .. Few realised that when lecturing he found it necessary to wear an elbow support to enable him to raise his arm to write on a blackboard.[55]
Heilbron (Sir Ian Morris)	Took a commission as Lieutenant in the RASC in 1910 and was posted overseas in the 52nd Division in 1915. During the period 1917-19 he served brilliantly, ultimately leading to the rank of Lieutenant-Colonel as Assistant Director of Supply at GHQ Salonika.[56]

Name	Posted abroad
Hewitt (John Theodore)	Received a commission as 'Major, General List attached to the Royal Engineers' and with H.R. Le Sueur had quickly acquired a uniform and started for the Dardanelles.[57]
Moseley (H.G.J.)	Granted a commission in the Royal Engineers, and later made Signalling Officer in the 38th Brigade of the First Army, leaving for the Dardanelles on June 13th. He took part in the severe fighting at the Suvla Bay landing on August 6th and 8th, and was instantaneously killed on the 10th by a bullet in the head, when in the act of telephoning an order to his division when the Turks were attacking on the flank only 200 yards away.[58]
Richardson (Archibald Read)	At the outbreak of War in 1914, went on active service with the British Expeditionary Force in France, rising to the rank of Lieutenant-Colonel.[59]
Spath (Leonard Frank)	Called up for Military Service in 1916 and served as a Private in the British Expeditionary Force in France and Belgium in the Middlesex Regiment.[60]
Stradling (Sir Reginald Edward)	In spite of his poor sight commissioned in the Royal Engineers. After the usual period of training he went to France with the 16th Division in 1915 and served continuously until the end of 1917, by which time he had reached the rank of Captain when his health failed and he returned to civilian life. His administrative abilities found their first real outlet during this period and at the time of his breakdown he had been for some time Adjutant, Divisional RE. His service was recognised by the award of the Military Cross and he was twice Mentioned in Dispatches. The Home Office ... formed the Air Raid Committee of which Stradling was a key member.[61]
Stratton (Frederick John Marrian)	Became OC Signals of the 20th Divisional Signal Company RE. Took his Company to France in the summer of 1915 to join the BEF where it formed part of the 14th Corps (which saw action in the Somme). In 1917 he was promoted to Lieutenant-Colonel and became Assistant Director Signals (later designation CSO) of the newly formed 19th Corps of the BEF under the command of Lt-General Watts. A fellow officer was Brigadier R.A. Bagnold FRS.[62]

Figure 4.9. Some Fellows posted abroad

5 Too old / too young / academic research/ Reserved Occupations

Those Fellows who were children during World War I played significant roles in World War II (and will appear in the follow-up book concerning the Fellows active in World War II due for publication 2014). Of course some were already retired and were re-engaged with their former activity if the need required their unique skills or knowledge. The remaining Fellows fell into one of several groups:

- remained in their current academic post
- remained in the institute where they were working
- remained in their industrial occupation
- were working abroad during the War

War Badges for Reserved Occupations

The Government had a procedure enabling key individuals to remain in post, known as Reserved Occupations. The Royal Society formed their own Reserved Occupations Committee which recommended certain individuals to receive a War Service Badge exempting them from call up. A circular was written, shown below.[1]

Ministry of Munitions
Badge Department
6, Whitehall Gardens
London S.W.
CIRCULAR BADGES

The Minister of Munitions is prepared to issue War Service Badges to firms engaged in munitions work or other work for War purposes (hereinafter referred to as 'war-work') upon the following conditions:-

(1) Badges may be issued on application duly received from firms engaged in the manufacture of munitions of War in other urgent war-work, for distribution to skilled workmen employed by them on such work, i.e., draughtsmen or other

technical assistants, supervising staff, skilled or, where they can be shown to be indispensible, other classes of workmen.

Where application is made in respect of men eligible for Military service proof must be afforded that every effort has been made, by application to a Labour Exchange or otherwise, to find substitutes.

(2) Firms applying for badges for the first time must forward to the above address two copies of the enclosed schedule (M.M. 37B) made out in respect of all their male employees over 16, underlining in column (a) the names of those for whom badges are desired. If any of these men already has a badge certificate this must be shown in column (d) of the return. A copy of this form with specimen entries is also enclosed.

Firms requiring additional sheets of the above schedule may prepare them themselves or obtain them by applying to this Department.

If the application is granted, one copy of the schedule will be returned with the individual numbers of the badges granted inserted against those men to whom the issue of badges is approved. This schedule will form the register (to be kept at the works) which every firm receiving War service badges is required by the Minister under Section 11 of the Munitions of War Act, 1916, to be kept up to date. When the register has been established, the firm to whom badges have been issued will ordinarily be justified in refusing to supply in any other form statistical information on the points and for the purposed covered by the register.

(3) Firms applying for badges must also fill up in duplicate the accompanying schedule (M.M. 40) showing in summary the nature and duration of their War contracts with other information as to the grounds on which their application is based.

(4) An employer on handing his badge to a man must also hand him the corresponding certificate. Should a man already possess a badge certificate, his new badge number and the name of the firm should be endorsed on the back of it.

(5) The badge must in every case be given up to the employer by a man who either (a) is definitely taken off war-work, or (b) leaves the firm through which the badge was issued to him. The certificate, however, is to be retained by the man. In such cases the badge number and firm's name should be crossed through in red ink, leaving them legible.

(6) An employer may at the same time apply for new certificates to replace any which he is satisfied have been accidentally lost, rendered illegible or destroyed. In such cases he must specify the circumstances in which the certificate has been lost, defaced, or destroyed. If, however, the original certificate is valid as a certificate of exemption under the Military Service Act, 1916 (i.e., was rightfully held on March 1st, 1916, by a single unattested man, who would otherwise be liable for military service under the Act), application for a renewal of the certificate must be accompanied by a fee of one shilling in accordance with the provisions of the Military Service Act, 1916.

(7) Attention is called to the enclosed Rules made under the Munitions of War Act 1915, providing penalties for the unlawful procuring or possession of badges. These Rules should be brought specially to the notice of any workman to whom a badge may be issued. In view of the fact that in certain cases badge certificates are valid as certificates of exemption under the Military Service Act, the attention both of employers and men is also drawn to Clause 3 (4) of that Act:

> 3 (4) 'If for the purpose of obtaining exemption for himself or any other person, or for the purpose of obtaining the renewal, variation, or withdrawal of a certificate of exemption, any person makes any false statement or false representation he shall be liable on summary conviction to imprisonment for a term not exceeding six months, with or without hard labour.'

For completeness a copy of form M.M.40 is shown below. Figure 5.1.

STRICTLY CONFIDENTIAL
Ministry of Munitions,
Badge Department,
6, Whitehall Gardens,
London, S.W.

TO BE FILLED AND RETURNED IN DUPLICATE.
WAR SERVICE BADGES.
Date ....
Name of Firm.......................................
Address of Head Office ....
Address to which Badges should be sent ....

You are required to fill up and return two copies of the enclosed Schedule (M.M. 37B) and to supply the following information in support of your application:-

1. Principal Contracts.

(a) Government Department or firm with which each contract is held.	(b) Nature and amount of contract.	(c) Duration of contract.	(d) Proportion delivered.	(e) Value of contract.

Figure 5.1. Form M.M.40

Reserved Occupations

The Royal Society Reserved Occupations Committee's first interim report is dated 22nd January 1918.[2] This document comments on the origin of this Committee:

> ... The formation of this committee arose out of a deputation consisting of Lt.-Col. Crossley, Professor Frankland, and Dr. M. O. Foster, as delegates of the Chemical Section of the Royal Society (War) Committee, to Mr. McLeod, of the Board of Trade, which took place on November 23, 1915.
>
> As the result of this interview 'Analytical, Consulting, and Research Chemists' were, in the national interest, placed on the Schedule of 'Research Occupations'. The Reserved Occupations Committee was appointed by the Council of the Royal Society to investigate the claims of Chemists seeking exemption under this Schedule of the Military Service Acts ...

The Royal Society Council formally constituted the Committee on 20 January 1916.

The Committee membership was: Sir Joseph J. Thomson FRS (President in the chair), Sir Arthur Schuster FRS (Secretary of the Royal Society), Dr. A. Scott FRS (President of the Chemical Society), Sir James Dobbie FRS (President of the Institute of Chemistry), Mr. A. C. Chapman FRS (President of the Society of Analysts), Dr. C.C. Carpenter (President of the Society of Chemical Industry), Professor P.F. Frankland FRS, Professor A.W. Crossley FRS, Professor P.F. Donnan and members of the Royal Society Sectional Committee for Chemistry.

The Committee held seven meetings over a two year period on the following dates: 21st January 1916; 18th February 1916; 17th March 1916; 3rd May 1916; 22nd November 1916; 11th May 1917; 30th May 1918.

During the first meeting, the Committee resolved:[3]

- that Professor P.F. Frankland and Sir Arthur Schuster (Secretary of the Royal Society) as a Secretary of the Society, had power to deal with straightforward cases brought before the Society
- that Professor P.F. Frankland and Sir Arthur Schuster have power to give immediate assurance to applicants who should appeal directly to the Society in cases in which it is obvious that the Society would not consent to their being enlisted.

The Committee's first interim report provided a table of the numbers of individual cases they examined, Figure 5.2.

	Before November 22, 1916.	Between November 22, 1916, and May 11, 1917	Since May 11, 1917	Total
Applications received	330	103	80	513
Applications refused	94	33	15	142
Exemption recommended under Resolution 2	55	4	1	60
Exemption recommended under Resolution 1	149	32	29	210
Exemption recommended under Resolution 3	32	4	6	42
Cases reviewed	-	30	29	59
Total	330	103	80	513

Figure 5.2. Applications from Research, Analytical and Consulting Chemists dealt with by the Reserved Occupations Committee

It is inappropriate here to discuss the individual cases. Interested readers can view some of the details at the Royal Society's website,[4] and input the relevant reference number.[5]

Sir Arthur Schuster FRS was an interesting scientist. Born in 1851 in Frankfurt am Main, Germany, Sir Arthur would have been 65 when this Committee was formed. Although a resident of St. John's College, Cambridge (1878) he relocated to Yeldall, Twyford, Buckinghamshire (in retirement, Sir Arthur was Professor of Physics at the University of Manchester (1888-1907)). He was President of the British Association (1915) whilst on this Committee and also Secretary of the Royal Society. He was knighted in 1920.

Of course placing someone on the Reserved Occupations list was only part of the overall administration of the process. There were also badges to issue. The Ministry of Munitions handed 145 badges to the Committee, which oversaw their distribution to men working for the Royal Society on tar testing and other projects. As this work drew to a close, some of the badges were returned to the Royal Society and which had to be fully accounted for and the proper procedure followed concerning their return. A register was kept in the Royal Society keeping details such as the names, addresses, badge numbers, ages, etc. of badge holders.

Initially some of the information was held by the institutions undertaking the work, requiring further paperwork to solicit the information. As one might expect there were some lost badges, two in fact.

Some of the Fellows working in Reserved Occupations have already been mentioned. As one might expect there were many Fellows helping with the War effort in other ways, see Figures 5.4-5.7.

Figure 5.3 Sir Arthur Schuster. (© The Royal Society. Reproduced with permission)

Those involved

Those individuals over the military recruitment age were normally left in post so that as much of the civilian infrastructure as possible functioned as best it could. In some cases the Fellows were seconded as either civilians or into the military. Figure 5.4 details some of the Fellows working in non-academic institutes who remained in post. It is not to say that they did not contribute to the war effort, merely that they were deemed to be of value to the effort by remaining in their pre-war posts, perhaps undertaking war-work from their normal occupation. Figure 5.5 details a few of the industrial based Fellows and 5.6 those in academic posts.

There are some Fellows, however, who defy categorisation. Arguably Sir Henry Solomon Wellcome FRS falls into this category. Born in Almond, Wisconsin, USA on the 21st August 1853, Sir Henry spent some of his early years working in his family's pharmacy and for a pharmaceutical firm. Later on in his career, Sir Henry created the Wellcome Foundation and had many business interests including chemicals manufacture and also helped to establish medical research institutes.[6]

At least two Fellows were ordained:

- John Ernest Holloway FRS returned to New Zealand where he was vicar successively of Oxford (1912-15) and Hokitika (1916-1921). His career is described on the Royal Society website as 'Clerk in Holy Orders; lecturer in charge of the Botanical Department, University of Otago (NZ)'[7]. He was also elected FRSNZ (1921)[8]

- Alfred Young FRS was ordained in 1908 and accepted a curacy at Christ Church, Blacklands in Hastings. Part of his Fellowship citation reads:

> ... Distinguished for his researches on Algebra. During the last thirty-three years has published a connected series of extensive memoirs, chiefly in the Proceedings of the London Mathematical Society, on Quantitative Substitutional Analysis, a calculus based on permutational operators, of which he is the chief living discoverer and exponent ...

Clearly an accomplished individual.[9]

Name	Date of birth	Fellows in senior civilian occupations
Allen (Herbert Stanley)	29th December 1873	Honorary Secretary of the Physical Society (1916 to1921)[10]
Barlow (Sir Thomas)	4th Sep 1845	President of the Royal College of Physicians 1910-15[11]
Burne (Richard)	5th April 1868	Physiological Curator of the Department of Comparative Anatomy, Museum of the Royal College of Surgeons[12]
Calman (William Thomas)	29th December 1871	Assistant, First Class, Natural History Museum[13]
Dixon (Henry Horatio)	19th May 1869	Director of the Botanic Garden (1906) and later Keeper of the Herbarium[14]
Dye (David William)	30th December 1887	joined the staff of the National Physical Laboratory (1910)[15]
Dyson (Sir Frank Watson)	8th January 1868	Astronomer Royal[16]
Eddington(Sir Arthur Stanley)	28th December 1882	Director of the Cambridge Observatory (1914)[17]
Evans (Sir Arthur John)	8th July 1851	presided over the Society of Antiquaries (1914-1918) and over the British Association at Newcastle (1914-1919)[18]
Fritsch (Felix Eugene)	26th April 1879	Botanist who in 1914 described the collections of PA Methuen from Madagascar[19]

Name	Date of birth	Fellows in senior civilian occupations
Goodrich (Edwin Stephen)	21th June 1868	Zoological Secretary of the Linnean Society (1915-1923)[20]
Harmer (Sir Sidney)	9th March 1862	Keeper of Zoology in the British Museum (Natural History from 1909)[21]
Jackson (John)	11th February 1887	Chief Assistant, Royal Observatory, Greenwich (from 1914)[22]
Keith (Sir Arthur)	5th February 1866	President of the Royal Anthropological Institute (1914)[23]
Kettle (Edgar Hartley)	20th April 1882	worked in the Pathological Department of St Mary's Hospital[24]
Laidlaw (Sir Patrick Playfair)	26th September 1881	worked in Guy's hospital throughout the War[25]
Newton (Edward Tulley)	4th May 1840	on the staff of the Geological Survey[26]
Plummer (Henry Crozier)	24th October 1875	Andrews Professor of Astronomy in the University of Dublin and Royal Astronomer of Ireland[27]
Prior (George Thurland)	16th December 1862	Keeper of Minerals, British Museum (from 1909)[28]
Regan (Charles Tate)	1st February 1878	worked in the Natural History Museum[29]
Russell (Alexander)	15th July 1861	Principal, Faraday House[30]
Sampson (Ralph Allen)	25th June 1866	President of the Royal Astronomical Society[31]
Seligman (Charles Gabriel)	24th December 1873	President of Section H (Anthropology) of the British Association for the Advancement of Science[32]
Spencer (William Kingdon)	10th December 1878	appointed HMI for Ipswich, East Suffolk and Lowestoft and also Chief Inspector for England and Wales (1914)[33]
Topley (William Whiteman Carlton)	19th January 1886	Director of the Pathological Department of Charing Cross Hospital (1911-1922)[34]

Figure 5.4. Some Fellows in senior civilian occupations

In addition to those mentioned above, at least two Fellows inherited titles during World War I. Randal Thomas Mowbray Rawdon Berkeley FRS was an accomplished scientist who studied osmotic pressure of cane sugar solutions. He became Earl of Berkeley and succeeded to Berkeley Castle and the Berkeley estates in 1916.[35]

Robert John Strutt FRS became 4th Baron Rayleigh[36], and was active in many aspects of World War I, see Chapters 2 and 3. Other Fellows remained in industry in positions vital for the production of essential materials. Figure 5.5 outlines just a few of them.

Name	**Date of birth**	**Industry/position**
Bowen (Norman Levi)	21th June 1887	Moved for a time to the glass plant of the Bausch and Lomb Optical Company.[37]
Forster (Sir Martin Onslow)	8th November 1872	Chairman of the Technical Committee of Read Holliday and Sons (dyestuffs company) from 1915, Director from 1916. He was also a member of the Royal Society Sectional Chemical Committee.[38]
Gilchrist (Percy Carlyle)	27 December 1851	With his better-known cousin Sidney Gilchrist Thomas, developed the Thomas-Gilchrist converter, based on the Bessemer Process for mass-producing steel.[39]
Pyman (Frank Lee)	9th April 1882	Appointed Director of the Wellcome Chemical Research Laboratories at Snow Hill (1914).[40]
Rowe (Frederick Maurice)	11th February 1891	Worked at Messrs Joseph Crosfield and Sons Ltd (soap manufacturers from Warrington). Moved to the Dyestuffs Research Laboratory at the College of Technology in Manchester (1916). Helped to assist the firm of Levinstein Ltd to extend its range of dye manufacture.[41]
Taylor (William)	11th June 1865	Manufacturer of camera lenses and other things for the government.[42]

Name	Date of birth	Industry/position
Twyman (Frank)	17th November 1876	Optical glassmaker. The Managing Director of Chance's Optical Department at the time wrote of Twyman 'owing to the shortage of chemicals, even the standard glasses, which had been produced in this country for years had to be changed, and by such a procedure the annealing range was altered, so that every type of glass produced for War purposes had its annealing temperature determined by Mr Twyman and on the instrument devised by him'.[43]

Figure 5.5. Some Fellows in Industrial Wartime Positions

Undoubtedly the majority of the remaining working Fellows occupied positions in academic establishments. In most cases the names of their respective academic institutes and their positions is documented in their Royal Society biographical memoir. There are a few whose memoir does not record this information. This does not detract from the memoir, it merely makes the inclusion of the following Fellows into Figure 5.6 incomplete. Some of these Fellows are therefore shown here:

- Hector Munro Macdonald FRS – Honorary Fellow of Clare in 1914, a Royal Medallist of the Royal Society in 1916 and Presidency of the London Mathematical Society in 1916-18[44]
- Léon Charles Albert Calmette Foreign Member – during the occupation of Lille, Calmette came under suspicion because he kept pigeons in his laboratory … his wife was removed to Germany as a hostage … Calmette was elected Sub-Director of the Pasteur Institute in 1917, but he did not take up his duties until 1919[45]
- Leonard James Rogers FRS – during his serious illness in 1917, he laid on his back paralysed for months[46]
- Sigmund Otto Rosenheim FRS – wrote a series of communications on the galactosides of the brain culminating in 1916 in a paper in which constitutions were advanced for phrenosin and kerasin which are close to those now accepted[47]
- Sir Arthur George Tansley FRS – botanist and ecologist, founding editor of the Journal of Ecology from 1917[48]
- Sir John Ambrose Fleming FRS – electrical engineer who wrote books on modern developments from 1915 onwards[49]
- Sir William Matthew Flinders Petrie FRS – wrote three books during the War years[50]

The vast majority of the Fellows working in academia do have the relevant details recorded in their biographical memoirs. It would add no purpose here to document all of the Fellows employed in this way, however a selection will be documented below in Figure 5.6.

Name	Date of birth	University/Institute
Bryan (George Hartley)	1st March 1864	In his later years Bryan found the ties with his university duties rather irksome and sought an opportunity for unfettered research. This was provided for him in 1917 with a three year grant devoted to the dynamics of aeroplane motion.[51]
Dixon (Alfred Cardew)	22nd May 1865	Professor of Queen's College (1901-1930), became the University of Belfast in 1908.[52]
Ewart (James Cossar)	26th November 1851	Regius Professorship of Natural History at Edinburgh (1882-1927).[53]
Forsyth (Andrew Russell)	18th June 1858	Chief Professor of Mathematics at Imperial College of Science and Technology (1913-1923).[54]
Hickling (Henry George Albert)	5th April 1883	Controlled the department of Geology at Manchester University.[55]
Jackson (Sir Herbert)	17 March 1863	Daniell Professor of Chemistry at King's College (1914-1918), also worked for the Ministry of Munitions developing glass formulations for thermometers, glass for artificial eyes, vitrite for capping electric lamps, and heat resistant glass comparable to Pyrex.[56]
Joly (John)	1st November 1857	Professor of Geology in Trinity College Dublin (from 1897).[57]
Lees (Charles Herbert)	28th July 1864	Professor of Physics, Queen Mary College the University of London (1912) and Vice-Principal of the College (from 1917).[58]
Marshall (Francis Hugh Adam)	11th July 1878	In 1908 he returned to Cambridge as University Lecturer in Agricultural Physiology … .in 1919 he became Reader in Agricultural Physiology a position he held until his retirement in 1943.[59]

Name	Date of birth	University/Institute
Miers (Sir Henry Alexander)	25th May 1858	Vice-Chancellor of Manchester University (1914- 1926).[60]
Newall (Hugh Frank)	21st June 1857	Admitted to the newly created Chair of Astrophysics in Cambridge (1909) and held the post until 1928 when he retired.[61]
Nicholson (John William)	1st November 1881	Appointed Professor of Mathematics in the University of London, King's College (1912).[62]
Oliver (Francis Wall)	10th May 1864	Became Quain Professor at the early age of twenty six, a position which he retained for thirty-nine years.[63]
Perkin (Arthur George)	13th December 1861	Appointed Professor of Colour Chemistry and Dyeing at the University of Leeds in 1916.[64]
Poulton (Sir Edward Bagnall)	27th January 1856	Elected to the Hope Professorship of Zoology at Oxford in 1893, a post he held for 40 years.[65]
Seward (Sir Albert Charles)	9th October 1863	Master of Downing College, Cambridge.[66]
Smith (Sir Grafton Elliot)	15th August 1871	Chair in Anatomy, Manchester (1909-1919).[67]
Sollas (William Johnson)	30th May 1849	Professor of Geology and Palaeontology at the University of Oxford (from 1897).[68]
Watts (William Whitehead)	7th June 1860	Chairman of the Board of Studies in Geology, Senator and Dean of the Faculty of Science (1913-1919) at the University of London.[69]
Whittaker (Sir Edmund Taylor)	24th October 1873	Professor of Mathematics, University of Edinburgh (1912-1946).[70]
Wynne (William Palmer)	13th February 1861	Professor of Chemistry at the University College (1904-1931).[71]

Figure 5.6. Some Fellows in Academic posts during World War I

A relatively few number of Fellows found themselves abroad working on projects started before the War. Some moved abroad either before or during the War. There is a category of Fellowship specifically for those born overseas, that of Foreign Member. Mention has already been made of some. Figure 5.7 documents just a few of the many Fellows caught up in the War in other countries.

Name	Date of birth	Worked abroad during WWI
Babkin (Boris Petrovitch)	17th January 1877	Professor of Physiology in the University of Odessa (1915-1922).[72]
Barnes (Howard Turner)	21st July 1873	Macdonald Professor of Physics and Director of the Laboratory of McGill University (Montreal, Canada).[73]
Benham (Sir William Blaxland)	29th March 1860	Professor of Biology and Curator of the Museum at the University of Otago, Dunedin, New Zealand.[74]
Butler (Sir Edwin John)	13th August 1874	Imperial Mycologist in India.[75]
Cartan (Elie Joseph)	9th April 1869	Professor in the Faculté des Science.[76]
Du Toit (Alexander Logie)	14th March 1878	Du Toit was seconded to the Defence Force (South Africa) where he drilled for water sources in the Kalahari.[77]
Fields (John Charles)	14th May 1863	Professor in the Department of Mathematics at the University of Toronto (from 1914).[78]
Matthew (William Diller)	19th February 1871	Department of Vertebrate Palaeontology in the American Museum of Natural History in New York (1895-1927).[79]
Perkins (Robert Cyril Layton)	15th November 1866	Consultant entomologist to The Hawaiian Sugar Planter's Association (from 1912).[80]
Plaskett (John Stanley)	17th November 1865	First Director of the Dominion Astrophysical Observatory in Victoria, Canada (1917) having spent the three previous years involved with its construction.[81]
Roux (Pièrre Paul Émile)	17th December 1853	Director of the Pasteur Institute (1904 - 1933).[82]
Sommerfeld (Arnold Johannes Wilhelm)	5th December 1868	Professor of Theoretical Physics in Munich (from 1906).[83]
Stephenson (John)	6th February 1871	Principal of Government College in India (1912-1919).[84]
Willis (John Christopher)	20th February 1868	Director of the Botanic Garden in Rio de Janeiro (1912-1915) then retired.[85]

Name	Date of birth	Worked abroad during WWI
Wood (Robert Williams)	2th May 1868	Full Professor of Experimental Physics at Johns Hopkins University (1901-1955).[86]
Young (William Henry)	20th October 1863	First Hardinge Professor of Mathematics in Calcutta and first Professor of the Philosophy and History of Mathematics in Liverpool. He lectured in Calcutta in the winter months and Liverpool in the summer.[87]

Figure 5.7 Some Foreign Members and Fellows living abroad

Some Fellows had either retired before the outbreak of War, or during it. For example:

William Cawthorne Unwin FRS was born in Coggeshall, Essex, on 12th December 1838. An engineer, Unwin was involved in harnessing the water power from Niagra Falls. He was[88]:

- Professor of Hydraulic Engineering, Royal Indian Engineering College, Cooper's Hill, Egham (1872-1885)
- Professor of Engineering, Central Institute, City and Guilds of London (1884-1904)
- President, Engineering section, British Association

Unwin retired in 1904 and died in Kensington, London on 17th March 1933.

William Mitchinson Hicks FRS was born in Launceston, Cornwall on 23 September 1850. He was:[89]

- Professor of Physics and Mathematics, Firth College, Sheffield (1883-1892)
- Principal of Firth College, Sheffield (1892-1897)
- Professor of Physics, University of Sheffield (1892-1917)
- Principal of University College, Sheffield (1897-1905)
- First Vice Chancellor, University of Sheffield (1905)
- Fellow of St John's College, Cambridge

Hicks retired from the Chair of Physics at Sheffield in 1917 and died on 17th August 1934.

Victor Herbert Veley FRS was born on 10 February 1856. A chemist by training, Veley was too old for War service and so joined the Marylebone Borough Council and helped to keep the organisation going, particularly his involvement in the finances. Veley died on 20th August 1933.[90]

6 Enemy detection / Allied concealment

Wars are fought on many fronts. Some fronts are physical locations such as trenches, others rely on technological improvements. World War I was unusual in that aeroplanes, submarines, tanks and wireless telegraphy/radio were all in their infancy. There were issues to resolve in range-finding both submarines and aircraft from many perspectives not least the need of the armaments community.

One of the first issues to be addressed was that of intelligence gathering from German radio signals. Sir Winston Churchill FRS recognised the need for a unit dedicated to understand the implications of decoded interceptions in a letter dated 8th November 1914. Stored in the National Archives[1], Sir Winston's letter is reproduced below:

> C.O.S.
>
> An officer of the War Staff, preferably from the I.D. should be selected to study all the decoded interceptions, not only current but past and to compare them continually with what actually took place in order to penetrate the German mind re movements and make reports. All these intercepts are to be written in a locked book with their decodes and all the other copies are to be collected and burnt. All new messages are to be entered into the book and the book is only to be handled under direction from C.O.S. The officer selected is for the present to do no other work. I shall be obliged if Sir Alfred Ewing FRS will associate himself continuously with the work.
>
> W.S.C.
>
> 8.11.14

Who was Sir Alfred Ewing FRS and what did he do during the War?

Room 40

Most of Sir Alfred's work and that of his unit were kept secret for many years after World War I was over. As far as can be determined Lord Balfour was the first to mention the existence of 'Room 40' in a speech he made some time in 1927. Lord Balfour's speech mentioned Sir Alfred Ewing FRS, following which Sir Alfred was invited to the Edinburgh Philosophical Institution to describe some of his work.

Unable to attend Sir Alfred's talk, Lord Balfour wrote the following letter on 1st December 1927.[2]

C.E. 56320/51

Copy of lecture to the Edinburgh Philosophical Institution, December 13th, 1927 entitled "SOME SPECIAL WAR-WORK" by the late Sir James Alfred Ewing.

The following letter from the Earl of Balfour to the Secretary of the Institution was read by the Chairman, the Hon. Lord Sands:-

----

4 Carlton Gardens, S.W. 1.
December 1st, 1927
Dear Mr. Miller,

I had promised myself the pleasure of being present to hear Sir James Alfred Ewing's address to the Edinburgh Philosophical Institution; but alas, I shall be kept in London over Parliamentary business for at least a week after the date of his lecture.

It would have given me very peculiar satisfaction to hear his account of the work in which he took the principal part during the critical period when I was at the Admiralty. To 'Room 40' where he was the leading spirit, the country owes an immense debt of gratitude – a debt which – at the time at least, could never be paid. Secrecy was of the very essence of the work, and never was secrecy more successfully observed. I deeply regret that I cannot be present on 13th, when the veil will be partially removed from the labours in which your distinguished lecturer took so important a part.

Yours sincerely,
(Signed) BALFOUR.

A copy of Sir Alfred's speech still exists. His wife, Lady Ewing, wrote the following letter to an unknown recipient.[3]

9, ADAMS ROAD,
CAMBRIDGE
TEL: 3890
Dear Sir;

I am venturing to approach you with a request for advice on the chance that you will be able and willing to give it.

It concerns my husband – the late Sir James Alfred Ewing FRS who was Director of Naval Education at the outbreak of the First World War and undertook, as his special war-work, the task of dealing with intercepted wireless

Figure 6.1. Sir James Alfred Ewing FRS. (© The Royal Society. Reproduced with permission)

messages from the Enemy. It came to be known as 'Room 40' of which you may have heard and of which there is no need for me to write now. The object of this letter is to tell you of what happened after the late Lord Balfour had publicly acclaimed my husband as the originator and guide of the organisation which had grown into an important and very secret concern. My husband maintained this secrecy absolutely till after Lord Balfour's speech and after various friends had urged him to divulge the true facts and so refute misrepresentations of him and his work that were being made. He therefore gave a lecture on some parts of 'Room 40', entitled 'Some Special war-work', to the Edinburgh Philosophical Institution on December 13th, 1927.

I have the typescript of this lecture by me, and it seems to me that it still contains that which may be very interesting and even useful to certain workers in the Admiralty. If you think this might be so, could you advise me to whom I should offer the typescript for, perhaps perusal only? I should be grateful for any pronouncement from you.

I am
yours faithfully
Ellen L. Ewing (signed)

The full transcript of Sir Alfred's talk appears as Appendix V.

Sir Alfred was born on 27th March 1855 in Dundee, Scotland, Figure 6.1. He was:[4]

Figure 6.2. The entranceway to the 'Room 40' building. (Author's photograph)

- Professor of Mechanical Engineering, University of Tokyo, Japan (1878-1883)
- Professor of Engineering, University College, Dublin (1883-1890)
- Professor of Mechanism and Applied Mechanics, University of Cambridge (1890-1903)
- Principal and Vice-Chancellor, University of Edinburgh (1916)

Sir Alfred's talk mentions little of the location of 'Room 40' or of the rest of the workers. Some surviving documents in the National Archives mention the building which housed the unit, which surprisingly was in London. It is still in use and located close to most of the other Central Government buildings. Figure 6.2 is a modern picture of the entrance to the building. The author was only allowed to take one picture by the security staff, who was concerned that too many photographs might compromise security. For that reason the exact location will not be provided here.

The National Archives document some of the names of those involved. The following may not be a true reflection of the number at any one time as there may have been some personnel movement, Figure 6.3.[5]

Adcock	W. H. Anstie	M. Ball
M. Bayley	Bickersteth	Birch
E.J. Bolton	D. Bond	H. Boulton

H.R. Bowlby	E. Bullough	A.M. Burton
C.S. Somers Cocks	A.G. Denniston	D.M. Denniston
Victoria Thornton Down	G.H. Dummett	H.R. Ford
G.H. Fowler	Fraser	Dr. Chas Gough
De Grey	Green	E.M. Gunning
C.W. Hardisty	Jean M. Harvey	L.C. Henderson
Herschell	Hippesley	J.B. Henderson
Dorothy A. Holcroft	J. Hooper	G.L.N. Hope
Philippa Hope	V.N.E. Howard-Vincent	J.H. Inskip
May E Jenkin	R.P. Keigwin	Knox
Leslie Lambert	Gerald Lawrence	H. Lawrence
D.H. Loch	Lord Lytton	G.P. Mackeson
Molyneux	Lord Monkbretton	W. Montgomery
H.A. Morrah	E. Nickerson	Norton
Dorothy O'Connor	R.N. Page	Capt. R. Orr Paterson
B.S. Faudel Phillips	Sybil M Pugh	G.S. Rawson
Miss Reeks	Olive Roddam	C.J.E. Rotter
Francis E Sandbach (Birmingham University)		Esme Winthrop Smith
F.S. Le Blanc Smith	Bettine M Spier	Talbot
J.F. Toye	E.M. Tribe	Gilbert Waterhouse
Willoughby	L. Wix	G.S. Woods

Figure 6.3. Some members of 'Room 40'

By modern standards their work might seem dated, yet in its day these individuals used cutting edge techniques to decipher many transcripts.

The above list of names has been compiled from several documents one of which relates to the salaries paid to some individuals. Interestingly, even in this most secret department the information was compartmentalised. There were probably few people who were aware of the extent of the overall operation. For example, a letter from W. Graham Greene to Sir Alfred Ewing dated 28th September 1916 suggests a further activity, the rest of the documents for which are not stored in the same location in the National Archives – if they exist at all![6]

Sir Alfred Ewing,

I am to acquaint you that their Lordships have approved your proposal that Mr. George Young M.V.O. should be definitely recognised as supervising, under you, the branch of your special work dealt with in Room 47 Old Building, together with the Ladies Section.

2.- The work of this Section should, as in the case of Room 40, be kept in touch with the Intelligence and Operations Divisions of the War Staff, and the Director of Intelligence Division is to be consulted with regard to it in the same manner as hitherto. The Intelligence Division is to continue to be the connecting link between this Section and the Foreign Office.

3.- The question of some additional remuneration to Mr. Young is deferred for the present.

By Command of their Lordships

(Sd) W. Graham Greene.

Setting aside the organisational structure of Room 40, there were thousands of intercepts which were decoded. One of which appears below.[7]

L.W. February 24th 1pm 1917

Balfour handed me this translation of a cipher message from Zimmermann, the German Secretary of State for Foreign Affairs, to a German Minister in Mexico, which was sent via Washington and relayed by Bernstorff on January 19th.

You can probably obtain a copy of the text relayed by Bernstorff from the cable office in Washington. The first group is the number of the telegram, 140, and the second is 13042, indicating the number of the code used. The last bit is 97556, which is Zimmermann's signature.

I shall send you by mail a copy of the cipher text and of the decode into German, and meanwhile I can give you the English translation as follows:

> ... we intend to begin on the 1st February unrestricted warfare. We shall endeavour in spite of this to keep the United States neutral. In the event of this not succeeding we make Mexico a proposal of alliance on the following basis:
>
> We make war together – make peace together. Generous financial support and an understanding on our part that Mexico is to reconquer the lost territory in Texas, New Mexico and Arizona. The settlement in detail is left to you.
>
> You will inform the President of the above most secretly as soon as the outbreak of War with the United States is certain and add the suggestion that he should on his own invitation invite Japan to immediate adherence and at the same time mediate between Japan and ourselves.
>
> Please call the President's attention to the fact that the ruthless employment of our submarines offers the prospect of compelling England in a few months to make peace.
>
> Signed
>
> Zimmermann.

The receipt of this information has so greatly exercised the British Government that they have lost no time in communicating it to me to transmit to you in order that you may be able, without delay, to make such dispositions as may be necessary in view of the threatened invasion of our territory.

(The following paragraph is strictly confidential)

Early in the War the British Government obtained possession of a copy of the German cipher code used in the above message and have made it their business to obtain copies of Bernstorff's cipher message to Mexico, amongst others, which are sent back to London and deciphered here. This accounts for their being able to decipher this message from the German Government to their representative in Mexico and also for the delay from January 19th until now in their receiving the information.

This system has hitherto been a jealously guarded secret and is only divulged now to you by the British Government in view of the circumstances and their friendly feelings towards the United States. They earnestly request that you will keep the source of your information, and the British Government's method of obtaining it, profoundly secret, but they put no prohibition on the publication of Zimmermann's telegram itself.

The copies of this, and other telegrams, were not obtained in Washington but were bought in Mexico. I have thanked Balfour for the service his Government has rendered to us and suggest that a private official message of thanks from our Government to him would be appreciated.

I am informed that this information has not yet been given to the Japanese government but I think it not unlikely that, when it reaches them, they will make a public statement on it in order to clear up their position regarding America and prove their good faith to their Allies …

Enemy detection

It is doubtful that information from Room 40 was passed on to more than a handful of individuals. However, there would have been increased urgency placed on all those active in protecting our shores, particularly the military. Arguably Lord Fisher and Sir Winston Churchill knew of the heightened threat of submarines. Fortunately, some years earlier, Fisher launched the Admiralty Board of Invention and Research. He would undoubtedly have pushed the scientist in the BIR to deliver technology able to neutralise the threat.

It will add no value here to reproduce all of the reports produced from the anti-submarine section of the BIR. It might be instructive to look at one report in detail and some of the highlights of the work reported by Sir William Bragg FRS in his capacity of Head of the Hawkcraig Research Station mentioned in Section II of the BIR (see Appendix II for further details). Figure 6.4 details the dates and locations of the reports written by Bragg as Resident Director of Research[8], initially at Hawkcraig, although Bragg did move to other experimental stations when needed.

Location	Date
Hawkcraig	15th May 1916
Hawkcraig	27th June 1916
Hawkcraig	22nd August 1916
Hawkcraig	24th November 1916
Hawkcraig	6th January 1917
Harwich	25th March 1917
Harwich	30th April 1917
Parkerston Quay	1st May to 30th September 1917
Harwich	19th November 1917

Figure 6.4. Dates and locations of reports written by Sir William Bragg

These reports document an outline of the work of the research establishments which had many scientists working in them. Some were also Fellows of the Royal Society, such as Paul Langevin FRS; other scientists were equally successful, but were never elected Fellow. Perhaps the most well known non-Fellow scientist was R.W. Boyle who invented a form of quartz transducer in 1917 which was the prototype of the ASDIC, previously mentioned in Chapter 3 (see Board of Invention and Research Document 38164/17).

The first report mentioned in Figure 6.4 opens with the phrase:

> ...I have to report that on the day of my appointment as Resident Director at Hawkcraig Experimental Station I was actually on a visit to the Station, but was obliged to return to London to fulfil some public engagements. I returned to Hawkcraig on May 8th ...

Sir William goes on to outline work on:

- direction finders
- photophones
- sound shadows

Surprisingly, Sir William's 27th June report outlines some work undertaken in London.

> ... a special form of direction-finding apparatus, designed by Professor A.W. Porter FRS of University College, has been made and tested by him in Regent's Park, with the help of Mr. Young. It consists of a set of Broca tubes or magnetophones arranged in series and regularly spaced. Its action is supposed to be the inverse of that of an optical diffraction grating, and to give a sharp directional maximum.

Some success has been obtained, but trials are not complete. If an instrument can be found to give a sharp maximum, it will have advantages over the 'converted drifter' set, because the latter gives the sharpest definition at the minimum sound. It is feared, however, that Professor Porter's apparatus will be cumbrous ...

A photophone was a device for transmitting speech by means of a beam of light. Alexander Oliver Rankine FRS designed one which was extensively tested. A comment in his biography reads:

... he was assistant in the Department of Physics in University College from 1904 – 1919, except for a period of War service from 1917-1918. He worked under W.H. Bragg (later Sir William Bragg) first at Aberdour on the Firth of Forth, then at Harwich as Deputy Resident Director under Professor (then Colonel) AS Eve, and finally as Director of a new station at Dartmouth, or rather Kingswater ... he also worked on acoustic and electromagnetic means of submarine detection. For his work in the War he received the OBE ... 9

Despite Professor Bragg's comment, this report does indicate that progress was being made. By 19th November 1917 there was progress on all of the technologies:

SECRET.
This paper is the property of
H.M. Government and is subject to the
provisions of the Official Secrets Act.
BOARD OF INVENTION AND RESEARCH.
Victory House,
Cockspur Street, S.W.1.
B.I.R. 38581/17.
Report of the Resident Director of Research at Harwich, November 19th, 1917.

Portable Hydrophones

The successful use of the xylonite baffle plate has considerably increased the rate of production of the Mark 1. P.D.H., which may now be considered fairly satisfactory. For some weeks the issue of tested instruments has amounted to about 70 in each week. The xylonite baffles are much more reliable and reproducible than the wood-lead baffles formerly used. A number are being supplied to A.S.D. for use in the Nash 'fish'.

At various times comparative tests have been made of the various directional instruments now in use, the American C Tube, the Perrin Trumpet, and the Mark 1. and Mark 11. designs. The sensitiveness is found to be of the same order in all four. The C Tube being somewhat less sensitive than the others, and the Trumpet rather more. The sense of direction is good enough in all of them, the Perrin Trumpet being reported to be the least effective in this respect. Mark 11. is the only one that has an ambiguity in direction, the other three being unidirectional. The C Tube is specially simple in its absence of electrical gear, and generally is distinguished for its simplicity of construction; on the other hand, no amplifying principle can be used. It has been pointed out that special precautions may be necessary to prevent injury to the ears from underwater explosions, but possibly the objection may be overcome. Mark 1. is perhaps the handiest of the four instruments.

Marine Sound Ranging

Some very interesting trials have been completed at Culver on the use of sound ranging methods for the purpose of enabling defence batteries to reply effectively to enemy ships firing under shelter of a smoke screen. It had been thought that the hydrophone could be used to good advantage for the receipt of concussions due to the explosion of a shell on striking the water, and so could give the location of the impact.

This could be proved to be quite correct; no doubt the principle could be used to find where any shell fired from shore out to sea lands on the water, at any rate if it explodes. But the full application of the principle would require that the enemy ship should also be located through a concussion wave starting from the ship when it fired and eventually reaching the hydrophones. This effect was found to be too feeble to make use of, as has indeed been thought probable. Simultaneously with the underwater experiments, trials were made with an ordinary sound ranging apparatus in order to test the capacity of air-borne sound to attain the object desired. It was found that both the explosion of enemy gun and of a defence shell could probably be heard at the full distance required, though the number of shots available was too small to test the effects of wind and weather. It may be pointed out that the latter are likely to be greater hindrances to accurate work than any disturbing effects found in the water. But, as already said, the water method fails to hear the concussion of the enemy gun.

The general conclusion is that ordinary sound ranging methods should be tried; and a report has been sent in to the military authorities recommending that this should be done at once, in a single instance and on a full scale.

As regards the application of sound ranging methods to the location of underwater explosions, it has been decided by the Admiralty that two full-sized stations should be set up at once, one near Flamborough and the other near Aberdeen. The designs are now under way.

Submarine Feeler

The 'feeler' has made considerable progress, and fortunately in the direction of an increase in simplicity. The towed apparatus has been reduced until it consists now of two insulated cables of different lengths without floats or attachment of any kind, except a certain amount of braided metallic covering which is mounted on the end of each cable and put into electric communication with the core. The inboard ends of the cables are connected to an amplifier; the output end of the latter is joined up to a telephone in the usual way.

It is found that these cables will stand the strain of being towed at any speed up to 25 knots at least, the electrodes keep well in the water. No sound is heard from the towing boat, provided that the cables are kept close together on the ship and over the side. It is advisable that the two bare ends of the cables should be 50 to 100 yards apart. With this arrangement a submarine can be heard when under way at distances of up to 400 yards, depending on the excellence of the amplifier and on the amount of noise emitted by the submarine, which varies considerably from boat to boat.

The hearing is equally good at all speeds of towing, so far as is known, and there is no need for the towing vessel to stop her engines while listening.

It is most likely that the same method can be used from airships, since the trailing part of the apparatus is so very light.

It may also prove convenient to use the 'feelers' for a simpler system of signalling, based on the leakage current system which has been investigated at this station.

Loop Detectors

The method of observing the passage of ships by the currents induced in a coil lying at the bottom of the sea has also made great progress during the last few weeks. The first trials of this method were made in 1915 by Professor Crichton-Mitchell for the Royal Society of Edinburgh, but were discontinued as no use could be found for it at the time.

The method is now applicable in two ways. In the first it can be used as a means of deciding the right moment to fire a group of observation mines. Coils have been specially laid at the mouth of Harwich harbour for this purpose by Captain Fraser, and full records have been kept of the observations made, the whole forming a highly instructive series. The most convenient instrument for recording the currents is found to be a fluxmeter, because it follows exactly the movement of the vessel under observation. When the vessel under observation has passed wholly or partly across the loop, and has thus made a definite change in the magnetic induction through the loop, either because of its own permanent magnetism or the magnetism which is induced in the ship by the earth, the fluxmeter records the amount of the change which has occurred, and keeps registering that amount if the vessel remains stationary, any further movement of the vessel causing a corresponding movement of the needle. This makes the apparatus most convenient to the use of the observer. Moreover, the system is independent of weather conditions, unlike the magnetophone system in use hitherto, and is also to be preferred on account of the exactness of its indications and its clear definition of the location of the passing vessel.

The application of the method to deeper waters than those of Harwich may introduce difficulties not felt as yet, but as far as can be anticipated there will be no real difficulty in overcoming them.

The second way in which the principle of the loop can be put into immediate use is in connection with the observations of the passage of shipping through a channel even of considerable width, the method being able to furnish indications of the type of vessel, its speed, course and position, and under certain circumstances to do this very accurately. For this purpose it is convenient to register photographically the current fluctuations due to each passing vessel. This has been regularly carried out at the harbour mouth with very interesting results. Each vessel gives its own characteristic curve, and indications are given also which, in the hands of a practised observer, will lead to the acquirement of quite a fund of information. For the purpose mentioned, it is also required that more than one loop should be paid. Preliminary tests of this system are to be made on the Clyde, and the necessary preparations are well in hand.

Towed Listening Apparatus

Much work has been done on the design of a small towing body able to travel at some speed and at the same time to carry microphones, the latter to give direction if possible, whether by phase difference or otherwise. Distinct advances have been made, but the results are not yet sufficient or successful enough to describe generally.

Underwater Vision

The collection of bubbles on a glass plate inserted in the bottom of a vessel was referred to B.I.R. by Commodore Heneage, who had found it a source of trouble. Experiments here showed that as long as the glass was flush with the bottom of the vessel, the bubbles did not collect.

Thermal Detection of Submarines

Investigation has been made of the possibility of detecting the passage of a vessel such as a submarine by means of temperature changes in the water, such as would be caused by the mixing of layers of water of unequal temperature. Suitable electrical resistance thermometers were constructed, capable of registering a minute fraction of a degree; but the method proved abortive because it was found that the temperature of the water was singularly independent of depth. Since the opposite is notoriously a feature of the Mediterranean waters, the apparatus has been sent to the French for trial at Toulon.

Periscope Signalling Device

A system of signalling from a submarine showing only a portion of its periscope, by means of a beam of light transmitted through the latter, has been worked out at the suggestion of an officer attached to the submarine flotilla. It is found that signals can be conveniently made in broad daylight at 1,500 yards without glasses.

Supersonic Vibrations

Dr. Boyle has continued his work on supersonic vibrations, to which added interest has been given in consequence of the remarkable increase in the power of the supersonic beams, which has been attained by the original observers at Toulon.

W. H. BRAGG,
Resident Director of Research.
Admiralty Experimental Station,
Parkeston Quay, Harwich.

This somewhat lengthy report has been produced in full in order to demonstrate just how much progress this unit made. Not only is there a discussion of the various types of portable hydrophones, but also of the different versions, implying that there was an introduction earlier on in the year which was improved and implemented – progress indeed. There is also a discussion of other instruments, all adding to the ability to detect submarines.

The scientists working on aircraft detection had one advantage over their counterparts working on submarines. Enemy aircraft that were shot down were not always destroyed, some of the instrumentation was recovered from the wrecks. There is a comment on page 26 in the *Report of Proceedings of the Board of Invention and Research to 31st December 1916*.[10] It states:

> … Airship Instruments – at the request of the Admiralty various instruments recovered from wrecked enemy airships were repaired and reconstructed by Mr. W Duddell FRS, who forwarded a most valuable report and drawings of the individual instruments concerned …

William Duddell FRS was an interesting scientist. Born on 1st July 1872, Duddell was a Whitworth Scholar and a consulting electrical engineer. He was elected to Fellowship on 2nd May 1907 aged 35, a very young age for this. He received gold medals at the Paris (1900) and the St Louis Exhibitions, went on to win the Hughes Medal 1912. Sadly Duddell died on 4th November 1917 and was awarded a posthumous CBE later in the year. Although he died at a very young age he was active in many aspects of the war effort and is mentioned in various earlier Chapters.

The BIR report mentioned above also comments on aeroplane photography (page 26):

... at the request of the Admiralty the Board undertook to investigate improvements in apparatus for photography from aircraft, and a special Sub-Committee was formed for the purpose. This Sub-Committee have forwarded a new type of plate-changing box which has been adopted. They have also obtained five types of camera for various purposes, which have been generally successful, and will be adopted in most cases. Great assistance in this matter has been given by the French Inventions Department ...

The report goes on (page 27):

Anti-aircraft work – during the latter part of 1915, before the transfer of London anti-aircraft defences to the Military authorities, the Board carried out a series of experiments at the Gun Station in Green Park with various instruments designed by the Board. These instruments comprised range-finders, spotting instruments, sight attachments, sub-target practice devices etc. etc. and results obtained were of value.

Exciting sparks in Hostile Airships – trials were carried out by Sir Oliver Lodge FRS with a view to exciting sparks in hostile airships by means of Herts vibrators, but were unsuccessful.

Explosive and Incendiary Bullets early in the year 1916 a considerable number of experiments were carried out with incendiary projectiles for anti-aircraft work, and very promising results were obtained, but the work ceased on the transfer of the London anti-aircraft defences to the Military authorities.

As the flying services now require an incendiary shrapnel, it is probable that this work will not be wasted ...

... Analysis of metals used in Construction of Hostile Airships – various metals recovered from wrecked hostile airships have been analysed by Sir Henry Carpenter FRS, and reports forwarded to the Admiralty ...

Sir Henry Carpenter was the Professor of Metallurgy in the Imperial College of Science and Technology, South Kensington. His citation for election to the Royal Society included the following:[11]

... Distinguished for his researches in Metallurgy and more especially for his work on High-Speed Tool Steel, Iron, Carbon, and Copper Alloys. Ex-Investigator to the Alloys Research Committee, and one of the founders of the Institute of Metals. Member of the Board of Invention and Research. Member of Sub-

Committee on the Erosion of Propellers, the cause of which was definitely ascertained. In July, 1915, dealt with a problem for the Government in connexion with cartridge metal arising out of shortage of zinc. Chairman of the Corrosion Research Committee on Condenser Tubes. Chairman of a Committee on the Corrosion of Aeroplane Parts under the Air Board ...

Of course there were other Fellows who had experience of metals. Sir Horace Darwin FRS was a scientific instrument maker, who co-invented the Darwin-Hill Mirror Position Finder, an instrument to record the flight of aeroplanes.[12] A son of Charles Darwin FRS, Sir Horace bought a partnership in the Cambridge Instrument Company when it formed in 1878. Sir Charles became its chief shareholder when it became a limited company in 1880. The Science Museum in South Kensington holds a mirror from a Darwin Hill Position Finder. It is described as a balloon tracking mirror, made of metal, brass and glass measuring 12 x 79 x 79 cm and is object 1919-269 in their catalogue.[13]

Sir Ralph's Obituary Notice (footnote 11) also mentions some of the membership of the Anti-Aircraft Experimental Section of the MID (specifically page 66) as being:

G.T. Bennett FRS, T.L. Wren, R.A. Herman, C.E. Haselfoot, C.W. Hartree, J.G. Crowther, W.E.H. Berwick, D.R. Dean Pollard and C. Mayes. Geoffrey Thomas Bennett was a Fellow and Lecturer of Emmanuel College, Cambridge and a distinguished mathematician. Little is known of the other mentioned scientists. Appendix VI lists some of their work.

The National Archives has produced a PDF file in which is listed

a miscellaneous collection of reports from the MID's Anti-Aircraft Experimental Section (at Rochford and at Orfordness) and Acoustical Research Station (at Imber Court) re sound location and allied subjects, complemented by material compiled later by Science Museum staff relating to echo-sounding, sound ranging, hydrophones, etc.[14]

Figure 6.5 lists some of the titles of these reports showing the breadth of the research.

Report number	Date	Title
/7	1917 January 15	207. Tests of accuracy of sound-locating trumpets on moving aircraft. Preliminary report. 20p.
/8	1918 February 18	220. Direction of searchlights to aeroplanes by means of sound-locating trumpets. 5p. + 4p.

Report number	Date	Title
/8a	1918 February 24	Report A/82 on value of a tetrahedral prism for indicating to a searchlight whether a machine it has picked up is hostile or friendly / Capt. F.W. Musson, O. i/c No. 1 Section, Major B.M. Jones, Chief Experimental Officer, Lt. Col. A.C. Boddam-Whetham O.C. A.E.S., Royal Flying Corps. 2p.
/12	1918 January	206. Sound locating apparatus used for position plotting and height finding. 3p.
/13	1918 March 15	232. G.T. Bennett FRS plane acoustic height and position finder / C. Jakeman. 4p.
/15	1918 August	Experiments made to determine suitable sound detection means for faint sounds / 'by Sgt. Major Maxwell'. 5p.
/16	1918 September 25	Notes on the proportions of trumpets for sound locators / C. Jakeman. [Bears ms. name 'Lt, MacAlister'] 5p.
/17	1918 September 25	Notes on Professor Stewart's paper on the use of long trumpets / C. Jakeman [Bears ms. name 'Lt. MacAlister'] 3p.
/37	-	230. Summary of a report on a pair of Darwin listening trumpets by Admiral Sir Henry Jackson FRS 3p.
/38	1916 September 4	M.I.D., Princes St., Westminster. The Hartree height-finder (patent). 8p. + blueprint
/48	1907 November	401. Sound location / Lord Rayleigh FRS, [from] New Quarterly, No.1, 3-16. [Ts. transcription circulated by Major A.V. Hill, Director A.A.E.S. on 3 January 1919] 14p.
/49	1920 March	The theory of receivers for sound in water / H.A. Wilson, [from] Physical Review, XV, 178-205
/50	1922 February	Sound-ranging / E. Lancaster Jones, [from] Proceedings of the Musical Association, 77-79

Figure 6.5. Some report titles for anti-aircraft research

The Royal Society lists a physicist Harold Albert Wilson (1874 – 1964) amongst its Fellowship, who was a lecturer in Physics at King's College, London and a Fellow of Trinity College, Cambridge. Unfortunately there is no information to associate this Fellow with the author of the report on the theory of receivers for sound in water.

In addition to the work at the various government research establishments, there were also sound ranging tests undertaken at the Front. Harold Roper Robinson FRS was involved in such an activity.[15] Robinson obtained a commission as a Second Lieutenant in the Royal Garrison Artillery and in August 1915 went to France where he measured the location of the German guns by measuring the relative time it took for the sound from enemy artillery to arrive at various fixed positions. He was promoted Captain and acted as Adjutant of the 1st Field Survey Battalion, RE to which he had been attached while sound ranging.

Various units and individuals worked on sound direction. Born in Lille, France on 30 September 1870, Jean Baptiste Perrin was elected a Foreign Member in 1918. During the War he was an officer in the engineer corps during which he devised a method and constructed an apparatus for determining the direction of the sound from an aeroplane. He was later awarded the Nobel Prize for Physics (1926).[16,17]

Allied Concealment

Arguably most of the work concerning Allied concealment during this War related to the development of smoke screens of various types. On page 26 of the 'Report of proceedings of the Board of Invention and Research to 31st December 1916' the summary statement concerning smoke screens is interesting:[18]

> Smoke screen and surface smoke – at the request of the Admiralty various experiments have been made in the production of smoke for screening fleet advances, retirements from submarines and for the detection of submarines passing through nets. As a result of these experiments, phosphorous filled shells, suggested by Sir Richard Threlfall FRS, are being supplied in quantity to the fleet. Phosphorous smoke pots, Brock smoke pots, and sulphur-chloride and ammonia apparatus are also being supplied in quantity. Trials of smoke apparatus for detecting submarines are proceeding …

Arguably, Thomas Slater Price FRS made a significant contribution to the Zeebrugge Raid. His Royal Society Obituary Notice states the following:[19]

> … Slater Price was first allocated to superintend in his own laboratories the large scale preparation of various organic chemicals to be used later in the manufacture of drugs, but in 1916 he was given the commission of Lieutenant in the Royal Naval Volunteer Reserves in order to take up special work of a secret nature at the Royal Naval Experimental Station at Stratford. Later, when this work

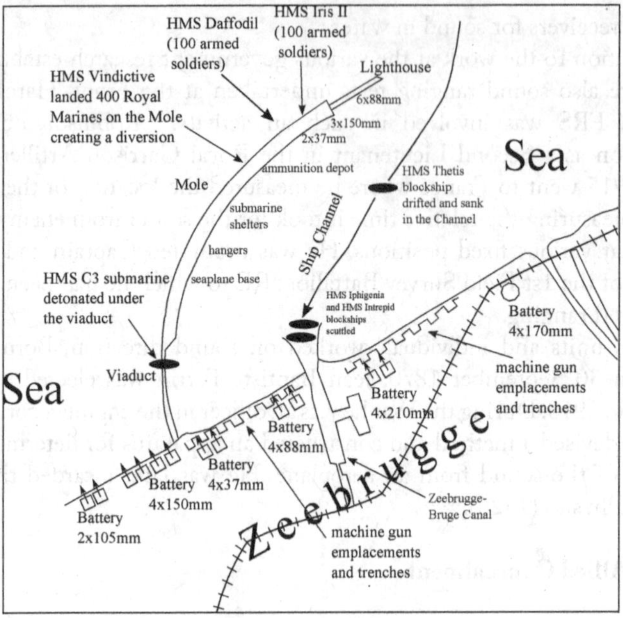

Figure 6.6. The Zeebrugge Raid. (Author)

> expanded – the number of naval ratings at the station rose finally to about 1,000, most of them science graduates – he was put in charge of a great variety of chemical and technical problems and promoted to the rank of Lieutenant-Commander … among the many topics of investigation … was the design and filling of suitable apparatus for the formation of smoke screens at sea, and Slater Price was responsible for the supply of material employed with great success in the raid on Zeebrugge, where the production of the smoke screen under cover of which the attack was made was entrusted to selected ratings of the Royal Naval Experimental Station who had undergone special training at Dover …

The Zeebrugge Raid took place over the 23rd and 24th of April 1918. The basic idea was to sink 'blockships' in strategic places in Zeebrugge harbour thereby preventing the Canal being used as a safe haven by German ships. Figure 6.6 outlines the plan.

Bruges was some fourteen miles inland and used by German U-boats and Torpedo boats as a harbour, accessed via the Zeebrugge Canal. The destruction of the jetty was to involve ramming an old 'C' class submarine loaded with six tons of explosives into the viaduct, thereby isolating the jetty, whilst also sinking HMS Thetis, Iphigenia and Intepid in strategic places. The drawback to the plan was the size of the German defences. Cover of darkness was not sufficient to protect the troops, hence the need for smoke deployed by the specially trained ratings.

Born on the 4th October 1872 at Tundiani Fort, India, Admiral Roger George Bowlby Keyes planned and directed the Zeebrugge Raid. Keyes was made a baronet after the Armistice, and later elevated to the peerage (1943) as the 1st Baron Keyes of Zeebrugge, and of Dover, in the county of Kent, and a Baronet.[20] Eleven Victoria Crosses were also awarded.

Unfortunately, the Germans, made a new channel round the two ships, and within two days their submarines were able to transit Zeebrugge. Destroyers were able to do so by mid-May.

7 Munitions / Gas attacks

Simplistically at least, the issues of munitions might be thought of as a two-fold problem, perhaps two *main* problems might be a better phrase. Arguably, delivery and content drive most munitions. In other words making sure that the material of choice is delivered to its required location. Whilst timing might be important there are only a handful of cases reaching the public consciousness where only one bomb or one bullet was required to complete the mission – at least in warfare. Oftentimes many shells are fired over prolonged periods, particularly so in the trenches.

Of course there are exceptions where an individual or group develops a weapon or defensive mechanism that is not a classic armament. For example Henry Selby Hele-Shaw FRS, Figure 7.1, was born in Billericay, Essex on the 29th July 1854. Part of his citation for Fellowship reads:[1]

> ... Harrison Professor of Engineering, University College, Liverpool. Senior Whitworth Scholar, 1876, and Miller Scholar of the Inst CE. Distinguished for his acquaintance with Engineering and Mechanical Science. Inventor of integrating and power transmitting mechanism. Was the first Professor of Engineering at Bristol and afterwards at Liverpool ...

His Obituary Notice, however, contains the following:[2]

> ... took part in the development of the flamethrower and seeking a readily detachable slightly flexible joint for the oil container invented one which was later exploited commercially and with great success as the 'Victaulic' joint ...

The use of flamethrowers increased throughout the War, two being modified and installed on HMS *Vindictive* and used in the Zeebrugge raid. Remarkably, one of the flamethrowers survives and is on display in the Imperial War Museum North, Figure 7.2.

Miles Walker FRS was Professor of Electrical Engineering in the Faculty of Technology, University of Manchester. His main research involved pioneering work in dynamos and alternators. His Obituary Notice contains the following:[3]

Figure 7.1. Professor Hele-Shaw. (© The Royal Society. Reproduced with permission)

Figure 7.2. A modified flamethrower. (Author's photograph)

> ... one of his inventions was a shield to be carried by about six men for use in no-man's land (provisional application 2661-15). It was successfully tested by soldiers carrying it over a large pile of builder's rubbish, but was never tried in actual warfare ...

Some of the other Fellows were involved in the administration of munitions, for example John Fletcher Moulton FRS, was created a Baron in 1912, KCB in 1915 and GBE in 1917. He was appointed Director General of Explosives, Ministry of Munitions in 1915 and in that position oversaw many improvements to traditional weapons. Lord Moulton has already been mentioned on several occasions, see Chapters 1 and 2 for example. Other Fellows working in the Board of Invention and Research were involved in some of the following munitions activities:

Extracts from the Report of Proceeding of the Board of Invention and Research to 31st December 1916, from pages 26, 27 and 28:[4]

> Mining the Air – this question was investigated, at the request of the Admiralty, by a Sub-Committee of the BIR, and experiments were made with specially light balloon mooring wires, with a view to increasing the height attained by captive balloons. As a result of these experiments, the height attained was increased from

about 3,000 feet to about 5,600 feet, but it was found impossible to raise the captive balloons to the heights at which hostile aircraft usually fly, and the matter was therefore abandoned.

Submarine Howitzers – The Director of Naval Ordnance requested information concerning special designs of howitzers for throwing heavy bombs with large explosive charges to ranges of 1,000 yards for attack of submarines. Stick mortar bombs and howitzers of the Sutton type were suggested, and trials have been made by the Department of the Director of Naval Ordnance. It is understood that difficulties have arisen in taking up the recoil on the light scantlings of trawlers, but that the trials are still proceeding. BIR also suggested the use of 9.2 inch Davis type guns for this purpose, and designs were obtained from Messrs Armstrong, Whitworth Limited. These designs are still under consideration by the Admiralty.

Noxious gases – various trials have been made with J.L. gas manufactured by Flight Lieut. Brock, which have been uniformly successful, and results have been forwarded to the Admiralty.

Deck Piercing Bomb – Designs were drawn up by BIR of deck piercing bombs carry asphyxiating gas for attack of enemy ships. Trials were made to obtain satisfactory flight of these bombs and it is hoped to carry out further trials against steel deck targets as soon as bomb-dropping sights produce more accurate results, and size of target required can be made more reasonable.

Effect of Bombs on Ships' Decks – two series of trials have been carried out by Major B. Hopkinson FRS at the request of the Board to ascertain the effect of heavy bombs on ship's structures. Detailed reports from Major Hopkinson are available.

Fuse setters – an experimental fuse setter, designed by Lieut. Brock for the Board, has been tried at Whale Island, and was fairly successful. It is being slightly modified, with a view to further trials by officers of HMS 'Excellent'. Another type of fuse setter is under manufacture, and it is hoped that this will shortly be ready for trial.

Bomb dropping at Rossington Main Colliery – at the suggestion of the BIR arrangements were made for the use of a vertical mine shaft, 22 feet in diameter and 3,000 feet deep, for measuring actual velocities of bombs and other falling bodies. These trials were carried out by the Air Department, and produced results of considerable value to the Royal Naval Air Service and the Royal Flying Corps.

> French Fabric Fuse – at the request of the Admiralty, designs of a new type of fabric fuse were obtained from the French Inventions Department, but were not considered superior to those now in service.
>
> 37mm guns for mounting in aircraft – requirements for guns of this type were discussed and decided with representatives of all the various Government Departments concerned and designs are being obtained.

Further in the BIR report were proposals put forward by inventors and other members of the general public. The report commented:

> As a general rule proposals coming under this sub-head have not been found of much value. Numerous investigations and trials have been made and are still in progress in certain cases. The most important subjects investigated and considered useful for His Majesty's Service are as follows:
>
> - 37mm and rifle calibre automatic guns
> - apparatus for setting fuses in guns with breech closed
> - attack table for anti-aircraft guns by Lieutenant Wilson
> - blinding lights and star shells etc.
> - boats and torpedoes controlled by wireless telegraphy and selenium devices
> - bomb sights of various types fire director systems
> - gyroscopic bomb sight
> - machine gun sights for use in aeroplanes, and rockets for use in aeroplanes by Lieutenant De Vaisseau Le Prieur, of the French Inventions Department. Both adopted by the Royal Naval Air Service and the Royal Flying Corps
> - mines to be dropped from aircraft
> - rockets of various types
> - use of compression of liquids for throwing projectiles and for absorbing recoil of guns

In addition to the general work described above, there was some work which was undertaken by a very select group of chemists. Chapter 2 mentioned a special committee working on topics mentioned in a secret document S8468. It is speculation to suggest that the following is in any way connected with S8468, however there is no other document filed in the National Archives with the other BIR material.[5]

> SECRET
> This paper is the property of H.M. Government and is subject to the provisions of the Official Secrets Act.
> BOARD OF INVENTION AND RESEARCH
> Victory House, Cockspur Street, SW

Report of the Sub-Committee for the Utilisation of New Raw Materials for Explosives.

Toluene from Solvent Naphtha. – Solvent naphtha may not be marketed if it contains more than 10 per cent. of toluene. A number of samples of commercial solvent naphtha were examined by the Sub-Committee and found to contain varying proportions of toluene up to 40 per cent., so that it was concluded that the above regulation was not being rigorously enforced. Representations on this matter were made to the Ministry of Munitions, and it is understood that steps have been taken to prevent the undue leakage of toluene into the solvent naphtha. The irregularity was apparently due in the main, to pressure on the available distilling plant.

Trinitroxylene. – In view of the necessity for increasing the possible output of high explosive it appeared desirable to investigate the available sources and methods of manufacture of substances similar in properties to picric acid and trinitrotoluene, the high explosives most generally used at present. The inquiry thus suggested led to the discovery that the Borneo petroleum "Straight Run", of which 5,000 tons per month enters this country, contains about 13 per cent. of meta-xylene; this latter hydrocarbon yields a trinitro-derivative, which was found to possess practically the same value as trinitrotoluene as a high explosive.

Considerable samples of trinitroxylene were prepared from Borneo petroleum and submitted to Lord Moulton FRS (Director General of Explosives, Ministry of Munitions 1915) for examination in the Research Laboratory of Woolwich Arsenal ; the laboratory reported very favourably on the explosive properties of the material, but indicated that its high melting point, 182 deg C., prevented it from being washed free from acid in the molten condition with hot water in the manner practised with trinitrotoluene, which melts at 82 deg C. This objection was removed by the manufacture of a mixture of forty parts of trinitroxylene melts at 60 deg to 65 deg C., and pours easily at 80 deg C.

This new high explosive, T.N.T.X., is being manufactured at the Government Works at Sandycroft and Queensferry. The current import of Borneo petroleum is all in the hands of one firm, the Asiatic Petroleum Company, and is sufficient to yield about 80 tons per day of T.N.T.X.

The Sub-Committee is now engaged with the problem of utilising the xylene contained in coal-tar and in coke-oven tar in a similar manner.

Dinitrobenzene. – The Borneo petroleum "Straight Run" was found to contain between four and five per cent. of benzene, and a method was devised for converting this into meta-dinitrobenzene; this substance can thus be prepared from this source in quantities of about ten tons per day. After examination of the product the Ministry of Munitions decided that the dinitrobenzene, mixed with four times its weight of ammonium nitrate, could be advantageously used as a high explosive, and plant was erected for its manufacture. It is possible, however, that this plant will now be fully utilised in the manufacture of the large quantities of T.N.T.X. referred to above.

Picryl Chloride. – Dinitrochlorobenzene is prepared on a large scale in this country with a view to its conversion into picric acid; the process offers, however, certain difficulties, and the Sub-Committee has therefore devised a method for converting dinitrochlorobenzene into picryl chloride, a compound which the Germans have apparently already used as a high explosive during the present war. The low melting point of picryl chloride, 83°C., renders it more easy to manipulate than picric acid, which melts at 122°C. A large sample has been handed to Lord Moulton for examination.

Trinitrobenzene. – The 1:3:5-trinitrobenzene, if obtainable in quantity at an economical rate, would be much preferable to trinitrotoluene as a high explosive. A method has been worked out for preparing trinitrobenzene from picryl chloride, and the Sub-Committee has submitted a large sample for examination at Woolwich.

Hexanitrooxanilide, Hexanitrodiphenylamine, Octonitrodiphenyldiaminoethane. – Considerable samples of these three substances have been prepared and submitted for examination at Woolwich. The first two exhibit no advantages over high explosives already in use, and the third, a previously unknown compound which might possibly replace the more costly trinitrophenylnotramine as a primer, proved to have too high a melting point and to be sparingly soluble to admit of its satisfactory purification on a large scale. The investigation of octonitrodiphenyldiaminoethane is still being prosecuted with a view to surmounting this difficulty.

(Signed) PERCY F. FRANKLAND.
WILLIAM J. POPE.
M.O. FORSTER.
10th April 1916.

Some aspects of Professor Frankland's War record have already been mentioned, but what of the other two authors of the above report? During part of the War, Sir William Jackson Pope FRS, Figure 7.3, was a Chemistry Professor at Cambridge University. He worked on the synthesis of mustard gas as well as explosives. Previously he was Head of the Chemical Department of the Goldsmiths' Institute. Some of his work is mentioned in Chapters 1, 2 and 3.[6]

Figure 7.3. Sir William Jackson Pope. (© The Royal Society. Reproduced with permission)

Sir Martin Onslow Forster FRS was a member of the Royal Society's Sectional Chemical Committee. Some of his pre-War research was whilst working with Professor Meldola FRS of the War Committee – see Chapter 2. Sir Martin was also a Member of Council of the Chemical Society.

Chemical payload

Whilst there were many people involved in chemical activities, two committees had oversight of the effort. Members of both committees met several times during a series of planned meetings. The Chemical Advisory Committee and the Anti-Gas Committee held a series of joint meetings the main agenda item from which involved ways to counter German chemical weapons. The National Archives hold some of the minutes from these meetings. For example:[7]

Joint Meeting of the Chemical Advisory Committee and the Anti-Gas Committee held on 3rd July 1916

Present: Colonel Horrocks (in the Chair)
Fleet Surgeon Hewitt
Colonel Atkins
Colonel Crossley[8]

Colonel Smithells
Colonel Starling
Major Harrison
Professor P.F. Frankland FRS
Professor A.R. Cushny FRS
Sir George Beilby FRS
Professor H.B. Baker FRS
Sir Boverton Redwood
Professor Cadman FRS
Professor Sir Thomas Thorpe FRS

The Chairman having made a brief statement, the committee proceeded to discuss the question of the methods of overcoming the trouble caused by lachrymators (tear gas) in shell holes, dug-outs and trenches at the Front. Colonel Starling gave a statement as to the work that has been carried out in this direction by the RAMC. For S.K. bleaching has been found a fairly effective absorbent.

Major Harrison stated that the French had covered the lachrymators in shell holes with petrol and ignited the mixture, and he suggested the use of Flammenwerfer for this purpose. This was thought to be impractical on account of the short duration of the discharge. Fleet Surgeon Hewitt stated that the Russians had used fine sprays of water for the purpose. It was considered that as far as shell holes are concerned, the most effective treatment consists in covering the material over with earth. The question was left open for further experiment. As regards dug-outs, Major Harrison stated that experiments had shown that the special dug-out with earth filter had proved effective up to a certain point against benzyl bromide.

The Committee decided:

- that there are no purely chemical methods available for the destruction of lachrymators
- that experiments should be conducted by the RAMC on the use of a fan drawing air through a box of charcoal, for supply to a dug-out

Professor Cadman undertook to furnish a suitable fan. If these experiments are successful, the suggestion will be further tested at Porton.

It was also decided to try at Porton this method of rendering a dug-out tenable during the discharge of artillery shells filled with SK.

Professor Cadman raised the question of the supply of respirators for use in Works, and Colonel Horrocks agreed to send a man to the different Works with a supply of suitable respirators in order that their adjustment might be explained to the work people.

Decided to hold a joint Meeting of the Chemical Advisory Committee and the Anti-Gas Committee at 2:30 and fortnightly thereafter.

The History of Imperial College London, 1907-2007 makes reference to S.K.[9]

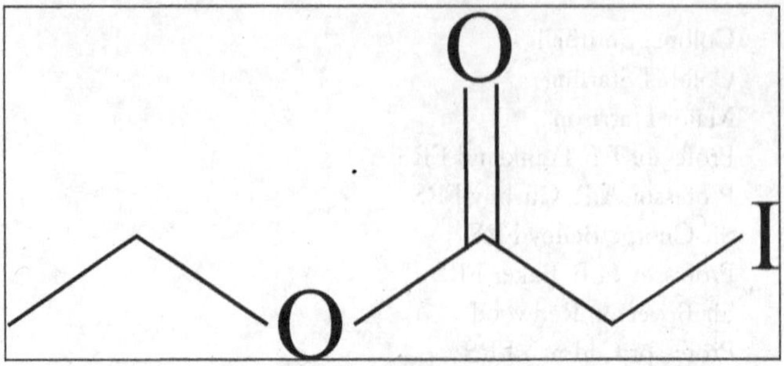

Figure 7.4. The chemical formula for S.K. (Author)

> … one of these was ethyl iodoacetate, the lachrymator codenamed S.K. (for South Kensington where it was first made). See J.F. Thorpe 'History of S.K. (typescript, 10 February 1919) PRO/MUN5/385/1650/7. On one occasion Baker was summoned to the War Office to give a demonstration of chemical warfare preparations to the King and the Prince of Wales. Baker noted in his diary that when the Prince of Wales appeared rather bored with chlorine tanks and respirators, he gave him a first-hand demonstration of the S.K. lachrymator. The Prince of Wales had asked to be exposed to the gas and was given just enough to make him weep …

Just as with the chemical structure of mustard gas mentioned earlier, Figure 2.2 in Chapter 2, S.K. looks equally innocuous, Figure 7.4 – it isn't.

There is little to be gained by reproducing all of the minutes of these meetings, even though there were many issues this joint committee addressed. Perhaps the minutes of the meeting of 31st July 1916 helps to illustrate the breadth of the issues relating to chemical warfare.[10]

Joint Meeting of the Chemical Advisory Committee and the Anti-Gas Committee Held on Monday July 31st 1916

Present: General Jackson (in the Chair)
Fleet Surgeon Munday
Colonel Cummins
Colonel Horrocks
Lieutenant-Colonel Starling
Lieutenant-Colonel Smithells
Major Harrison
Professor H.B. Baker FRS
Sir George Beilby FRS
Professor J. Cadman FRS
Professor P.F. Frankland FRS
Sir Thomas Thorpe FRS

1) Soda-Lime-Permanganate Granules and Charcoal – experimental work on. Progress was reported. Major Harrison described the tests which he had already carried out with different varieties of charcoal, including those supplied by Professor Greenish; the tests are carried out by means of air mixed with the vapour of P.S.

Colonel Cummins drew attention to the need for research on the production of charcoal of uniformly good quality, and Professor Baker undertook to carry out experiments in his laboratory.

2) Box respirator against hydrogen cyanide. Tests on infantry. Major Harrison's report noted.

Professor Cadman drew attention to the slipping of the nose clip which occurs when the wearer perspires.

3) Gas shells. Colonel Starling's memorandum on the employment of gas shells was communicated, and the Chairman read the instructions for the use of chemical shell and instructions for the use of S.K. shell prepared by Ch.A.C.

It was decided that Colonel Starling's memorandum should be referred to the Ch.A.C. and the matter can be discussed when the Ch.A.C. will have the opportunity of considering the memorandum,

4) Directions for the treatment of accidental cases of poisoning by:

- P.S.
- Two Red Star
- White Star
- Nitrous fumes

and provisional notes on treatment of cases of poisoning by gas and vapours. Received. It was noted that these instructions may be amended from time to time.

5) Colonel Starling's report on experiments with S.K. shells at Porton. Referred for consideration by Ch.A.C. Colonel Starling withdrew the determinations of concentrations quoted in this report.

6) Colonel Starling's report on the ventilation of a gas-proof dug-out. Received.

7) Instructions regarding the protection against new type of gas shell. Received.

8) 'K' shells – Captain Allmand's report on the effect. Received.

9) Captain Jones' report on German hand grenade containing lachrymatory liquid. Referred to the Ch.A.C. for consideration of the possible use of bromine derivatives of methylethylketone.

10) Captain Wyeth's report on abnormal type of gas shell used by Germans on the night of 14th-15th July. Received

11) Reports from Captain Hicks and Schwabe on defensive organisation in the Russian Army. Received.

12) Instructions for the use of chemical means for War purposes published by the Russian General Staff. Received.

Note: It is presumed that Ch.A.C. is the Chemical Advisory Committee.

Many of the Minutes of the Chemical Advisory Committee are more concerned with the movements of chemicals.[11]

Meeting of the Chemical Advisory Committee Held Tuesday 28th November 1916 at 10:30am12

Present: Professor H.B. Baker FRS
Sir George Beilby FRS
Professor J. Cadman FRS
Colonel Crossley
Colonel Matheson
Sir Boverton Redwood
Sir Thomas Thorpe FRS

1. The minutes of the previous meeting were read and confirmed.

2 Applications, forwarded by the War Trade Department, for licences to export acetic acid, sodium prussiate, cylinders, red potassium prussiate, white phosphorous, phosphorous sesquisulphide and cayenne, were considered, and recommendations made as shown on File VI C 226.

3. W.T.D.

- 682713. Application of Messrs R.T. Turnbull & Co for extension to the end of January of their licence to export 25 gallons of carbon bisulphide to New Zealand. No objections.
- 687936. Application of Messrs. May and Baker Ltd for extension to the end of December of their licence to export 500 lbs of acetic acid to Calcutta. No objection.
- 685686. Application of Messrs May and Baker Ltd for extension to the end of December of their licence to export 250 lbs acetic acid to Calcutta. No objection.
- 684985. Application of Messrs May and Baker Ltd for extension to the end of December of their licence to export 224 lbs acetic acid to Calcutta. No objection.

4. The Committee considered and approved the draft of their weekly report.

5. Professor Cadman communicated verbally his supply report for the week ending 27.11.16.

6. The Committee discussed:

(a) The communication of reports to General Ozil (M.D.S./G/164) (Mins X, 88, 4b). Decided that the weekly reports should not be forwarded but only the detailed reports of experiments in which the French authorities are interested. The previous reports by Colonel Crossley on the discharge of Yellow Star were ordered to be forwarded

(b) The communication of weekly reports to Captain Moreland, (Mins. X, 90, 4d). Professor Cadman reported that he had referred the matter back to D.G.T.W.S.

(c) The suggested use of silicon tetrachloride (Mins. IX, 47, 7f). A resumé of the previous experimental work on this subject was read. Decided to enquire of D.E.S. as to the possibilities of obtaining supplied of sulphur trioxide at the rate of approximately five tons a week, for the use of silicon tetrachloride
(d) The use of opacite for smoke production (D.G.M.D./0/03) (Mins. X, 80, 5d). A repost from Professor Baker on the chemical shell fillings with which opacite can be mixed was read. Copy ordered to be forwarded to D.D.G.(S) on the above file with a minute stating that as yet there is no evidence as to the character of the smoke produced but that experiments are due to be carried out to determine this. Professor Baker, Colonel Crossley and Sir Thomas Thorpe undertook to prepare a program for trials of shell at Porton, containing opacite in the chemical filling
(e) The inclusion of a list of the members of the Committee in Whitaker's Almanack (Mins. X, 96, 4a). Agreed. Draft approved
(f) The suggested use of dimethyl sulphate (MID/24846) (Mins. X, 97, 4p). Decided to enquire of Mr. Cooper whether he had any evidence of sufficient supplies of the raw materials for the manufacture of this substance
(g) The proposed exchange with France of sodium cyanide for B.R. and opacite (M.D.R.S./296 B) (Mins. X, 97, 4q). Correspondence between Mr. W.T. Layton and Colonel de la Panouse re this exchange was read. Noted
(h) Professor Baker's report on the addition of glycerol to P.S. (Mins. X, 98, 4r). Decided to recommend to D.G.T.W.S. that, to the P.S. for use in Green Star, 0.5 per cent of its weight of glycerol be added to prevent the corrosive action of the P.S. on steel, instead of 5 per cent as previously recommended
(i) P.S. in shell. Professor Baker reported that a number of 4.5in container shell, filled with P.S. had been loaded at South Kensington, with different bursters and linings for the container. Decided that these shell be fired at Porton for observation on bursting, of the comparative merits of the different loadings and conclusions drawn as to the design of loading to be adopted for large scale trials; further, that these shells should have distinctive markings by which they might be recognised
(j) Suggested use of HCN with SK (Mins IX, 35, 6f) (D.G.M.D./C/824). Decided to inform D.D.G.(S) that these substances mix quite easily and that the mixture might be used at a later date if thought desirable
(k) Gas filled hand grenades (Mins. IX, 47, 7c). Sir Thomas Thorpe reported that designs of the modified MSK grenade and the egg

shaped grenade (loc. cit.) were in hand. Professor Cadman suggested that lots of six MSK grenades be obtained for trial filled with mixtures of Red Star with a) disulphur dichloride, b) carbon tetrachloride, c) acetylene tetrachloride, d) sulphur dioxide and e)opacite. Approved

(l) Report MIL 8753 on a gas attack delivered against the Russians on 22nd October 1916. Noted

(m) Minute from Captain Lister forwarding designs of the 4in CI Stokes shell filled CG, PS, JL and SK. Referred to Sir Thomas

(n) The design of chemical shell. A draft memorandum by the Secretary on this subject was read. Ordered to be circulated, referred for further discussion

7. The Secretary reported that Colonel Newton had enquired whether, on account of the large number of double diaphragm shell being manufactured and of the shortage of the container type, some other filling in addition to SK could not be approved for use in this type of shell. Decided to inform Colonel Newton that the Committee recommend the use of double diaphragm shell with CBR under these circumstances, with the smoke mixture as a constituent of the explosive charge, as in the SK shell

8. Sir Thomas Thorpe undertook to attend the MID meeting at 3pm this day in the absence of Colonel Crossley.

Signed Sir George Beilby FRS

This small group seemed to be *the* group that decided on the type of chemical warfare used in these armaments.

Of course many scientists worked on gas production, deployment or protection against an attack. Figure 7.5 shows just some of them, all of whom are either Fellows or Foreign Members.

Name	Activity
Allmand (Arthur John)	Seconded from Regimental duties to 'Gas' Services RE as Assistant Chemical Adviser to the Third Army. He was awarded the Military Cross in 1916. In that year he was made Chemical Advisor to the Fourth Army, in 1918 he held the same appointment with the Second Army … he was demobilised with the rank of Major in 1919.[13]
Baker (Herbert Brereton)	Asked (by Sir Alfred Keogh, Director of Medical Services) to go to the Front and determine which gas had been used. Secret Service information came through that the gas was phosgene so Baker spent some time working on phosgene absorbents.[14]

Name	Activity
Barcroft (Sir Joseph)	Appointed Chief Physiologist at Porton (January 1917) for special duties in connection with the medical aspects of gas poisoning. Shortly afterwards he was joined by Captain R.A. Peters, Captain (later Major) A.E. Boycott FRS, Captain J Shaw-Dunn and Captain Hunt – all of the RAMC. Sir Joseph remained a civilian.[15]
Dudley (Harold Ward)	Detailed for special work on the protection against the new chemicals of War ... ... he also took part in an advisory mission to the United States (early 1918) to the new anti-gas organisation of the US Army and also its mechanisms of supply.[16]
Freundlich (Herbert)	Made proposals concerning the best use of charcoal in anti-gas respirators.[17]
Gibson (Charles Stanley)	Joined Pope on the manufacture of mustard gas.[18]
Hill (Sir Leonard)	Was a member of, and for a considerable time Chairman of, a Committee appointed by DGAMS which was concerned with the medical aspects of gas warfare.[19]
Mulliken (Robert Sanderson)	His first job was in a laboratory for research on poison gases, at an American university in Washington DC presided over by Lt. James B. Conant of the Chemical Warfare Service.[20]
Raper (Henry Stanley)	Invited by Starling, he joined the Anti-Gas Department ... in the researches which the Chemical Warfare Department was then undertaking ... including respirator manufacture (towards the end of the war).[21]
Simon (Sir Franz Eugen)	Had the unenviable distinction of being one of the earliest poison gas casualties of the War. He was twice wounded, the second time only two days before Armistice.[22]
Smithells (Arthur)	Lectured to troops at the Command School of Instruction, training in measures of prevention. Major General Sir H. Cecil Lowther commented 'This GHQ has been fortunate in having the services of a distinguished Fellow of the Royal Society as Chemical Advisor'. Smithells ended the War a Colonel.[23]

Name	Activity
Whytlaw-Gray (Robert)	Appointed a civilian advisor to the Chemical Warfare Committee, and when the Germans started to use toxic smokes in 1917 he commenced investigations on particulate clouds which were soon of great practical value.[24]
Willstätter (Richard)	Awarded the Iron Cross for civilians in recognition of pioneer work, started about this time (1914) on the fillings for gas masks intended as a protection against chemical warfare.[25]

Figure 7.5. Some Fellows who worked on chemical warfare

Munitions delivery

Arguably it is somewhat surprising that *Whitaker's Almanac* was printed throughout the War. Those who have read the publication know of the detailed account it presents regarding many aspects of the day. Figure 7.6 details the various departments of the Ministry of Munitions, as reported in Whitaker's Almanac in 1916.[26] Chapter 3 covered the work of the Department of Munitions Inventions (MID), which was largely concerning the development of new types of equipment or munitions. However, the Ministry of Munitions, the Ministry into which the MID reported, had a much wider brief, including the delivery of armaments.

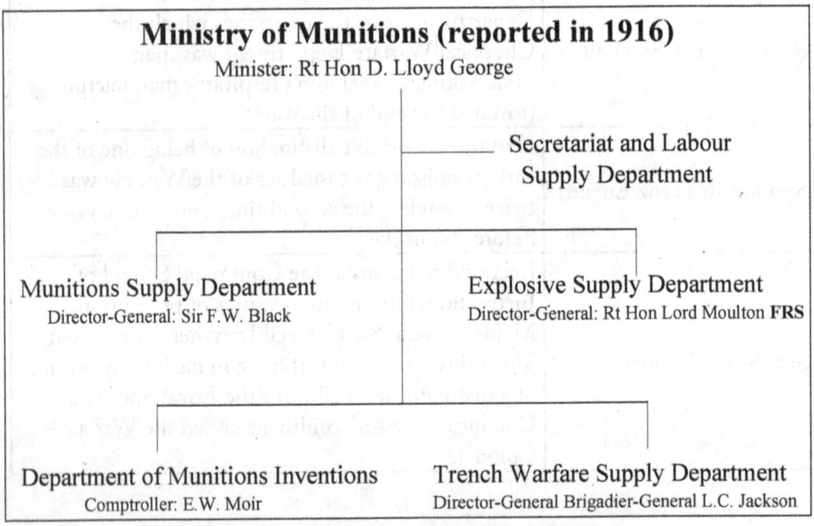

Figure 7.6. The Ministry of Munitions. (Author)

The 1916 edition also lists the following officers of the Royal Ordnance Factories:[27]

- General Staff, Woolwich: Chief Superintendent, Ordnance Factories, V.L. Raven (acting)
- Royal Gun and Carriage Factories: Superintendent, Colonel C.P. Martel
- Royal Laboratory: Colonel Sir H.W.W. Barlow
- Building Works Department: Superintendent, Major N.M. Hemming
- Mechanical Engineering Department: Superintendent, G.H. Roberts
- Medical Department (Royal Arsenal): Senior Medical Officer, Major P.S. O'Reilly
- Royal Arsenal Chapel: Reverend C.A. Berry
- Royal Gunpowder and Small Arms Factories, Waltham Abbey and Enfield Lock: Superintendent, Colonel F.T. Fisher

None of these individuals were Fellows of the Royal Society. The departments are shown here to place the sections of the Royal Ordnance Factories in context.

There were, however, Fellows working within these departments and at universities associated with Woolwich Arsenal. Of the chemists working at the Woolwich Arsenal, perhaps Sir Robert Robertson FRS is particularly noteworthy. Born in Cupar, Fife on 17th April 1869, Sir Robert was an established chemist with a long association with explosives. Indeed part of his citation for election to Fellowship reads:[28]

> … Assoc Mem of the Ordnance Committee. Research Chemist, Royal Arsenal, Woolwich. Has been connected with research work in the Government service 1902. Most of his work relates to explosives, described only in confidential reports or (official) secret patents. It is therefore necessarily unknown to scientific men generally, although its great value is known personally to the signatories. His work has been the means of enormous financial saving to the country, and of great scientific value and technical importance in connection with the present War. The following are some of the chief matters dealt with in his investigations: – Discovery of Mode Decomposition of Nitro-glycerine, of Guncotton and of Cordite (1907); Of Cause of Stabilizing Action of Mineral Jelly and other Stabilizers; of Principles of Stabilizing Guncotton (1902); Researches on Influence of Climate and of additions to Cordite; on Flamelessness in Guns (1914); On Calorimetry of Cordites (1906); On Significance of Abel Heat Test (1910 …

Such was Lord Moulton's concern for the supplies of TNT that he asked Robertson if he could produce TNT at Woolwich. Robertson called a meeting on Sunday 18th October 1914 during which he laid out the problem to his staff (there were eight at the outbreak of War). The necessary work was undertaken with all haste leading to a successful route to the synthesis and scaled up to the pilot plant quantities within a short time. At one point this method produced three tons per week of TNT which was used in shell filling as soon as it was made. It was a method which was transferred to larger scale facilities at Oldbury and later Queensferry. Robertson's equipment was later transferred to the War Museum as a historical relic.

As War progressed so did the size of Sir Robert Robertson's Department such that at the end there were 110 scientists in his department and he was restyled Director of Explosives Research. Sir Robert was created a KBE for his war-work in 1918.[29]

Figure 7.7 details the exploits of Fellows, arguably with a lower profile than Sir Robert.

Name	Activity
Bone (William Arthur)	Carried out various investigations and researches in chemical and fuel problems connected with the War and also trained skilled chemists for munitions work.[30]
Garner (William Edward (1889-1960))	Joined the scientific staff of Woolwich Arsenal where he worked for Sir Robert Robertson on the calorimetry of high explosives.[31]
Smiles (Samuel)	Chemist on the Small Arms Ammunition Committee of the Ministry of Munitions also carried out work on tracer bullets.[32]
Sugden (Samuel)	Joined the Research Department of the Royal Arsenal in Woolwich as a chemist under Sir Robert Robertson.[33]

Figure 7.7. Chemist Fellows working on munitions work

Not all of the chemists employed at Woolwich were involved in the synthesis of explosives, many were employed in the inspection department. Further chemists were also employed at universities as part of the inspection process. This is not so surprising as there were many samples to analyse and universities had the necessary resources and equipment. Some of these individuals were active in other aspects of the War effort. Figure 7.8 is reproduced from documents stored in the National Archives and details some of the university analysts employed up until June 1917.[34]

University	Name	Salary per annum	Duty	Whole or part time	Date commenced
Manchester	Professor H.B. Dixon FRS	£300	in charge	part	1/2/17
	F.P. Burt	£150	analyst	part	1/5/17
	Sir William Slater FRS[35]	£85	sampler	part	1/5/17
	F. Fairbrother	£150	sampler	whole	16/6/16
	W.A. Kirkby	£150	analyst	whole	16/6/16
	C. Campbell	£85	analyst	part	1/5/17
	F.A. Stocks	£150	analyst	whole	1/5/17
	W.R. Berry	£75	analyst	whole	1/5/17
	C. Core	£50	analyst	part	1/5/17
	A. Core	£50	analyst	part	1/5/17
Liverpool	Professor E.C.C. Baly FRS	£300	in charge	part	1/2/17
	Dr. Holt	Nil	if required		
	R.O. Griffiths	£150	analyst	whole	16/6/16
	W. Doran	£150	samples or analysis	whole	16/6/16
	G.G. Kirby	£150	samples or analysis	whole	16/6/16
	F.S. Smith	£150	analyst	whole	10/7/16
	W. Lawson	£125	analyst	whole	16/7/17
Leeds	Professor J.W. Cobb	£300	in charge	part	1/2/17
	H.J. Hodsman	£200	deputy	part	1/2/17
	D. Burton	£150	sampler or analyst	whole	16/6/16
	H.M. Wolfe	£150	analyst	whole	16/6/16
	W. Johnson	£150	analyst	whole	16/6/16
	T. Hanby	£125	analyst	whole	8/5/17
	C.A. Mountford	£125	analyst	whole	10/5/17
	H.S. Houlsworth	£150	assistant chemist	whole	1/12/16
Birmingham	Professor P.F. Frankland FRS	£300	in charge	part	1/2/17
	A. Parker	£150	samples or analysis	whole	16/6/16
	W. Wardlow	£150	analyst	whole	16/6/16
Edinburgh	Dr. S.A. Kay	£150	in charge	part	1/2/17

Figure 7.8. University chemists employed by the Woolwich Inspection Department

The physicists and mathematicians were also busy. Figure 7.9 details some Fellows and their exploits.

Name	Activity
Baly (Edward Charles Cyril)	Appointed one of the Deputy Inspectors of High Explosives working under the Chief Inspector Lt-Colonel C.D. Crozier. His area included Fleetwood, Lytham, Liverpool, N Wales and Bristol.[36]
Bennett (Geoffrey Thomas)	Worked in Professor AV Hill's team.[37]
Boys (Sir Charles Vernon)	Civilian member of the Ordnance Committee at Woolwich worked on problems of internal ballistics.[38]
Cox (Sir Ernest Gordon)	Worked on static electrification of explosives.[39]
Fowler (Sir Ralph Howard)	Worked in AV Hill's group on experimental gunnery.[40]
Hartree (Douglas Rayner)	Worked in Professor A.V. Hill's FRS team which was studying anti-aircraft gunnery. Hartree also made significant contributions to the official text book on anti-aircraft gunnery.[41]
Hill (Archibald Vivian)	Formed a group working on ballistics and operations research.[42]
Irwin (George Rankin)	Worked in the Naval Research Laboratory on penetration ballistics.[43]
Littlewood (John Edensor)	Devised a rapid and powerful method of calculating high angle trajectories avoiding the long process of 'small arc' integration.[44]
Love (Augustus Edward Hough)	Proposed 'Love's method' for the calculation of high angle trajectories by small arcs which was used for some time in Woolwich.[45]
Milne (Edward Arthur)	Worked in AV Hill's group, he was commissioned as a Lieutenant RNVR to prevent conscription.[46]
Pearson (Karl)	Pearson offered the services of his staff which was taken over by the Department of Munitions Inventions, for calculating gun trajectories and creating range tables.[47]
Sidgwick (Nevil Vincent)	Acted as an unpaid consultant to the Department of Explosive Supplies.[48]
Steele (Bertram Dillon)	Served as a Technical Director to the Explosives Branch of the Ministry of Munitions.[49]

Name	Activity
Kennedy (Sir Alexander Blackie William)	Was on the Panel of the Department of Munitions Inventions, Chairman of the Committee on Gunsights and range-finders, Vice Chairman of the Committee on Ordnance and Ammunition and Vice Chairman of the Anti-Aircraft Committee. Some of his War duties took him to the Western Front.[50]

Figure 7.9. Mathematician and physicist Fellows working on munitions problems

One could argue that all of these activities were different to the norm as regards war-work. Even within these War activities there were some Fellows whose activities need a special mention. The following few serve as examples of unusual activities arguably out of the norm even for the Fellows:

Archibald Barr FRS together with his business partner William Stroud formed Barr and Stroud Ltd in 1913. The company still trades, indeed Barr and Stroud binoculars are available from the largest online retail website. Their company website make the following comment:[51]

> … Archibald Barr and William Stroud had been associated from as early as 1888 when the two men were professors of, respectively, engineering and physics at the Yorkshire College (now the University of Leeds)
>
> … In 1914 they began extensions to the Anniesland works in order to meet the sharp increase in demand for their rangefinders that followed on the outbreak of the First World War. The War years saw the development of other products, including a torpedo depth recorder, a periscope rangefinder and a dome sight for aircraft.
>
> During WWI there was a problem with the supply of binoculars to the armed forces and apart from the British makers, binoculars were brought in from various sources. So it was only natural that the military would be looking to rectify this problem. At the time Zeiss was probably the leading manufacturer and the military thought this may cause a problem in the future …

Sir James Walker FRS was appointed Professor of Chemistry, University College Dundee, in 1894. The explosive TNT was in such short supply in 1915 that the Munitions Branch of the War Office formed the Lothian Chemical Company Limited of which Sir James was a member. Together with two colleagues (Cummings and Romanes), he set about turning a nearby facility into an explosives factory. The facility was in a populous part of the city which prompted the Ministry of Munitions to relocate the factory to the outskirts of the town in some disused quarries at Craigleith, the enterprise being known as

HM Factory, Craigleith.[52]

Sir Albert George Hadcock FRS went to France several times personally to inspect the new guns and mountings in use at the Front, after the War he was a member of the commission sent to Germany on behalf of the Government to inspect the dismantling of arms factories there. He was created a KBE for his war-work.[53]

Earlier comments concerning Sir Charles Vernon Boys FRS, Sir Charles Vernon Mallock FRS, Sir Robert Robertson FRS mentioned their involvement as civilian members of the Ordnance Committee. This Committee was staffed by career army personnel with civilians attached to it when the need arose. Minutes stored in the National Archives detail the Committee's work as being largely related to testing armaments, or formulations for them, that has passed the relevant criteria thereby requiring further testing.

8 Engineering / Transport improvements and their raw materials

The drive for transport improvements and new engineering solutions gathered pace in the early years of World War I perhaps like no other War in history. Fighting ships of all types were already in use, however submarine warfare was relatively new. Tanks were developed during the War as well as military aircraft.

Warships

Information concerning the total number of ships in the major fleets was already being compiled. Indeed, the 1916 *Whitaker's Almanac* documented the World's navies up to February 1914, Figure 8.1.[1]

Classification	UK		France		Russia		Germany		Australia		Italy		USA		Japan	
	Blt.	Bldg.	Blt.	Bldg.	Blt.	Bldg.	Blt.	Bldg.	Blt.	Bldg.	Blt.	Bldg.	Blt.	Bldg.	Blt.	Bldg.
Battleships	58	14	21	10	8	7	35	6	14	2	9	5	30	6	17	2
Coastal Defence – armoured													10			
Battle cruisers	47		24		12		9		2		9		17		15	
Light Cruisers	65	20	8		2	8	43	6	9	3	14	4	18		19	
Torpedo Vessels	25	1	3						11		3		2	2	3	
TBD	201	36	80	7	95	45	133	12	15	3	30	16	52	14	51	2
Torpedo Boats	106		153		25		80		58	27	94	1	21		33	
Submarines	69	27	50	26	25	18	24	14	6	5	18	2	29	18	13	2

Figure 8.1. Effective fighting fleets of the maritime powers (numbers)

Britain's future needs – at least in the short term – were documented in a secret paper written by Sir Winston Churchill FRS and printed for Cabinet. Dated December 1914 it is reproduced below.[2]

This document is the property of His Britannic Majesty's Government.

The new construction program approved by the Cabinet in 1914-15 was as follows, Figure 8.2:

Type	Number	Votes 8 and 9 Cost in £
Battleships	4	10,135,000
Light Cruisers	4	1,375,000
Torpedo-Boat Destroyers	10	1,750,000
Flotilla leaders	2	
Submarines	9	1,245,000
Small craft	-	280,000
Total cost		14,785,000

Figure 8.2. The proposed construction plan for 1914-15

The normal program, if there had been no War, for 1915-16 would have been, Figure 8.3:

Type	Number	Cost in £
Battleships	4	10,160,000
Light Cruisers	8	3,055,000
T.B.D.s	10	1,725,000
Flotilla leaders	2	
Submarines	10	1,255,000
Small craft		200,000
Total cost		16,395,000

Figure 8.3. The normal 1915-16 program (peacetime)

In order to compare the War new construction with what it would have been if peace had been maintained, it is better to add the two programs together. Thus we have normal programs, 1914-15 and 1915-16, Figure 8.4.

Type	Number	Cost in £
Battleships	8	20,295,000
Light Cruisers	12	4,430,000
T.B.D.s	20	3,475,000
Flotilla leaders	4	
Submarines	19	2,500,000

Type	Number	Cost in £
Small craft		480,000
Total cost		31,180,000

Figure 8.4. Normal programs 1914-15 and 1915-16

Instead of this, we have under War conditions dropped 2 of the battleships sanctioned in 1914-15, and we have proposed to lay down no new battleships in 1915-16. We have, however, acquired 2 Turkish ships by a partial payment of about 2,500,000l, and the Chilean Dreadnought at a cost of rather less than 3,000,000l. Whereas before the War we should have spent in these two years 20¼ millions on 8 Dreadnoughts, we are now spending 10½ million on 5. As against this saving, there are very large additional programs of smaller vessels under construction, and several new types have been bought or constructed.

The total new program now proposed for the two years is therefore as follows, Figure 8.5:

Type	Number	Cost in £
Battleships	5	10,563,620*
Light Cruisers	6	2,360,000
T.B.D.s	58	8,984,240
Flotilla Leaders	9	1,696,500
Submarines	75	12,278,200
Small Monitors	3	465,000
Large Monitors	4	2,207,000
Fleet Sweepers	12	826,200
Total cost		39,380,760*

Figure 8.5. The new construction program

The new commitment on account of War construction taken as a whole is therefore 8,200,760 in excess of what would have been the peace construction in these two years.

The distribution of expense between the years is, however, very different. Vessels which are purchased from Foreign States have to be paid for at once instead of being spread over two or three years of construction. All vessels under all programs are being accelerated to the utmost. It is not possible to give exact figures, but the following table is approximately correct, Figure 8.6.

	Normal Peace Program		War Program
	£		£
1914-15	1,954,890		12,595,300
1915-16	8,796,550	Includes new program 1915-16	24,468,340
1916-17	13,146,120		2,311,060
1917-18	7,146,340	Ditto, if no subsequent program	6,060
1918-19	136,100		-

Figure 8.6. War shipping costs

It will be seen, therefore, that while there is a very large increase in the money spent in new construction during 1915, the commitments for the years after the War are greatly reduced; and, as far as can now be foreseen, we shall at the close of the War be free to review the whole of our shipping policy. This position will, I hope, not be unsatisfactory to my colleagues.

To these liabilities it is now proposed to ask the Cabinet to add 8 more large Monitors, costing together approximately £3½ million, the whole of which charge will have matured for payment by next May, when these vessels can be completed.

Signed

Sir Winston Churchill FRS

Admiralty 14th December 1914

* Excludes 3,680,650l paid to Turkey on 2 battleships, not accepted as Admiralty liability

Understandably shipyards around the United Kingdom went into full production. Three shipyards are notable here as they were founded by Fellows of the Royal Society, namely Lord Armstrong FRS, Sir John Isaac Thornycroft FRS and Sir Alfred Fernandez Yarrow FRS.

Of all the Fellows included in this account of World War I exploits, William George Armstrong, Baron Armstrong of Cragside, is unique in that he died on 27th December 1900, fourteen years before the War. Born in No 9 (formerly No 6) Pleasant Row, Shieldfield, Newcastle upon Tyne, England on the 26th November 1810, Lord Armstrong was an engineer whose early interest lay in hydraulics. He invented a hydraulic crane which was used on the waterfronts of the Newcastle area, and installed a hydraulic lift in his home, Cragside, Figure 8.7.

Lord Armstrong later formed an armaments company, followed by a shipyard. He also founded companies involved with aircraft and motor cars. Some of his interests became Vickers-Armstrong Limited, which developed the Wellington bomber in World War II. This in turn, and after mergers and nationalisation issues, became part of BAE Systems which ceased tank

Figure 8.7. Cragside (2012). (Author's photograph)

production in their Northumbria factory in 2012. Of relevance here were the ships he built before his death which were still in use during World War I.

Figure 8.8 lists all was ships built before 1900 and registered as in use in the 1916 *Whitaker's Almanac*.[3]

Class	**Ship**	**Year built**
Battleships	*Caesar*	1898
	Canopus	1888
	Glory	1900
	Hannibal	1898
	Illustrious	1898
	Jupiter	1897
	Magnificent	1895
	Mars	1897
	Prince George	1896
Cruisers	*Amphitrite*	1900
	Argonaut	1899
	Ariadne	1899
	Diadem	1898
	Edgar	1893

Class	Ship	Year built
	Endymion	1893
	Europa	1898
	Gibraltar	1894
	Grafton	1893
	Royal Arthur	1893
	Terrible	1895
	Theseus	1894
Light Cruisers	*Astroea*	1894
	Brilliant	1893
	Charydbis	1894
	Diana	1897
	Dido	1897
	Doris	1897
	Eclipse	1896
	Fox	1895
	Furious	1898
	Hermione	1894
	Highflyer	1899
	Hyacinth	1900
	Isis	1897
	Juno	1897
	Minerva	1897
	Sappho	1893
	Sirius	1892
	Talbot	1896
	Vindictive	1898
Minesweeper	*Andromache*	1890
	Apollo	1891
	Intrepid	1891
	Iphigenia	1891
	Latona	1890
	Naiad	1890
	Pelorus	1897

Class	Ship	Year built
	Philomel	1891
	Proserpine	1898
	Pyramus	1899
	Thetis	1890
Torpedo vessels	*Antelope*	1894
	Circe	1893
	Dryad	1894
	Gossamer	1891
	Halcyon	1895
	Harrier	1895
	Hussar	1895
	Jason	1893
	Leda	1893
	Seagull	1890
	Skipjack	1891
	Spanker	1891
	Speedwell	1890
	Vesuvius	1874

Figure 8.8. Warships in use in 1916, but built before 1900

This list demonstrates the age of some ships in use during the War. To illustrate the contribution of Lord Armstrong, the Sirius was built in his yard some nine years before he died, and was still in service in 1916. There are two reference books documenting World War I Destroyers that detail some of the shipbuilding from all three Fellow shipyard owners.[4,5]

Lyon's book (note 2) documents many different shipyards, most of which are not relevant to this discussion as the information relates to other firms and owners. By way of an example to show the number of the ships involved with each shipyard and the costs/timescales, some examples of the Thornycroft yard is provided below. In each case the page reference refers those in Lyons book, Figure 8.9.

Class A Naval Destroyers (pp. 40-52) Ordered 27th June 1892 delivered 27th August 1893				
	Yard No	Laid Down	Launched	Complete
Daring	287	July 1892	25/11/1893	February 1895
Decoy	288	July 1892	07/2/1894	June 1895
Costs for the two vessels £66,948				
'27-knotters' 1893-1894 program Ordered 12th October 1893 for delivery in 13, 14 and 15 months				
	Yard No	Laid Down	Launched	Complete
Ardent	297	December 1893	16/10/1894	25/3/1895
Boxer	298	February 1894	28/11/1894	June 1895
Bruiser	299	April 1894	27/2/1895	June 1895
Tender £110,520 for all three. First costs £39,555, £39,505 and £39,406				
'30-knotters', 1894-1895 program Ordered 10th May (first three), 30th May (Mallard) for delivery ??				
	Yard No	Laid Down	Launched	Complete
Desperate	305	1/7/1895	15/2/1896	February 1897
Fame	306	4/7/1895	15/4/1896	June 1897
Foam	307	16/7/1895	8/10/1896	Jul 1897
Mallard	308	13/9/1895	19/11/1896	October 1897
First costs £54,579, £54,724, £54,432 and £54,715				
1895-1896 Program Ordered 23 January 1895 (313) for delivery ??				
	Yard No	Laid Down	Launched	Complete
Angler	313	21/12/1896	2/2/1897	Jul 1898
Ariel	314	23/4/1896	5/3/1897	October 1898
No costs recorded				
1896-1897 Program				
	Yard No	Laid Down	Launched	Complete
Coquette	319	8/6/1896	25/11/1896	January 1899
Cygnet	320	25/9/1896	3/9/1898	February 1900
Cynthia	321	16/7/1896	8/1/1898	June 1899
First costs £53,939, £53,746 and £53,884				
1897-1898 Program Ordered 7th September 1897				
	Yard No	Laid Down	Launched	Complete
Stag	334	16/4/1898	18/11/1899	September 1900

The Thornycroft shipyard also made ships for the Imperial Japanese Navy, for example *Murakumo, Shinonome, Yugiri, Shiranui, Kagerou, Usugumo, Shirakumo, Asashio,* and for the Royal Swedish Navy. Of course the above examples predate the War, below are examples of ships built during the War.

Thornycroft 'M' Class (p.32)
Mastiff 1914
Meteor 1914
Patrician 1916
Patriot 1916
Rapid 1916
Ready 1916
Thornycroft 'R' Class (p.40)
Radiant 1917
Retriever 1917
Rosalind 1916
Taurus 1917
Teaser 1917
Thornycroft 'S' Class (p.44)
Speedy 1918
Tobago 1918
Torbay 1919
Toreador 1919
Tourmaline 1919
Thornycroft 'V' and 'W' Class (p.48)
Viceroy 1918
Viscount 1918
Wolsey 1918
Woolston 1918
Thornycroft Modified 'W' Class (p.49)
Wishart 1918
Witch 1918
Admiralty Modified 'W' Class Thornycroft Type (p.52)
Shakespeare 1917
Spenser 1917
Wallace 1919

Figure 8.9. Thornycroft build warships

Thornycroft shipyards continued to produce many ships after the War and indeed built ships that were used in World War II. The Company no longer trades, having been split and amalgamated into several organisations over the years.

The Yarrow shipyard, founded by Sir Alfred Fernandez Yarrow FRS, was started in England prior to moving to the Scotstoun district of Glasgow. Remarkably, many ships built in the Yarrow yards survived the War. Volume 2 of Conway's *All the World's Fighting Ships* covers 1906-1921 and documents the following, Figure 8.10:[6]

Name	Launched	Stricken
Alagoas	29 July 1909	disarmed 1939
Amazonas	21 November 1908	1931
Mato Grosso	23 January 1909	1946
Para	25 May 1910	1944
Pará	14 July 1908	1933
Paraiba	18 May 1909	1944
Parana	27 March 1910	disarmed 1933
Piaui	07 December 1908	1944
Rio Grande do Norte	1909	1944
Santa Catharina	26 October 1909	1944

Figure 8.10. Some of the Yarrow ships built for overseas customers

Conway's book, however, lists some of the ships which were in service closer to home, Figure 8.11. All of these ships were built at the Yarrow shipyards in Poplar, London.

Name	Launched	Stricken
Gala	07 January 1905	collided with HMS *Attentive* and sank 27 April 1908 off Harwich
Garry	21 March 1905	sold for breaking up 22 October 1919
Ribble	19 March 1904	29 July 1920
Teviot	07 November 1903	sold for breaking up 23 June 1919
Usk	25 July 1903	sold for breaking up 29 July 1920
Welland	14 April 1904	sold for breaking up 30 June 1920

Figure 8.11. Some Yarrow-built ships made at the Poplar Shipyard

Of course the British Navy were at an advantage in that we had centuries of tradition and excellence in sea battles. Not so the relatively new transport system of aircraft.

Air Inventions Committee

The Royal Flying Corps (RFC) was only established in May 1912, comprising of naval and military wings with a Central Flying School at Upavon on Salisbury Plain. On 1st July 1914, the naval wing of the RFC became the Royal Naval Air Service (RNAS), the military wing by retaining the title Royal Flying Corps. At the outbreak of War the RFC possessed a total of 179 aircraft, with the Royal Air Force being formed in November 1918 then with a strength of nearly 291,000 officers and airmen. As the War progressed there was a clear need for an organisation tasked with issues relating to air and aircraft. Accordingly, the Air Board was established in 1916, the constitution for which was documented in May 1916.[7]

A document was prepared for Cabinet in May 1916:

WAR COMMITTEE

Extracts from the Proceedings of a meeting of the War Committee, held on Thursday 11th May 1916.

New Air Board

The War Committee recommend the formation of an Air Board constituted on the following lines:-

1) The Board to be composed of:

- The President, who shall be a Cabinet Minister
- One Naval representative, who shall either be a Member of the Board of the Admiralty, or shall be present at its meetings when matters connected with the work of the Air Board are under discussion
- An additional Naval representative, who need not always be the same individual
- One Military representative, who shall be a Member of the Army Council
- An additional Military representative, who need not always be the same individual
- A member of independent administrative experience
- A Parliamentary representative in the other House to the President

2) The Board will be an Advisory Board in relation to its President, i.e., the decisions will not be arrived at by voting

3)

(a) The Board shall be free to discuss matters of general policy in relation to the air, and in particular combined operations of the Naval and Military Air Services, and to make recommendations to the Admiralty and War Office thereon

(b) The Board shall be free to discuss and make recommendations upon the types of machines required for the Naval and Military Air Services

(c) If either the Admiralty or War Office decline to act upon the recommendations of the Board, the President shall be free to refer the question to the War Committee

(d) The Board shall be charged with the task of organising and co-ordinating the supply of material and of preventing competition between the two Departments

(e) The Board shall organise a complete system for the interchange of ideas upon air problems between the two Services and such related bodies as the (Naval) Board of Invention and Research, the Inventions Branch of the Ministry of Munitions, the Advisory Committee on Aeronautics, the National Physical Laboratory, etc.

4) The Board shall have a Secretariat to assist in the conduct of the business that comes before it.

Initialled H.H.A.

Having established the Air Board, a series of letters followed setting out the scope of the work it was to commission, and the interaction the Board would have with the Committees mentioned in Chapter 3. For example the following letter is stored in the National Archives in the same folder as the above minutes:

8th July 1916

Sir,

In reply to your letter of the 9th June, I am directed by the Minister to express his concurrence in the proposal to establish an 'Air Inventions Committee', to be attached to the Air Board, to investigate all aeronautical inventions and to relieve the Munitions Inventions Department of those portions of their present work which relate to such inventions.

He assumes that for this purpose some definition of the term 'aeronautical' will be agreed upon in conference with that Department before the announcement is made to the press, and that arrangements will be made for the division of work and the transfer of records to take effect from a date to be fixed.

With regard to the view of the present position which is stated in the first paragraph of your letter, it should perhaps be explained that the relations of the Munitions Inventions Department to the Air Service of the War Office correspond to those of the Naval Board of Invention and Research to the Air Service of the Admiralty and are based upon the principle that the earlier stages in the consideration of inventions fall to the Inventions Department or the Board of Invention and Research, and the later stages (in the case of those which survive the earlier) to the War Office or Admiralty respectively.

Again the allocation of work between the Inventions Department and the

Board of Invention and Research has been made upon broad lines which are well understood, and any remaining possibilities of overlapping are guarded against by an arrangement by which representatives of the Naval Board attend meetings of the Inventions Department and representatives of the Department attend meetings of the Board. The Advisory Committee on Aeronautics are mainly concerned with the experiments carried out at the National Physical Laboratory at the suggestion of the Department or of the Board.

I am Sir,
Your Obedient Servant
Edmund Phipps

The above letter setting out the process of communication helped to establish which resources were working on the many problems of the day. In practice the newly formed Air Inventions Committee comprised of some familiar names mentioned in Chapters 2 and 3. It goes without saying that most were Fellows. They would also have had a view on the duplication of effort across the Committees and Boards.

Air Inventions Committee

Sir Leonard Bairstow FRS	F.W. Lanchester FRS
Professor H.L. Callendar FRS	Professor Lees FRS
Sir Dugald Clerk FRS	J.P. Millington
Sir Horace Darwin FRS	Sir Joseph Petavel FRS
Sir Richard Glazebrook FRS	Major-General Ruck
Captain A.V. Hill FRS	Major G.I. Taylor
Sir Bennett Jones FRS	Lt. Commander Wimperis

Engine Sub-Committee (No 1)

Sir Dugald Clerk FRS	F.W. Lanchester FRS
Sir Joseph Petavel FRS	Professor Lees FRS

Aeronautics Sub-Committee (No 2)

Sir Leonard Bairstow FRS	Lt. Commander Wimperis
Sir Richard Glazebrook FRS	Sir Joseph Petavel FRS
F.W. Lanchester FRS	

Armament Bombs (No 3)

Captain A.V. Hill FRS	Major G.I. Taylor
J.P. Millington	Sir Leonard Bairstow FRS
Sir Bennett Jones FRS	

Instruments Sub-Committee (No 4)

Professor H.L. Callendar FRS	Lt. Commander Wimperis
Sir Bennett Jones FRS	Sir Richard Glazebrook FRS
Major G.I. Taylor	Sir Leonard Bairstow FRS

Procedure Sub-Committee (No 5)

Sir Joseph Petavel FRS	Sir Leonard Bairstow FRS
F.W. Lanchester FRS	

Chairman and Vice-Chairman to be ex-officio members of each Sub-Committee

There were many inventions to discuss, not least would have been the inventions proposed by other Fellows. For example, Arthur John Rowledge FRS, Figure 8.12, started the design of the Lion engine in 1916. Rowledge's biography comments:[8]

> … during World War I the Napier Company was initially engaged in building aircraft engines which had been designed in the Royal Aircraft Factory and also by the Sunbeam Company. As a result of experience gained in building these engines, Rowledge commenced in 1916 the design of the famous 'Lion' engine in which the cylinders were water cooled and arranged in three banks in a broad arrow formation. He had arrived at this configuration as the result of a study of the requirements of the military fighter of the day, and this led to the use of a propeller driven by a spur reduction gear … the Lion was the first to reach a height of six miles …

Later in the Biographical Memoir (p.217), there is a further comment:

> … in 1921 he resigned from the Napier Company and joined Rolls-Royce as Chief Assistant to Mr. F.H. Royce …

Of course Rowledge was not the only Fellow/engineer working on aircraft related activities. For example:

- George Frederick Charles Searle FRS worked at the Royal Aircraft Factory, Farnborough, where he developed a recording accelerometer for use in aircraft on the lines suggested by Lord Cherwell FRS (formally Frederick Alexander Lindemann FRS).[9]
- Henry Norris Russell FRS was a civil engineer and carried out research under the Division of Science and Research of the Bureau of Aircraft Production on the navigation of planes. He made observations at heights up to 16000ft and in aeroplanes flying at 105 mph.[10]

Other Fellows were active in other, arguably more traditional, pursuits

Figure 8.12. Arthur John Rowledge. (© Godfrey Argent Studio. Reproduced with permission)

including:

- William Ringrose Gelston Atkins FRS worked on problems connected with aeroplane dopes, balloon fabrics, fuels, lubricating oils and varnishes[11]
- Ludwig Prandtl ForMemRS studied dirigibles at Göttingen in a 300 horse-power wind tunnel project (1915-1917)[12]
- Charles Frewin Jenkin FRS was responsible for the preparation of specifications in regard to every kind of aircraft material[13]
- Charles Alfred Edwards FRS Chair of Metallurgy at Manchester University, mainly involved in the analysis of steels[14]
- Sir Horace Lamb FRS helped in those aspects of aircraft design connected with their intrinsic strength[15]
- Stanley Smith Cook FRS worked on the problem of cavitation, i.e., the erosion of propeller blades. He was appointed to the Board of Invention and Research Committee concerned with the subject[16]
- Herman Glauert FRS was appointed to the staff of the Royal Aircraft Factory, Farnborough in 1916[17]

For completeness, Frederick William Lanchester FRS has been mentioned on several occasions specifically in Chapter 3 as a member of the Board of Invention and Research. Lanchester was also a member of the Advisory Committee on Aeronautics under the Presidency of Lord Rayleigh on its formation in 1909 and remained a member until 1920.[18]

General Engineering

Three Fellows deserve mention for their contribution to general transport issues.

- Sir Alexander Gibb FRS accepted an appointment under Sir Eric Geddes as Chief Engineer, Ports Construction to the British Armies in France. Sir Alexander's responsibility was to prepare for the reconstruction of ports and railway junctions in Belgium which the Germans were expected to demolish in their retreat[19]
- Sir Charles Edward Inglis FRS designed a light tubular bridge, readily transportable and easy to erect, which the War Office adopted. From 1916 to 1919 he was in charge of the department responsible for the design and supply of military bridges[20]
- William Herbert Hatfield FRS worked in the iron founding firm of John Crowley and Co. Worked with a scientist called Brearley and together invented a type of steel resistant to corrosive gases first used for rifle barrels and then for lining large guns. In 1916 he joined Brown-Firth Research Laboratories, a post he occupied until his death[21]

Raw Materials

The above engineering activities drove the need for supplies of metals, timber and fuel. Figure 8.13 provides some of the Fellows active in geological matters during the War.

Name	Activity
Adams (Frank Dawson)	Appointed Logan Professor of Geology at McGill University in 1898 to 1924.[22]
Burrard (Sir Sidney Gerald)	Sir Sidney was kept in his post as Surveyor General after his 55th birthday in 1915 by the Indian Government.[23]
David (Sir Tannatt William Edgeworth)	On arrival in France he became Geological Advisor(GA) to the Controller in Mining in the First, Second and Third Armies. In September 1916 he met with a serious accident at Vimy, falling some 70 feet down a vertical shaft owing to the failure of the windlass … After convalescence he was attached to General Headquarters as GA to the Inspector of Mines and together with Captain W.B.R. King he was responsible for geological work relating to tunnelling and water supply in connection with the British Armies in France.[24]

Name	Activity
Fermor (Sir Lewis Leigh)	Investigated the coal resources of Korea State in Madhya Pradesh (1914-1915), acted as Mineral Adviser to the Indian Munitions Board (1916-1918). Here he worked out schemes for manufacturing calcium carbide and nitrogenous fertilisers in India. He also investigated the possibility of smelting aluminium ore in India as a War measure.[25]
Gibson (Walcot)	Was directed to an examination of the sources of iron ore in the coal measures.[26]
Goldschmidt (Victor Moritz)	Appointed (in 1914) to the post of Professor and Director of the Mineralogical Institute of the University (Oslo) aged 26.[27]
Gregory (John Walter)	Continued to work on corals and bryozoa, on ore-deposits and on general geology but still found time to undertake expeditions to India in 1916.[28]
Hall (Arthur Lewis)	Assistant Director if the Geological Survey of the Union of South Africa (1910 – 1932).[29]
Lacroix (François Antoine Alfred)	Wrote some papers on the gold deposits of the French Colonies in 1917.[30]
Lenox-Conyngham (Sir Gerald Ponsonby)	Would normally have expected to become Surveyor General, however it was decided his boss Burrard should remain in post during the War years in India.[31]
Rogers (Arthur William)	Appointed Director of the Union Geological Survey in 1916 (the union of the four South African provinces).[32]
Sinnatt (Frank Sturdy)	Lecturer in applied chemistry specialised in coal deposits, their extent and location.[33]
Thomas (Herbert Henry)	Took part in the preparation of a series of reports on the Mineral Resources of the country and acted as a technical advisor to the Research Department of the Admiralty, also served on a committee appointed by the Home Office to investigate the nature of dust in mines.[34]

Figure 8.13. Some Fellows involved in Geology and Surveys

There was also a need for metallurgists and their specialist skills of determining the composition of alloys etc.

- Sir Henry Cort Harold Carpenter FRS has been mentioned on several occasions, particularly his work for the Board of Invention and Research in Chapter 3. Sir Henry was appointed to a Chair at Imperial College in October 1914 and gave advice on metallurgical problems of many kinds during the War. In collaboration with L. Taverner, he published (in 1917) a detailed study of the influence of annealing temperatures on the rate of softening of cold-rolled aluminium sheet.[35]

Finally, and for completeness, a brief discussion of Robert Scott Troup FRS and his timber survey work was outlined in Chapter 3. Troupe is referenced here as his work on establishing exactly what timber and quantities were available in the United Kingdom helped with supplies of wood for war-work. At the time Troupe was Assistant Inspector of Forests at the Government of India's headquarters, and on the formation of the Munitions Board in 1917, under Sir Thomas Holland, he also held the post of War Controller of Timber Supplies.[36]

9 Our Health and Well-being

No amount of food and drink will compensate for fear, lack of sleep, missed loved ones and the death of close relatives or friends. Make no mistake life was tough. The conditions during this wartime are impossible to truly understand almost one hundred years since World War I began.

Behind the scenes Local and Central Government, scientists, engineers, doctors and nurses were working with specialists concerned with agriculture, the environment, farmers etc. to provide the best available living conditions. Often the basic diet of bread, fresh vegetables and other staples were all available, at least for the first two years of the War. Indeed our reliance on imported wheat and wheat products remained constant for the first two years of the War, Figure 9.1.[1]

Country	Season 1913-1914 August 1st to July 31st*	Season 1914-1915 August 1st to July 31st
United Kingdom	27	26
Italy	5.7	7
Germany	9.1	0.4
Belgium	6.4	3
France	7.5	8
Holland	2	3.8
Smaller European countries	11	8
Extra European countries	12	6
Total	80.7	62.2

* expressed in millions of quarters of 480lb of imported wheat

Figure 9.1. The principle importers of wheat and wheat flour

Then as now, the Board of Agriculture and Fisheries oversaw land and its productive use. The President, Rt. Hon. Earl Shelborne, was ably supported by a department that included Fellows. For example:

- Sir John Claud Fortescue Fryer FRS – Entomologist, Director of the Board's Plant Pathology Laboratory, Secretary to the Agricultural Research Council.
- Sir James Johnston Dobbie FRS – Chief Agricultural Analyst

Director of the Science and Art Museum, Edinburgh.

- Lt. Colonel Sir David Prain FRS – Technical Advisor in Botany to the Board and Director Royal Botanic Gardens, Kew – his wartime occupation, formerly Superintendent, Royal Botanic Gardens, Calcutta Professor of Botany, Medical College, Bengal Director of Botanical Survey of India, Government Quinologist and Director of Cinchona Cultivation in Bengal.

The titles under the Fellows' names are occupations held before, during or after their time working for the Board of Agriculture and Fisheries.

Figure 9.1 might imply that nothing was being done to address the issue of importing food. Nothing could be further from the truth. Whitaker's Almanac also records the area under crops for the UK excluding the Channel Islands and the Isle of Man, Figure 9.2.[2]

	Acreage 1914	Acreage for 1915
Wheat	1,904,930	2,334,090
Barley	1,871,170	1,523,980
Oats	3,877,960	4,148,050
Potatoes	1,197,010	1,202,520
Turnips and Swedes	1,752,570	1,617,460
Mangolds	515,860	500,490
Clover, Sainfoin etc. for hay	2,902,900	2,839,920
Permanent grass for hay	6,489,880	6,420,360

Figure 9.2. Areas under crops

Clearly there was more land being used for cereal crops and less for animal feed. Figure 9.3 shows the livestock changes during the same time.

Description	1913	1914	1915
Cattle	11,963,600	12,144,560	12,131,370
Horses	1,874,264	1,842,560	1,699,640
Pigs	3,305,771	3,939,890	3,783,780
Sheep	27,629,206	27,886,090	28,181,540

Figure 9.3. Livestock

There is also a comment concerning Fisheries of the United Kingdom. In 1911 the industry employed 102,000 men and boys, 3,155 steam vessels and 21,827 sailing ships. The total value of the fish landed in 1913 was £14,229,000 (excluding salmon and shellfish), the weight being approximately 24,660,000cwt.

Whatever the food position at the start of the War, by 1916 there was a need to consider many issues. Responding to requests by the Board of Agriculture and Fisheries the Royal Society appointed two committees, Grain Pests and Food (War). The initial emphasis was protecting produce already in barns and other storage containers. The Committee, called the Grain Pests (War) Committee, was appointed in June 1916. The Board of Agriculture and Fisheries wrote to the Royal Society asking for help 'in relation to damage done to grain by insects'.

The Royal Society Grain Pests Committee

The Committee was composed of:

Professor V.H. Blackman FRS, Professor A. Dendy FRS, Dr. Gertrude Dixon of the Wheat Supplies Commission, Mr. J. Hartley Durrant, Dr. Edkins, Sir John Claud Fortescue Fryer FRS, Professor Stanley Gardiner FRS, Sir William Bate Hardy FRS (Secretary), Professor Sir William Abbott Herdman FRS (For. Sec. and Chairman) Figure 9.4, Mr. A.E. Humphries, Mr. Edward Paul, Professor R. Newstead FRS and Mr. O. Robinson.

Born in Edinburgh on the 8th September 1858, Sir William was a Demonstrator of Zoology at the University of Edinburgh (1880) and the Professor of Natural History at the University of Liverpool throughout the War (1881-1919). He was also a Professor of Oceanography and established a marine biological station at Port Erin, Isle of Man. He was created CBE in 1920 and knighted in 1922.

Mr. Oswald E. Robinson was a representative of the milling trade and Sir John Claud Fortescue Fryer FRS, as mentioned above, worked for the Board of Agriculture. The Liverpool Grain Trade was represented by Mr. Edward Paul, and the Incorporated National Association of British and Irish Millers by Mr. A. E. Humphries.

The Committee forged links with Overseas Committees in Australia, Canada, New Zealand, South Africa and Russia. Unusually, the Committee Members also decided to divide the work between London and Liverpool.

The London work was initially carried on at two centres, namely:

1. Natural History Museum (which was at the time part of the British Museum), under the direction of Mr. J. H. Durrant. Professor Newstead was appointed Chairman of the Executive Sub-Committee and Dr. Gertrude Dixon acted as Honorary Secretary during the first year of work
2. King's College Department of Household and Social Science, under the direction of Professor Dendy FRS

Later in the War, some of the London work was transferred to the Zoological Department of King's College (Professor Dendy) and the Physiology Department of the Bedford College for Women (Dr. Edkins). The work was

Figure 9.4. Sir William Herdman. (© The Royal Society. Reproduced with permission)

divided thus:

- British Museum: Mr. Durrant, with some assistance, investigated samples in order to identify which pests were involved
- King's College: Professor Dendy, with the assistance of Mr. Billinghurst, investigated the bionomics and life-histories of weevils and other imported insects. They also undertook a statistical investigation of samples with a view of determining the amount of damage caused by the pests in question
- Bedford College: Dr. Edkins investigated the life conditions of the flour moth (Ephestia kuhniella) and the possibility of controlling this pest by fumigation with various gases

The Liverpool work was carried out first in the laboratories of Tropical Medicine at the University, but later transferred to the Department of Zoology. This work consisted of

Professor Newstead, with the assistance of Miss H.M. Duvail, B.Sc., undertaking an investigation of mites as grain and flour pests from all points of view.

Dr. Gertrude Dixon resigned her position as Secretary to the Sub-Committee in consequence of her appointment under the Royal Commission of Wheat Supplies (January 1917). Also at this time the statistical work had established fact that:[3]

> … a very considerable amount of damage to grain was sustained be the action of the pests, and that the Committee was justified in recommending further investigation on faunistic, bionomic, developmental and experimental lines at the various laboratories concerned …

The Committee Report also concluded:

> … As the result of some of these reports and discussions on the Committee memoranda have been prepared on:
>
> 1. The protective treatment of stored grain by the application of heat and other methods
> 2. The investigation of acarids in relation to grain and flour
>
> The first of these memoranda was sent as a provisional report to the Royal Commission on Wheat Supplies at their urgent request. It was subsequently circulated amongst members of the Committee for further additions and amendment …

This Committee's findings were widely circulated. In keeping with their correspondence with various Committees around the world a copy of the report was sent to equivalent representatives in Australia, Canada, Cyprus, Italy, Malta and the United States. They were also sent to many trade organisations such as the Royal Commission on Wheat Supplies, the Imperial Institute, and some members of the trades concerned.

The Committee Report summarises in the following way:

> … Under Mr. Durrant, at the British Museum, samples of grains have been examined for insect pests, and statistical results have been accumulated as to the relative numbers of different species and the proportion of injured and uninjured grains in a sample, their respective weights, and the amount of damage done by the various insects. The work at the British Museum has thus been both faunistic and statistical.
>
> At King's College, with the aid of a grant of £10 from the Grain Pests Committee, a range of incubators has been installed in a special room and Professor Dendy has been engaged in experiments on the life-histories and bionomics of the various grain insects. Owing to the appointment of Dr. Dixon to the Royal Commission on Wheat Supplies grain work at the Household and Social Science Department of King's College for Women has ceased, the incubator installed there having been transferred to King's College. Faunistic work has been carried on by Miss Courtauld. Owing to pressure of other work Mr. Billinghurst has been able to do very little grain work during the past term, but he is keeping his insect cultures under observation and assisting Professor Dendy from time to time. It is hoped that a Report on Professor Dendy's investigations

will be ready for publication almost immediately.

At Bedford College, Dr. Edkins, assisted by Miss N. Tweedy, has been conducting physiological experiments as to the effect of various gases upon the insect pests of grain, especially flour. After trying and rejecting for various reasons formaldehyde, sulphur dioxide, ammonia and extracts of pyrethrum in ether and methylated spirit, he is now engaged in a series of experiments testing the effects of ozonised air upon the flour moths, their larvae, and other flour pests. The experiments are not yet complete, but they indicate that if a chamber of about 18 litres capacity be swept by a current of dry air, amounting to about 100 litres per hour (i.e., renewal of air about once a minute) for broken periods aggregating 15 hours, such air containing 100 parts of ozone in a million, moth are destroyed entirely larvae are only partially destroyed, beetles are affected but not killed. The difference between a chamber containing moths thus treated and a chamber containing moths ventilated with dry air only is very striking. It may be pointed out that such a proportion of ozone in air would not be permissible in to be breathed by human beings, and such ventilation could only be adopted in closed channels.

At Liverpool University investigations on the acarid pests of stored grain and flour are being undertaken by Miss H. M. Ducall, B.Sc., under the direction of Professor Newstead. The work carried on is faunistic, bionomic and experimental. The species so far found have a wide range and their occurrence is reported in all temperate wheat-producing countries. They have been detected in newly arrived cargoes of Canadian wheat in this country, generally in small quantities only. The investigations so far have proved:--

1. That flour suffers more deterioration than wheat when attacked by mites, and that the effects of such attacks are less readily combated; and
2. That moisture content is, at the temperatures at which in this country wheat is stored, the primary factor determining the presence of mites in harmful numbers …

Royal Society Food (War) Committee

The Food (War) Committee was appointed by the Royal Society Executive of the Council on 16th December 1915 to deal with questions of food supply of the nation. The Committee was reconstituted as the Food Committee on 18th December 1916. At that time the Committee membership included:

Sir Alfred Kempe FRS (in the Chair) figure 9.5, Dr. H. B. FRS, Professor R.H. Buffen, Professor A.R. Cushny FRS, Sir Henry H. Dale FRS (Representing Medical Research Committee), Sir Arthur D. Hall FRS, Sir William B. Hardy FRS, Sir Frederick G. Hopkins FRS, Mr. A. J. W. MacFadden, Professor D. N. Paton FRS, Captain S. G. Tallents (Representing Ministry of Food), Professor W.H. Thompson, Dr. A. D. Waller and Professor T. B. Wood FRS.

Figure 9.5. Sir Alfred Kempe FRS. (© The Royal Society. Reproduced with permission)

Sir Alfred Kempe FRS led an interesting life. He was called to the Bar at Inner Temple and was a Barrister on the Western circuit, specialising in ecclesiastical law. Later in his career he was elected to Fellowship (2nd June 1881) for his work in mathematics. An accomplished man indeed!

Arguably this Committee was the most active, or at least published the most reports of any of the Royal Society Committees. For example there is a document summarising the main proceedings of the Food Committee for the years 1915-1919. It would add no value here to reprint the entire report, however a summary of topics covered may provide an insight to the varied topics the Committee considered.[4]

Summary of Main Proceedings of the Food (War) Committee of the Royal Society (1915-19)

1. Energy Requirements of Hand Workers by Greenwood (undated)
2. The Food Supply of the German Empire
3. Restriction of Imports of Fruit – February 1916
4. Manufacture of Alcohol – November, 1916
5. Food Supply for the United Kingdom – October, 1916
6. Rationing of Meat – January, 1917
7. Saccharin – January, 1917
8. Sugar Rationing – January, 1917
9. Bread and Meat Rationing – January, 1917
10. The Primary Importance of Bread – February, 1917

11. Alcohol Production and the Saving of Tonnage – February, 1917
12. Bread Rationing – February, 1917
13. Soya Bean – February, 1917
14. Supply of Yeast and Reduction in Alcohol Production – March, 1917
15. Voluntary Bread Rationing – March, 1917
16. Bread Rationing – March, 1917
17. National Food Policy. Primary Importance of Bread – March, 1917
18. Conservation of Supply of Summer Milk – March, 1917
19. Consumption of Meat – March, 1917
20. Food from the West Indies – April, 1917
    (a) Bananas
    (b) Sweet Potatoes
    (c) Rice
21. Supply of Fats – April, 1917
22. Maximum Prices – April, 1917
23. A Limited Measure of Food Distribution – April, 1917
24. Nutritive Value of Maize – April, 1917
25. National Food Policy – April, 1917
26. Some Industrial uses of Cereals – May, 1917
27. Comments on Correspondence from the Wheat Commission – May, 1917
28. National Food Policy – May, 1917, Price Fixing
29. Food Value of Cocoa – May, 1917
30. Estimation of the Cereal Needs for 1917 – 1918 – June, 1917
31. Food Supply of the Nation in 1917 – June, 1917
32. The Food Supply of the United Kingdom – An H.M.S.O. Publication, Cd. 8421, 1917
33. The Food Supply of the United Kingdom in 1916 – July, 1917
34. Food Value of Pickled Herring by T.H. Milroy – August, 1917. Analyses of various types of herrings
35. West Indian Food Products – October, 1917
36. Permits for Pure Wheaten Flour for Invalids – October, 1917
37. Potatoes as Substitutes for Cereals – October, 1917
38. Distribution of Milk – November, 1917 by Drs. Hutchinson and McFadden
39. The Use of Potatoes by the Home Army, Munitions Workers, etc. – November, 1917
40. The Use of Potatoes to Conserve Cereals – November, 1917
41. Report on Compulsory Rationing Scheme – December, 1917
42. Economies in Meat Consumption – December, 1917
43. Report on Dried Meat Powder by S.W. Cole – December, 1917
44. National Food Supply – December, 1917

45. The Necessity of an Adequate Food Supply to the Nation – January, 1918
46. The Effect of an Inadequate Diet – February, 1918
47. Digestibility of Breads – No date
48. Influence of the Percentage Extraction and of Admixtures of Flour on Yeast Activity – March, 1918
49. The Relative Order of Importance of Foodstuffs – March, 1918
50. The Pig Question in Germany – March, 1918
51. Practical Suggestions for the Conservation of Meat and Fats. By Noel Paton – March 1918
52. Rate of Cooling on Metabolism – May, 1918
53. The Availability of Fatty Acids for Man – May, 1918
54. Replacement of Fruit by Swede Turnips by Sir Leonard Hill – October, 1918
55. Digestibility of Cocoa Butter – December, 1918
56. Food Requirements of Man – March, 1919
57. The Composition of Potatoes Grown in the United Kingdom – April, 1919

All of the above verbatim titles are from reports written by Food Committee Members. Documenting all of these reports here will add little value. A better approach might be to look at the context which led to them. Figure 9.6 is a small table of reports kept in the National Archives. The first column is the Archive reference number and the next column the report subject. The first of these reports outlines the Government's position on some of the staple foods.

National Archives reference	Report title
CAB/24/3_0008	Report by the Food Controller on bread, meat and sugar January 1917
CAB/24/3_0017	Restriction of Brewing – Memorandum by Lord Devonport 5th January 1917
CAB/24/7_0096	Food (War) Committee of the Royal Society – The National Food Policy 16th March 1917
CAB/24/11_0012	Minutes and memoranda on matters affecting alcohol supplies 5th April 1917
CAB/24/11_0050	Food (War) Committee of the Royal Society – The National Food Policy 24th April 1917
CAB/24/3_0049	Re-distillation of potable spirits for munitions etc. April 1917
CAB/24/14_0067	Alcohol supplies for War purposes May 1917
CAB/24/27_0041	War Cabinet note on Lord Rhondda's memo 28th September 1917

National Archives reference	Report title
CAB/24/34_0089	Food (War) Committee of the Royal Society – The distribution of milk 20th November 1917
CAB/24/34_0077	Second Interim Report from the Committee of the Production and Distribution of Milk, 2nd December 1917
CAB/24/34_0099	War Cabinet – Supply of milk for young children and mothers 7th December 1917

Figure 9.6 A brief list of Food-related reports

The first report was written for the War Cabinet, and was stamped SECRET at the time:[5]

Report by the Food Controller on bread, meat and sugar January 1917
To the Right Hon. D. Lloyd George, MP.

I have now had the opportunity of making a personal investigation into the conditions which govern the importation of three of our staple food products, viz. bread, meat and sugar. My enquiries have covered:

1. the sources of supply
2. the buying of various commodities
3. their transport to destination
4. financial considerations: and most important of all
5. the statistical position of each in relation to consumption at the moment and in the future

STATISTICAL POSITION.

Bread.

In the opinion of the Royal Commission on Wheat Supplies, it is essential to secure economy of wheat by a considerable reduction in its consumption in this country. There is no evidence of economy. In fact, such evidence as there is points in the other direction. The imports of wheat and flour at the principal English ports in the calendar year 1916 exceed the corresponding imports in 1915 by about 2,000,000 quarters, of which increase half was imported as, and still constitutes, a reserve; the remaining 3,000,000 quarters represent excess of sales of imported wheat in 1916 compared with 1915 to the extent of, say, two weeks' imports:. The home-grown stocks are short, the amount available for consumption being estimated at 6,460,000 quarters, of which about 3,780,000 quarters are estimated as still remaining on the farms. As you are well aware, owing to the vicissitudes of the harvest, the crops of the northern hemisphere were poor; and in consequence by far the major portion of our requirements have to be imported from the more distant points, in Australia, &c. In their estimate of requirements of wheat and/

or flour for importation to the United Kingdom from the 1st November, 1916, to the 31st August, 1917, the Royal Commission have estimated that an economy of 5 per cent, on the normal importations will be realised by the effect of the Manufacture of Flour and Bread Order, 1916, increasing the extraction of flour from the wheat milled. In view of all the circumstances, the Royal Commission consider that an economy of 5 per cent, is entirely inadequate. Further, with the existing tendency towards an increase in consumption, they doubt whether any actual net economy will be realised unless some further State action is taken. The estimated stocks of wheat and flour in the United Kingdom this year and the two preceding years are given below. You will notice that while the total stock is slightly lower than 1915, and considerably lower than 1914, a portion of this stock is Government reserve, which it was decided should be maintained at 1,000,000 quarters; and the fact that it is now less than this figure is the effect of the local demand for supplies, Figure 9.7.

	Quarters	Weeks' Supply	
December 21, 1914	11,145,000	17⅓	
December 20, 1915	9,036,000	13⅔	
December 13, 1916			
Trade stock	7,727,000	11⅘	13⅕ weeks' supply
Government reserves	900,000	1⅖	

Figure 9.7. Estimated Stocks of Wheat and Flour at Ports, in Millers', Bakers', and Farmers' Hands

The quantity afloat for United Kingdom direct is about the same now as in 1915 and 1914 at this time. If these figures are considered from a statistical, standpoint alone it may be urged that there is a sufficiency of wheat supplies in hand, and on the way, to justify the present uncontrolled distribution of bread (and flour) continuing ; but assuming that the policy to be aimed at is to bring about at the earliest moment a curtailment of the national consumption in order to husband supplies against 'unforeseen contingencies,' this end can only be attained by some system of rationing. I may add that the Wheat Commission are not anticipating any insurmountable difficulty in continuing to maintain supplies at the present level. Even if supplies of wheat should fall below the present level by as much as 15 per cent., the deficiency could be made up by still closer milling of the wheat and by the addition of other cereals. In view of this, and of the fact that the great variation in bread consumption among different classes of the community (from 3 to 6 lbs. per head per week) makes rationing almost impossible, I recommend that no such system be introduced at present.

If altered circumstances should warrant rationing at a later date, I should recommend that a maximum allowance per head, per week, of 4 lb. of bread should be enforced. My enquiries have been made through the most reliable distributive channels of the co-operative and other organisations throughout the country in order to get as near a figure as possible of the average consumption at the present time. Further, I have consulted the War Food Committee of the Royal Society, through Professor T. B. Wood, now on my staff, as to what quantity per day or per week of bread, and of other foods with which I am dealing, is necessary for the maintenance of efficiency in different classes of the community.

To Increase the Supply of Bread-stuffs.

I have had prepared and have personally tested several batches of loaves made from Government regulation flour, to which was added 5 per cent, and 10 per cent, of flour made from maize, rice, barley, and oats. Both the loaves containing 5 per cent, admixture and those containing 1.0 per cent, were of excellent quality, palatable, and nutritious, and with no objectionable characteristics of any kind. At a recent conference of representative millers and bakers, it was admitted that an admixture up to 10 per cent., so far as barley and rice are concerned, presents no milling difficulties, but that other cereals could not be milled with the existing plant without considerable alterations. I took the opportunity of discussing at the same time the possibility of further increasing by 5 per cent, the extraction of flour from wheat up to 81 per cent, instead of 76 per cent., the average extraction enforced by the regulation issued a few weeks ago. I am satisfied that this further extraction will not unduly depreciate the character of the loaf. I have issued an Order making it compulsory on all millers (a.) To increase the percentage of flour extracted from the wheat from the present 76 per cent. to 81 per cent.; or (b.) To add not less than 5 per cent, of flour from maize, rice, barley, or oats.

In both cases it will be permissible to add a further 5 per cent, of flour from maize, rice, barley, or oats. The result will be a further economy of at least 5 per cent, and probably 10 per cent, of wheat.

The effect of these operations will be (a.) To further economise wheat; (b.) To widen the basis of the supply of breadstuffs ; (c.) To economise tonnage.

Meat

As regards meat, the main sources of supply of meat are:

(a) From Australia

(b) From South America (shipped mainly from Buenos Aires (Argentine) and Montevideo (Uruguay))

(c) From home production

I am informed that the imported supplies of beef and mutton in the past ten months for civilian consumption amount to about 221,000 tons, equivalent to 22,100 tons per month, and, taking home supplies as being the same as in 1913. We have a further 96,000 tons a month available. As evidence of the diminution of imported meat for civilian consumption, the home supplies, which formed nearly 64 per cent, of the whole in 1913, now represent about 82 per cent, of the whole.

Taking the civilian population at the two periods, and correcting for the varying consumption according to age and sex, the quantity of beef and mutton available has fallen from 2.84 lb. per adult man per week in 1913 to 2.42 lb., a decrease equivalent to nearly ½ lb. per week per adult man.

In order to control distribution and/or further reduce consumption by State action, there are the alternatives of a meatless day or days and rationing.

I do not support the idea of meatless days. I think in the main it would be ineffective, would lead to compulsory waste of good food and evasion. Further, it would tend, on the day fixed, to create an abnormal demand for fish and other foods, which it might not be possible to meet. This would lead to disappointment and public irritation.

Rationing, on the contrary, if and when necessary to adopt, would give what is wanted to ensure diminution of meat consumption. In effect it would produce meatless days or their equivalent, and each household could suit its own convenience and predilection.

I have carefully discussed with Sir Thomas Robinson the immediate and future outlook as to his power to maintain imported supplies, and he is quite sanguine that this can be done. He informs me that the Australian meat available for export will be greater this season. New Zealand expects to exceed last season's shipments, and from the River Plate we could draw additional meat if more refrigerated tonnage were available. On the whole, the quantity of meat offered us is certainly in excess of what was available twelve months ago, but in every case our imports are limited by the amount of tonnage available.

Steps are being taken by myself, in association with Mr. Prothero, to stimulate the home production of meat by measures which will ensure larger and cheaper supplies of feeding-stuffs, and so obviate the danger of reduction of home stocks, already threatening, by reason of the dearness and scarcity of feeding-stuffs.

The head of live-stock in the country at present is slightly above normal, and the high prices of all feeding-stuffs is sufficient evidence of their scarcity. By compulsory regulation of slaughter of cattle and sheep at a certain stage of fatness, great economy of feeding-stuffs would be effected, and the feeding-stuffs saved could be diverted to the immediate production of pork. A given weight of pork can be produced in about one third of the time and with the consumption of much less fodder than is required to produce the same weight of steer beef.

Considered purely from the statistical position, there is apparently no immediate necessity for the curtailment of consumption by compulsory methods; but if policy dictates that the necessity has arisen, then rationing is essential.

Presuming that meat would be defined as including fresh meat, preserved meat, poultry, game, and bacon, I should recommend that a maximum allowance per head per week of 2lbs. should be enforced.

Sugar

I have ascertained from the Royal Commission on Sugar Supplies that the amount of sugar put upon the market by the Sugar Commission during the last six months has been in round figures 25,000 tons a week. This is appropriated through the regular channels of distribution covering:

1. Domestic consumption
2. Naval and military forces
3. The manufacture of jams, confectionery, biscuits, &c

These quantities ought to be amply sufficient to prevent anything like complaint, but, owing to the inequalities in distribution, certain areas and also certain individuals have, as a matter of fact, found difficulty in obtaining reasonable supplies. As regards areas, the difficulty has arisen, partly from delays in transport and partly from movements of the population.

In order to ensure an equivalent of distribution so far as the supplies permit, I have come to the conclusion that this can only be achieved by a system of rationing. Rationing, if for no other reason, is justifiable in order to prevent that section of the community with greedy instincts from using such influence as they can command to securing for themselves an excessive supply of sugar, disregarding the deprivation it causes to others less fortunately circumstanced.

As regards the statistical position, if a fair and equal distribution could be secured, there would be available a sufficiency of supplies to ensure each individual in the country getting an adequate supply ; but under the present circumstances that appears to be unattainable, hence I recommend that an allowance per head per week of ¾ lb. of sugar be enforced.

System of Rationing.

I suggest that the first operative action as a preliminary to the establishment of the essential organisation to bring effective rationing into operation, which of necessity will take some time to improvise, will be to proclaim by Order under the Defence of the Realm Regulations the articles of food to which rationing is to be applied, stating the fixed maximum ration, and that to exceed these quantities is illegal; and, further, that infringement will be punishable by fine or imprisonment; also the date when the Order will become effective.

I have prepared a rough draft of a further announcement which I think should be issued by the Food Controller to the public, explaining why extended rationing may become necessary. The announcement would set out the quantities of the various foods that should be consumed per head per week, and appeal for a whole-hearted observance of these.

The great merit of these two acts would be:

(a) To immediately bring rationing into action

(b) The probable curtailment of the excessive consumption of foods generally

This would be in effect putting the nation upon its honour pending the decision to set up full rationing machinery, involving a system of official food-tickets, which would take some time to complete.

DEVONPORT. January 11th 1917.

The Royal Society Committee responded with their Report thus:[6]

FOOD (WAR) COMMITTEE.
ROYAL SOCIETY.
March 16, 1917.
THE NATIONAL FOOD POLICY.

I.-THE PRIMARY IMPORTANCE OF BREAD.

1. Bread is the prime foodstuff of the working classes, and it is by the consumption of bread that the mass of people are enabled to produce their daily output of work. It is impossible to ration bread without the gravest danger to the health and efficiency of the poorer element of the population, as is shown by German experience during the present War. While the average consumption of wheat flour in peace time was equivalent to 5¼ lbs. of bread per head per week, the consumption in the poorer labouring classes has always been much higher, and at the present time rises as high as 10 lbs. per head per week in families which include men doing heavy physical work on low wages. A considerable number of working men consume individually as much as 14 lbs. per week. The poorer the individual or family, the greater is the actual consumption of bread, as well as the proportion it bears to the total dietary. While among the middle classes bread supplies less than one-third of the energy of the total food they consume, with the poorer families of the working classes bread alone has to furnish more than half of the energy of their dietary.

Practically no other food is as cheap as bread; that is, no other food generally available will enable a man to do as much work for the money he spends on food as bread will. The poor man is unable to replace deficiencies in bread by other foods, because all other foods he is accustomed to use will cost him more. As a matter of experience it is found that as bread and other foods rise in price, the poor man actually buys more bread than before, because it remains still the cheapest food available to him.

The Committee wish, therefore, to insist that the first aim of the national food policy should be to maintain the supply of bread at its highest possible point, and to leave its consumption unrestricted.

II.-THE PROBLEM OF SUPPLY.

2. In considering the various problems connected with the supply and distribution

of foodstuffs during the War we have been compelled to reconsider principles which are undoubtedly valid in normal times. The considerations which ordinarily justify confidence in the stimulus of high prices on supply and their restraining effect on demand are, we recognise, to a considerable extent inapplicable at the present time. The availability of supplies is conditioned even more by the difficulties of transport from the countries of production to the countries of consumption than by the offer of an attractive price for the goods in question.

3. The position of this country is very different from that of Germany. Germany is limited to the quantities of the several foods which it can itself produce, supplemented by the limited quantities it can obtain from occupied territories and contiguous countries. This country, on the other hand, has a large measure of choice, not only as between food and imports other than food, but also as between the several forms of food. It is limited as to the total amounts which can be procured mainly by considerations of the tonnage available for transport. Until recently tonnage has been adequate for the maintenance of normal supplies of most varieties of food materials. Should the anticipation of a further shortage of shipping be realised, we are of opinion that the rationing of food materials generally should not be resorted to until unessential imports, whether of foodstuffs or of other goods, have been completely eliminated. Attention should be concentrated on those articles that are vitally necessary. The first and by far the most important of these is wheat. In the case of most other food materials their distribution among the population can be left to the effects of price, provided that the supply of the fundamental food, bread, can be maintained.

4. A few months ago the reports of the probable quantities of wheat available during the harvest year indicated that the North American supplies would be so much reduced from the level of recent years that it would be necessary to have recourse to the supplies of the Southern Hemisphere in an unusual degree, in spite of the great disadvantage presented by the longer voyage involved. Since then, however, an important revision of the Canadian figures has been made which increases the available supplies from that country – both from the crop of 1915 and from the crop of 1916 – the aggregate increase amounting to 3,000,000 tons.[7] Further, the quantities which it has been found possible to obtain from the United States have been greater than appeared probable from the harvest estimates of that country, and visible supplies at United States centres are still reported as of substantial magnitude and little less than at the same, period in 1914.[8] It would consequently appear probable that the aggregate wheat supplies of that part of the world now open to maritime trade are adequate to its needs. Moreover the necessity for drawing on very distant sources to the extent that had previously appeared unavoidable may be considered as removed.

5. Our supplies ought no longer to be affected by the shortage of tonnage so far as that was due to the necessity for sending to Australia for wheat, since it now appears that this can be obtained in North America, It is true, that in order to

secure Australian supplies, contracts were entered into between the Imperial and the Commonwealth Governments, but we would urge that, rather than carry out those contracts at the expense of an adequate supply of wheat, an effort should be made to arrange a basis of pecuniary compensation to the Australian interests affected, so as to avoid the necessity of taking delivery of wheat in Australia so long as adequate supplies can be obtained at much less distant points. In our view the problem of compensation should present less difficulty than the problem of transport. Full advantage should, therefore, first be taken of the available supplies of wheat at the nearer sources. When the shipping at our disposal has been employed as advantageously as possible for this primary purpose, it may be feasible to employ such cargo space as may not be thus disposed of to obtain barley, maize or rice, also from nearer points of supply. The admixture of these other cereals with wheat for the purpose of bread-making to a substantially larger extent than has hitherto been prescribed should, we think, be adopted before any reduction in the quantity of bread consumed is decided upon.

6. An additional supplement to our supply of breadstuffs may be secured by further reducing their use for feeding animals and for the manufacture of alcoholic beverages. So far as these cereals have been used as foods for livestock, there is room for immediate economy by drawing more heavily upon our home meat supplies for the Army in training in this country and for civilian use; thus releasing tonnage which otherwise would be required to transport refrigerated meat, and, in addition, the tonnage needed to keep up the food supply of our livestock. Since the outbreak of War the herds of cattle and flocks of sheep have grown,[9] and when the choice lies between a moderate reduction in the present numbers of our stock and a reduction in bread supply we think there should be no hesitation in deciding in favour of the former alternative. Immediate slaughter would doubtless involve the difficulty that the preparation of animals for slaughter has only taken place in the customary proportion, so that to add to the number slaughtered would not be to add quite in the same proportion to the meat produced. The final stage of the preparation of animals for the market improves appearance and flavour much more than meat yield.

In the last stage of fattening, 15 lbs. of dry food, 4 lbs. of which are imported, are consumed for the production of each additional pound of fat. We do not desire to suggest that a reduction in our supplies of meat-yielding animals should be made on the scale on which this was done in Germany in 1915, but, without proceeding to that extreme, it appears possible to add very substantially to our meat supplies from home sources.

7. The prevalence of the idea that there is a special merit in reducing the amount of meat consumed constitutes a real danger, inasmuch as it is likely to cause an increased demand for cereal foods, to make up for the smaller consumption of meat. Thus economy in meat is likely to increase the strain on tonnage rather than to decrease it.

8. It has already been announced that a further reduction is to be made in the beer and quantity of beer produced; and this reduction, together with the reduction in the spirits, output of potable alcohol, should furnish a contribution towards providing the supplies of cereals by means of which the quantity of bread available may be maintained even if the quantity of wheat imported should not be fully maintained. In our opinion no spirit at all should be manufactured in this country during the War beyond what is necessary for munitions purposes and for the provision of such a supply of yeast – unobtainable as we understand from other sources – as is absolutely necessary for bread-making. So far, moreover, as the former purpose is concerned, very serious attention should be directed to the possibility of converting to this use some part of the stock of spirit already in existence. The question of cost is altogether subordinate to the question of food supply and transport.

9. We have referred above in a general way to the desirability of restricting imports of the less essential commodities, whether foodstuffs or not, and in this connection we are of the opinion that, unless there be grave counter-balancing considerations, the prohibition of the import of fruit, which has been announced, should be strictly maintained since, bulk for bulk, its nutritive value is far below that of wheat. In any case the licences which may be granted should be limited as far as possible to cases in which no other return cargo is obtainable. Similar considerations apply, in our view, in the case of other restrictions on imports included in the list recently made public; and we would particularly direct attention in this connection to the items of paper, wood pulp and timber. By a rigid limitation of the use of paper and by a vigorous development of our domestic resources in timber there appear to be possible important economies in the demand for shipping space for imports, and no effort should be spared to realise them.

10. It appears desirable to examine the magnitude of the problem involved in the maintenance of the bread supply. In recent weeks the usual information as to imports and stocks at ports has not been made public; but from what was published up to the middle of February[10] it would appear that the stock of wheat and flour actually in this country at the present time is by no means inconsiderable in relation to the requirements of the period between now and the new harvests in the Northern Hemisphere. Taking into account the effect of the milling orders, and allowing for a probable economy in the uses of wheat and flour for purposes other than human food, the quantity required to provide for a supply of bread per head equal to that consumed prior to the War would appear to be not more than 550,000 quarters per week. Between now and the end of August there are about 25 weeks, the requirements for which on this scale would be somewhat under 14,000,000 quarters, or 3,000,000 tons, a figure approximately equal to the excess of the new over the old estimate of the resources of Canada.

11. The estimates which have been put forward by trade organs[11] suggest that

there may not improbably be in the hands of farmers and millers and in port warehouses as much as half of the requirements of the next six months. Those figures may perhaps be somewhat exaggerated, and it must be remembered that such stocks cannot be wholly used up, except on condition that we are faced by imminent starvation.[12] It must not be overlooked, however, that there are also stocks of some magnitude in the hands of bakers and in private households.

12. In the six months March to August of last year, the weight of all imports recorded in the monthly trade accounts was well in excess of 21,000,000 tons;[13] and even though it should be supposed that during the next six months that weight might be reduced by as much as 25%, the aggregate imports of the six months would exceed 15,000,000 tons, or five times the weight of the wheat required for consumption in that period. It would consequently appear that if the maintenance of the supply of wheat becomes the primary consideration which governs policy, normal supplies should not fail to be provided.

III.-THE PROBLEM OF DISTRIBUTION.

13. A proposal to ration the nation with respect to bread involves one set of problems if it is confined to a restriction of quantity, and an additional set of problems if associated with a regulation of price.

The restriction of quantity is involved in peculiar difficulties because of the fact that bread is the chief source of nutrition for the great mass of the people. The requirements of nutrition vary with sex, age, and the character of the occupation. An absolutely uniform individual ration would be satisfactory only on condition that the people lived in families so constituted that a redistribution of the total family allowance according to needs could be effected by household management within each group. But such a redistribution is impossible with the existing differences in the constitution of families and the existing differences in the distribution of industries. Accordingly, a country which introduces a bread ration soon finds itself urged to grant supplementary rations to heavy workers and to adolescents. The administrative difficulties in determining who shall receive the supplementary rations are evidently considerable, and Germany has found itself compelled to distinguish further between 'laborious' and 'very laborious' employments. And if, with changing conditions of anticipated supply, the administration finds itself compelled, as in Germany, to reduce very considerably the number of supplementary rations, this is bound to give rise to discontent.

14. Moreover, there are obvious reasons why it is hardly possible for a Government to enforce a system of bread rations without going much further – rationing first meat and then all the other important foods. Bread occupies the dominant position in working-class households because it is not only the cheapest but also the most convenient form of food. Where it is bought already baked, as is the more general practice in this country, it requires no further cooking or preparation. Even when it is baked in the household the operation

takes place at intervals of a few days. In consequence of its food value, combined with economy of labour and fuel, bread occupies a progressively larger place in the household budget the poorer the family. In families of the upper middle class it accounted before the War for less than 10% of the total expenditure on food; among skilled artisans it was about 15% ; among the bulk of the working classes it was over 21%.[14]

15. If the consumption of bread is rationed, there therefore quickly arises a popular complaint that the staple food most nearly approaching bread in nutritive value, viz., meat, is relatively too dear to be resorted to by the working classes in substitution, so that a restriction of bread alone is in effect a favouring of the more well-to-do classes. The German Government has, of course, found it necessary to yield to these representations and to ration meat also. Yet it is unavailing to fix the worker's ration at so many pounds of bread and so many pounds of meat if the worker is unable, owing to the price, to purchase the quantity of meat nominally at his disposal..

16. This result will follow the more quickly when the working classes find it difficult to obtain potatoes in the accustomed quantity. Potatoes, though not comparable, weight for weight, in nutritive qualities with bread or meat, come next to bread in their prominence in working-class consumption in the United Kingdom. In bulk they are much more important than any other item except bread. Failing bread, the working-class mother will seek to give her family potatoes. Any difficulty in obtaining them will intensify the demand that the more expensive foods shall be controlled.

17. If the restriction as to bread is one of quantity only, and price is left to supply and demand, the distribution of the available supply can also be left to the existing agencies and the operation of the usual business motives. Granting that some restrictions were deemed necessary, it would probably be wise in this country to go no further for the time being than a restriction of quantity. Rationing could reduce the consumption, and therefore probably the price (or at any rate keep it below what it would otherwise become), without reducing it sufficiently to lessen the zeal of the farmer or importer to increase the supply.

18. It must frankly be recognised that reliance cannot be placed on increase of price to check consumption in the case of bread to anything like the same extent as in maximum the case of other foodstuffs. Bread is one of the most important examples of inelastic demand, i.e., of a demand which does not readily increase or diminish as price falls or rises. Owing partly to the circumstance already referred to that, until very high prices indeed are reached, bread is the cheapest form in which nutriment can be obtained, and partly to ingrained habit, working-class families will cut down all other forms of food before they will dispense with their customary weekly purchase of bread. And it must be conceded that this consideration strengthens the argument in favour of maximum bread prices. Yet the experience of Germany has shown that it is impossible to abide by a system

of maximum retail prices and not be compelled step by step to fix wholesale and growers' prices, then to eliminate the merchant, and finally to take possession of the whole supply. German experience also shows that such action has invariably deceased production and checked supply. For the State to decide exactly when the farmer shall deliver his corn involves grave risk of miscalculation and much irritating interference with the farmer's operations. On the other hand, to permit an increase of price on corn delivered in later months may end, as in Germany, in corn being unduly held up. And if the Government takes over the supply, it has to take over the whole business of milling, distribution, and transport.

19. If a full normal supply of bread can be maintained the difficulties of the poorest class of consumers would appear to be capable of being substantially mitigated by measures less open to objection than general rationing. The situation would, for example, be much improved for this class if the children under five years consumers, of age, who are largely dependent upon milk, can have a greater assurance of supplies. The measure which it is understood is about to be introduced by the Local Government Board with reference to maternity and infant welfare centres would enable Local Authorities to provide or assist in providing milk and other foods for mothers and young children in any areas where this was required. Some of these centres are already being used to ensure the necessary provision of sugar for such young children as are brought to them. Such means of dealing with the distribution of foodstuffs of special importance to children would, if suitably developed, tend to mitigate the hardship resulting from leaving the distribution of foodstuffs as a whole to be determined by considerations of price.

20. So far as bread is concerned, the greater part of the population would be unlikely to increase their consumption of bread substantially even if the price were notably reduced. Those who have adequate incomes, including those whose earnings have increased owing to the great demand for labour for War purposes, are in a position to secure, by payment, the supplies of bread which they deem necessary to their welfare. With regard to that section of the population who, because of inadequate incomes, may be subjected to great hardship owing to the high price of bread, it would appear that the problem of adequate provision for them is one which, being of much more moderate magnitude than the control of supply for the entire population, may be attempted with greater probability of successful handling. It is, further, to be noted that the experience obtained in the handling of this more limited problem would be of great assistance should it be found inevitable, at a later date, to undertake a control of the distribution of food for the entire population.

SUMMARY

In view of the considerations set out above, the Committee emphasise the following points as the guiding principles of the National Food Policy:

1. That an unrestricted supply of bread should be maintained, whatever sacrifice

of other imports may be necessary for the purpose.

2. That no restriction should be placed on the consumption of meat.
3. That home-grown meat should be used for the Army, Navy and civilians wherever possible

The Royal Society mentioned in paragraph 6: '... An additional supplement to our supply of breadstuffs may be secured by further reducing their use for feeding, animals and for the manufacture of alcoholic beverages ...'

Alcohol production was tightly monitored as there were many wartime uses, Figure 9.8.[15]

	Monthly consumption (gallons)
Propellants	1,025,550
T.N.T. purification	60,200
Acetone (Crosfield's)	26,500
Transport services	20,000
Industrial trade (70 per cent, War services)	450,000
Chemists and druggists	117,500
Rectifiers (gin)	106,250
Bulk gallons	1,806,000
Proof gallons	3,010,000

Figure 9.8. Monthly alcohol for wartime needs

Alcohol production on this scale required almost 40,000 tons of grain and molasses. Clearly the wartime need for grain impacted the ability to produce sufficient wheat for bread. The problems were complex to say the least. The Royal Society Food Committee also issued a Private and Confidential Memo concerning milk distribution.[16]

Food (War) Committee of the Royal Society – The distribution of milk 20th November 1917
FOOD (WAR) COMMITTEE.
ROYAL SOCIETY.
November 20, 1917.

THE DISTRIBUTION OF MILK.
Draft drawn up by Dr. Hutchison and Dr. MacFadden and amended and approved by the Committee.

The Committee have been assisted in considering the questions referred to them by Major Astor by the memoranda on the subject received from medical members of the Committee, by the examination of such published figures as were available bearing on the consumption of milk in this country in pre-war periods, and by information as to the present and prospective state of our milk supply. Concerning the last, it may be said at once that although any marked diminution in the milk supply in the immediate future is not anticipated, local shortage of more or less acute character may occur.

Circumstances obviously demand that the questions put by Major Astor should be considered not only from the point of view of what is physiologically desirable, but also, in view of a possible future diminution of supplies, from what is physiologically necessary. Between these two extremes, conditions of supply may leave room for a number of intermediate adjustments of the scale of rationing, each calling for expert guidance from the medical aspect. It is anticipated that such adjustments of this kind as might be called for would be local rather than general.

In considering these questions in connection with an emergency like the present, it is necessary also to keep in mind the past habits of the population in regard to milk consumption. However desirable it may be from the point of view of public health to increase the consumption of milk among our poorer classes from the very inadequate pre-war figure to an amount which is more in accordance with their physiological needs, the present does not seem a propitious time to attempt such a reform on any great scale. The value of milk is not well understood by the people, and there might be danger of waste if supplies on a fully adequate scale were provided for them. The most that could well be expected at a time when there is a prospect of some diminution in supplies would be to ensure that the people generally did not suffer from lack of milk more than in normal times and that where milk was physiologically necessary it was supplied in adequate amounts.

As regards pre-war consumption of milk, figures given in the Board of Trade's 'Report on the Cost of Living of the Working Classes, 1908' (Cd. 3864), indicate that the weekly consumption of fresh milk in urban workmen's families in 1904 averaged only 1.8 pints per head. According to Professor Noel Paton the consumption of milk by the working-class families of Glasgow averages about half a pint per 'man' per day.

The total amount of fresh milk calculated as being available in 1916 was 928,034,000 gallons. On a population of 45,200,000, this would yield a weekly allowance per head of 3.23 pints. ('Report of the Food (War) Committee,' Cd. 8241, 1917.) The pre-war figures for Ireland give an average consumption of 3 pints per head per week.

I. The suitability of the Stockholm ration for the classes specified below. The ration referred to is:

Class 1 – 1 litre, or nearly 1¾ pints per day
Class 2 – ½ litre, or nearly 0.88 pints per day
Class 3 – ¼ litre, or nearly 0.44 pints per day

Class 4 – in accordance with a medical certificate

Taking the first of the questions put by Major Astor, the reports received from the medical members of the Committee agree generally that the amounts laid down by the Stockholm scheme are physiologically adequate and, indeed, liberal.

Class 1 of the Stockholm scheme, namely, children from birth to the age of 2 years: Sir Clifford Allbutt and Dr. Hutchison criticise the inclusion of infants from 0 to 2 years under a single ration, and most of the other reports refer more or less directly to this fault. The waste involved in this scheme would largely be avoided by altering the infant age grouping as follows:

Group 1 – 0 to 9 months (normally breast-fed) to receive milk on medical certificate up to 1½ pints per day

Group 2 – 10 to 18 months 1½ pints per day

As these groups include the section of the population for whom milk is a physiological necessity in approximately the amounts stated, the maintenance of this supply should be a first charge on the country's milk resources.

Class 2 of the Stockholm scheme, namely, children from the age of 2 to the age of 12 years, and old persons above the age of 65: Sir Clifford Allbutt and Sir Leonard Hill would extend the age period of this group to cover puberty. They doubtless had 'physiological desirability' in view when recommending this step. Others appear to be content with the Stockholm provision for this age group, viz., ⅞ of a pint per head per day. Having in view the amounts consumed by the working-class families as shown in the figures given above, it is clear that the argument for physiological necessity is much less strong at these ages. We think it would be desirable to sub-divide this class into two groups:

Group 3 – 19 months to 5 years … 1 pint

Group 4 – 6 to 14 years … 1 pint

This would ensure for the younger of these age groups priority over the elder, which would operate favourably for the younger in the case of diminishing supplies.

We would propose omitting the age group 65 upwards from this class, leaving such individuals in it as really require milk to obtain it on a medical certificate as arranged for the last group (6).

Class 3 of the Stockholm scheme, namely all other healthy persons (Group 5): There appears to be general agreement as to the amount, namely 0.44 of a pint, prescribed for this class in the Stockholm scheme being sufficient, but several of the reports suggest that as milk is unnecessary in this age group no allocation should be made for it. In administering a priority system of rationing this would obviously be the correct course to take if the necessity arose. It might be desirable on general grounds however to make a small allowance of milk to adults. In considering the needs of the last three groups, it should be remembered that milk is largely taken in the form of milk puddings or in making palatable other kinds of food.

Class 4 of the Stockholm scheme, namely sick persons and pregnant women (Group 6): Sir Leonard Hill and Professor Cushny criticise the proposal to deal with the requirements of invalids by means of a doctor's certificate, and the latter refers to the experience of the Ministry of Food in this respect in the case of bread. It is difficult to see however in what other way this class could be dealt with. The Ministry of Food would of course need to devise some means for limiting abuses, such as, for instance, a schedule of diseases which need a milk diet. On the understanding that this schedule is narrowly limited, this group should rank with groups 1 and 2.

The Groups suggested above are:

1. 0 to 9 months 1½ pints per day
2. 10 to 18 months 1½ pints per day
3. 19 months to 5 years 1 pint per day
4. 6 to 14 years, 1 pint per day
5. All other healthy persons, ¼ pint per day, or according to supply available
6. Sick persons and pregnant women, according to medical certificate

In allotting supplies to the different groups preference would be given in the order 1 to 5. Group 6 would rank with groups 1 and 2.

II. The relation of the Stockholm ration to the normal pre-war consumption of milk in the United Kingdom.

No figures are available to enable us accurately to compare the pre-war consumption of milk with that provided by the Stockholm scheme. It is fairly clear, however, that the latter represents a much larger consumption per head than exists in this country. As has been estimated, the total milk available in the United Kingdom, only allows of the consumption of about ½ pint per head per day. The figures of the Board of Trade report show that the average consumption among workmen's families did not reach 2 pints per head per week. As already pointed out these are facts which should be taken into careful consideration in any scheme of milk rationing.

III. The advisability of adopting a flat rate and the possibility of its adoption leading to a wastage or to unnecessarily high consumption of milk by certain classes at the expense of the remainder.

The Committee advocates a priority scheme rather than a flat rate. Anomalies can, to a large extent, be removed by careful sub-division of the age groups when such a food as milk is concerned. The revised sub-divisions suggested above have been made largely for this purpose. Even so difficulties will remain. The scheme for instance does not recognise the normally higher consumption of milk by the middle and upper social classes as compared with the working classes. We think, however, that any danger of waste, due to over reservation of milk for a given class, would be avoided by insisting on early notification of demands by customers within the limit of the quantities allotted to them on the priority scale.

IV. Suggestions for a lower scale, if the above allowance were unobtainable, or were thought to be considerably in excess of normal consumption.

We have already suggested modifications of the Stockholm scale. In the case of the six groups which we have suggested above, any diminution in the milk supply necessitating alteration in the allowances, should be met by a reduction, first of all, in groups 5 and 4, until the milk allotted to these groups was exhausted, and subsequently, if necessary, a reduction in the allowance of group 3.

One might be tempted to think that these reports were merely an academic exercise. Not so. The second interim report from the Committee on the Production and Distribution of Milk, had the following committee members:[17]

Major the Hon. Waldorf Astor, M.P	Chairman
Mr. J. F. Blackshaw	Board of Agriculture and Fisheries
Mr. J. B . Campbell	Department of Agriculture and Technical Instruction for Ireland
Major Gerald R. Leighton, M.D	Local Government Board, Scotland
Dr. A.W.J. MacFadden	Local Government Board, England
Sir George Newman, M.D.	Board of Education
Mr. Dermod O'Brien	Local Government Board. Ireland
Mr. James O'Grady, M.P.	
Mr. W. Anker Simmons	Ministry of Food
Sir Robert P. Wright	Board of Agriculture for Scotland
Mr. J. MacKintosh, Secretary	Food Production Department

The second interim report was presented to Parliament and contained the following statement:

IV. Preferential Distribution. The Committee examined the possibility of allocating the supplies of milk, if they became materially reduced, to different sections of the community on some system of priority according to their respective needs. They obtained the views of the Food (War) Committee of the Royal Society, as well as of the representatives of Day Nurseries, &c. They also had the advantage of studying the German War rations and the report of a scheme which had been adopted in Stockholm. In considering this question in connection with an emergency like the present, it has been necessary to have regard to the past habits of the population in regard to milk consumption. However desirable it might be from the point of view of public health to increase the consumption of milk particularly among the poorer classes, from the very inadequate pre-war figure to an amount which is more in accordance with their physiological needs, the present is not a propitious time to attempt such a reform on any great scale. The most that could well be expected at a time when there is a prospect of some diminution in supplies would be to ensure that people generally did not suffer from lack of milk more than in normal times and that where milk was physiologically necessary it was supplied in adequate amounts …

Those involved

Health and well-being covers a multitude of activities and disciplines, Figures 9.9 through to 9.12. The scientists mentioned in these figures are merely representative of the many who worked in the general field of well-being. All were affected by the War in one way or another even though they were, in the vast majority of cases, based in the United Kingdom.

Name	Activity
Andrews (Sir Frederick)	Made a careful and prolonged study of the serological races of dysentery bacilli.[18]
Cheyne (Sir William Watson)	Was Consulting Surgeon to the Royal Navy and in 1915 became temporary Surgeon-General RN being afterwards given the rank of Rear-Admiral and KCMG. He retired at the end of the War.[19]
Dobell (Clifford)	The Imperial College released Dobell for service with the War Office, to conduct protozoological investigations of dysentery of intestinal protozoal infections. He was engaged in this work from the end of 1915 until 1919 (based at the Wellcome Bureau of Scientific Research which was placed at the disposal of the War Office for this purpose).[20]
Dreyer (Georges)	He first worked with A.C. Inman perfecting the diagnosis of typhoid and paratyphoid fever in inoculated men. He pressed for the inoculation of all troops with typhoid-paratyphoid vaccine (TAB) instead of the ordinary typhoid vaccine, a procedure which was adopted after he appeared before the Pathological Advisory Committee of the Army Medical Service. Later he joined the RAF and took up certain problems connected with high altitude flying. He designed an automated oxygen dispenser which delivered different oxygen levels for different flying altitudes.[21]
MacBride (Ernest William)	Was made a member of the Committee appointed in 1913 by the Board of Agriculture and Fisheries under the chairmanship of Mr. H.G. Maurice to draw up a program for English fishery investigations.[22]

Name	Activity
Masterman (Arthur Thomas)	He served as an expert on the International Council for the Exploration of the Sea and his department took charge of the English investigations … rejected as too old for War Service but in 1917 was seconded to the Technical Department of the Air Ministry, to be transferred in 1918 to the National Salvage Committee.[23]
Middleton (Sir Thomas Hudson)	Worked in the Food Production Department.[24]
Newstead (Robert)	Appointed by the War Office (1915) to the charge of an Entomological Commission to deal with 'insect prophylaxis' in France and Flanders. He served on this Commission for six months, and a year later joined the late Sir John Fryer in the establishment, at the request of the Board of Agriculture, of the Royal Society Grain Pests (War) Committee.[25]
Pembrey (Marcus Seymour)	Member of the Advisory Board for Army Medical Services, Pembery was appointed to the Committee which between 1906 and 1909 enquired into the physiological effects of food, training and clothing on the soldier … This committee recommended the scale of rations for the troops on active service which was in operation at the beginning of the Great War. The scale of the rations had been drawn up for soldiers on active service and not in trench warfare conditions. The scale of the rations was thought to be excessive for trench warfare and were reduced with no detriment to the troops.[26]
Shearer (Creswell)	Worked at the Military Hospital at Devonport working on the growth of Meningococcus.[27]
Todd (Charles)	On the outbreak of War, Todd was appointed Director of the Hygienic Institute, of which the title was changed to Public Health Laboratories.[28]
Trotter (Wilfred Batten Lewis)	Remained in London working on a committee appointed by the Medical Research Council for the study of wound injuries of the brain and nerves.[29]

Figure 9.9. Government Committees

There were some medics who remained in private practice yet were fundamental to the War effort, Figure 9.10.

Name	Activity
Dakin (Henry Drysdale)	Invited by Dr. Flexner of the Rockefeller Institute to cooperate in a research program on the treatment of infected wounds which had been initiated in France by the late Alexis Carrel … . There, in cooperation with French military surgeons, Dakin developed the buffered hypochlorite solution which bears his name.[30]
Forster-Cooper (Sir Clive)	Like many other zoologists, was diverted to medical work on human animal parasites. The work was a symptomatic examination of the action of quinine on malaria, covering all possible methods of administration and each species of malaria parasite.[31]
Freud (Sigmund)	The War actually helped the progress of psychoanalysis by opening the eyes of the medical profession to the importance of psychogenesis in neurotic disturbances and in some of the early Freudian formulations such as 'flight into illness' suddenly became popular. The old cathartic method was used in treatment of a great many cases of so-called 'shell shock'.[32]

Figure 9.10. Wartime medical practice

Of course there was a constant need to train the next generation of medics and so the traditional academic posts remained occupied as in pre-war times. These departments were depleted of both staff and students, however they did carry on as best they could. There were some individuals, however, who combined their academic position with that of secondments to the armed forces. For example

> … Harvey Williams Cushing ForMemRS became the Moseley Professor of Surgery at the Harvard Medical School and Surgeon-in-Chief at the newly built Peter Bent Brigham Hospital. Cushing worked and taught in both institutions for twenty years, excepting his absences in France in the World War – for a brief time in the spring of 1915 and from May 1917 to March 1919. In the latter War period he was First Director of the United States Base Hospital No 5 attached to the British Expeditionary Forces and later was Consultant in Neurosurgery to the American Expeditionary Force[33] …

Some of the other Fellows are mentioned in Figure 9.11

Fellows	Activity
Albert (A. T.)	Director of the Institute Raoul Warocque.[34]

Bolton (Charles)	Director of Pathological Studies and Research, University College Hospital Medical School. Bolton also took charge of a special extension of the hospital for army patients particularly those with dysentery.[35]
Dixey (Frederick Augustus)	Bursar of Wadham College, Oxford University (1906-1927).[36]
Fletcher (Sir Walter Morley)	The first Secretary of the Medical Research Council in 1914, and member of the Sectional Physiology Committee of the Royal Society.[37]
Hardy (Sir William Bate)	Became Biological Secretary of the Royal Society and as such organised the Food War Committee and during those years came into close touch with the many problems of food values, supplies and transport.[38]
Hopkins (Sir Frederick Gowland)	Appointed Chair of Biochemistry at Cambridge in 1914. He also became a member of the Royal Society Food Committee.[39]
MacDonald (John Smyth)	Succeeded Professor Sir Charles Scott Sherrington[40] OM FRS as Holt Professor of Physiology in the University of Liverpool.[41]
Macleod (John James Rickard)	Professor of Physiology at the Western Reserve University, Ohio (1902-1918).[42]
Mellanby (Sir Edward)	Appointed to Chair of Physiology of the University of London in the King's (now Queen Elizabeth's) College for Women (1913).[43]
Murray (James Alexander)	Director of the Imperial Cancer Research Fund.[44]
Smith (Theobald)	Director of the Department of Animal Pathology of the Rockefeller Institute for Medical Research at Princeton (from 1915).[45]

Figure 9.11. Some medically-trained Fellows in academic posts, research facilities or hospital.

Some of the Fellows were involved with agriculture and/or botany. In some cases the botanists at institutes such Kew Gardens were asked to grow plants of pharmaceutical interest, others worked as crop inspectors, on food committees etc. Figure 9.12 shows just a few of these Fellows.

Fellow	**Activity**
Balfour (Sir Isaac Bayley)	King's Botanist in Scotland 1888-1922.[46]
Bateson (William)	Director of the John Innes Centre from (1910-19).[47]

Fellow	Activity
Biffen (Sir Rowland Harry)	Director of the Plant Breeding Institute at Cambridge (from 1912).[48]
Brooks (Frederick Tom)	Joined the staff of the Department of Food Production as Plant Pathologist (1917).[49]
Ewart (Alfred James)	Chair of Botany at Melbourne University.[50]
Imms (Augustus Daniel)	Acted as an additional crop pest Inspector and Reporter for the (then) Board of Agriculture throughout most of the War.[51]
Keeble (Sir Frederick William)	Controller of Horticulture in the Food Production Department of the Board of Agriculture.[52]
Kluyver (Albert Jan)	Appointed a consultant for the Dutch East Indies to the Department of Agriculture, Industry and Commerce (in 1916).[53]
Robinson (Gilbert Wooding)	Appointed Advisory Agricultural Chemist for North Wales (in 1912).[54]
Smith (Sir William Wright)	Deputy keeper of the Edinburgh Garden and continued to catalogue the collections from Forrest's expeditions.[55]

Figure 9.12. Some Fellows involved in either agriculture or botany.

As might be expected there were some Fellows that defied categorisation. They included:

- Arthur Felix FRS a medical practitioner who co-discovered the Weil-Felix reaction (diagnosis of rickettsial infections) in the autumn of 1915.[56]
- Frederick Wallace Edwards FRS worked for the British Red Cross Society (1914-1916) prior to resigning from his post and was granted special leave from his permanent job (with the London Museum) until April 1919 during which he worked as an agricultural labourer.[57]
- Marjory Stephenson FRS worked with the British Red Cross (October 1914 to September 1918) at first in France and then in Salonika.[58]
- Sir Alexander Cruikshank Houston FRS. Prior to the outbreak of the War, Houston was appointed the first Director of Water Examinations to the Metropolitan Water Board, a post he held until 1928.[59]
- Sir William Dampier FRS was asked to help in a food production campaign during which he inherited a small estate near Yeovil and used his own farms to try out his ideas. His surplus whey was used by Dr. Leonard Harding in developing a new method for making lactose which ultimately developed into a commercial process.[60]

10 Conclusion

It might be difficult, if not impossible, to undertake a detailed analysis of the impact the Royal Society as a corporate body and individual Fellows had on the course of the War. Equally difficult might be the relative contributions.

We know from three documents in earlier chapters and one in the appendices, that Royal Society Committees were held in high regard and the contents of their reports were read. Also minutes of government committees referred to them. For example:

- Board of Invention and Research launch meeting document
- Report by the Food Controller on bread, meat and sugar January 1917
- Committee on the Production and Distribution of Milk
- Minutes of a Meeting of the War Cabinet held at 10 Downing Street, S.W., on Thursday, December 13th, 1917, at 11 a.m.

These four government documents were used here to illustrate various points, but many other government documents could have been chosen making reference to the Royal Society War Committees.

Additionally we know the Government War Badge Committee were happy to allow the equivalent Royal Society Committee to act as an administrative centre for vetting certain chemists in their war-work.

We also know that various government departments and committees actively sought the inclusion of Fellows. Also many letters still exist in the Royal Society and National Archives from various Government officials and the Fellows.

There can be no doubt that the expertise and commitment of the Royal Society as a corporate body served the country well during the War.

Equally, at least for the Fellows mentioned in earlier chapters, we can assess the way the Fellows were recognised by the Government at the time. Arguably the easiest way to approach this might be to look at the honours invested in the Fellows either during the War, or shortly thereafter.

Of course before undertaking such a task it is worth briefly mentioning the honours system. Fortunately, the Government website explains the system in detail, and comments:[1]

> ... the honours system recognises people who've made great achievements in public life and people who've committed themselves to serving Britain. They will usually have made life better for other people or been outstanding at what they do. People get honours for achievements like:
> - changing things, with an emphasis on achievement
> - displaying moral courage and vision in making and delivering tough choices
> - enhancing Britain's reputation
> - improving life for people less able to help themselves
> - innovation and entrepreneurship
> - long-term voluntary service
> - making a difference to their community or field of work

There are various types of Honour. In the extreme there could be the award of a peerage. In the early 20th century peerages were hereditary and, then as now, the five types range from Duke (the most senior) through Marquis, Earl and Viscount to Baron (the lowest order). From there on the awards are (see note 1 for further details):

- Companion of Honour(CH)
  A major contribution to the arts, science, medicine, or government lasting over a long period of time
- Knight/Dame (typically KBE and DBE)
  A major contribution in any activity, usually at national level. Other people working in the nominee's area will see their contribution as inspirational and significant, requiring commitment over a long period of time
- Commander of the British Empire (CBE)
  A prominent but lesser role at national level, or a leading role at regional level. You can also get one for a distinguished, innovative contribution to any area
- Order of the British Empire (OBE)
  A major local role in any activity, including people whose work has made them known nationally in their chosen area
- Member of the British Empire (MBE)
  A significant achievement or outstanding service to the community. An MBE is also awarded for local 'hands-on' service which stands out as an example to other people
- British Empire Medal (BEM)
  Reintroduced in 2012, this rewards a sustained, local contribution or innovative, high-impact work of a relatively short duration (e.g., 3-4 years).

Then as now there is an established process of nomination and a series of committees overseeing the various nominations. There are always some high profile people serving these committees. It is useful to outline the process as any Fellows awarded such an honour must have had his or her nomination scrutinised for eligibility. Figure 10.1 shows those Fellows awarded a knighthood or above either during the War or shortly thereafter, their other honours (if they had any) are also shown for completeness.

Fellow	Honour
Anderson (John, 1st Viscount Waverley)	CB 1918; KCB 1919; GCB 1923; GCIE 1932; GCSI 1937; Viscount 1952; OM 1957
Arden-Close (Sir Charles Frederick)	CMG 1899; CB 1916; KBE 1917
Balfour (Arthur James, 1st Earl of Balfour)	OM 1916; KG 1922; Earl 1922
Bayliss (Sir William Maddock)	Kt 1922
Beilby (Sir George Thomas)	Kt 1916
Bragg (Sir William Henry)	CBE 1917; KBE 1920; OM 1931
Bruce (Sir David)	CB 1905; Kt 1908; KCB 1918
Burrard (Sir Sidney Gerald)	CSI 1911; KCSI 1914
Cadman (John, Baron Cadman of Silverdale)	CMG 1916; KCMG 1918; GCMG 1929; Baron 1937
Cheyne (Sir William Watson)	CB 1899; Bt 1908; KCMG 1915
Churchill (Sir Winston Leonard Spencer)	CH 1922; OM 1946; KG 1953
Clerk (Sir Dugald)	KBE 1917
Darwin (Sir Horace)	KBE 1918
David (Sir Tannatt William Edgeworth)	CMG 1910; DSO 1918; KBE 1920
Dobbie (Sir James Johnston)	Kt 1915
Dyson (Sir Frank Watson)	Kt 1915; KBE 1926
Fletcher (Sir Walter Morley)	KBE 1918; CB 1929
Garrod (Sir Archibald Edward)	CMG 1916; KCMG 1918
Gibb (Sir Alexander)	CB 1918; KBE 1918; GBE 1920
Glazebrook (Sir Richard Tetley)	CB 1910; Kt 1917; KCB 1920; KCVO 1934
Hadcock (Sir Albert George)	KBE 1918
Hadfield (Sir Robert Abbott)	Kt 1908; Bt 1917
Hall (Sir Alfred Daniel)	KCB 1918
Hankey (Maurice Pascal Alers, 1st Baron Hankey of the Chart)	CB 1912; KCB 1916; GCB 1919; GCMG 1929; GCVO 1934; Baron 1939
Harmer (Sir Sidney Frederic)	KBE 1920
Heath (Sir Thomas Little)	CB 1903; KCB 1909; KCVO 1916

Fellow	Honour
Herdman (Sir William Abbott)	Kt 1922; CBE 1920
Holden (Sir Henry Capel Lofft)	CB 1911; KCB 1916
Houston (Sir Alexander Cruikshank)	KBE 1918; CVO 1919
Jackson (Sir Henry Bradwardine)	KCVO 1906; KCB 1910; GCB 1916
Jackson (Sir Herbert)	KBE 1917
Keeble (Sir Frederick William)	CBE 1917; Kt 1922
Keith (Sir Arthur)	Kt 1921
Lenox-Conyngham (Sir Gerald Ponsonby)	Kt 1919
Lewis (Sir Thomas)	CBE 1920; Kt 1921
Lindsay (David Alexander Edward, 27th Earl of Crawford and 10th Earl of Balcarres)	KT 1921
Long (Walter Hume, 1st Viscount Long of Wraxall)	Viscount 1921
Lyle (Sir Thomas Ranken)	Kt 1922
Middleton (Sir Thomas Hudson)	CB 1913; KBE 1918; KCIE 1929
Moulton (John Fletcher, Baron Moulton)	Kt 1906; Baron 1912; KCB 1915; GBE 1917
Petavel (Sir Joseph Ernest)	KBE 1920
Pope (Sir William Jackson)	KBE 1919
Robertson (Sir Robert)	KBE 1918
Ross (Sir Ronald)	CB 1902; KCB 1911; KCMG 1918
Russell (Sir Edward John)	OBE 1918; Kt 1922
Russell (Herbrand Arthur, 11th Duke of Bedford)	KG 1902; KBE 1919
Rutherford (Ernest, Baron Rutherford of Nelson)	Kt 1914; OM 1925; Baron 1931
Schuster (Sir Arthur)	Kt 1920
Shaw (Sir William Napier)	Kt 1915
Sherrington (Sir Charles Scott)	GBE 1922; OM 1924
Strahan (Sir Aubrey)	KBE 1919
Tennyson D'Eyncourt (Sir Eustace Henry William)	CB 1915; KCB 1917; Bt 1930
Threlfall (Sir Richard)	KBE 1917; GBE 1927
Tomes (Sir Charles Sissmore)	Kt 1919

Fellow	Honour
Vincent (Edgar, Viscount D'Abernon)	KCMG 1887; Baron 1914; GCMG 1917; Viscount 1926; GCB 1926
Volterra (Sir Vito)	KBE 1921
Walker (Sir James)	Kt 1921
Woodward (Sir Arthur Smith)	Kt 1924
Wright (Sir Almroth Edward)	Kt 1906; CB 1915; KBE 1919
Yarrow (Sir Alfred Fernandez)	Bt 1916

Figure 10.1. Fellows honoured with a Knighthood or greater either during or just after the War

There are two comments to make beyond the large number of Fellows receiving knighthoods either during or shortly after the War. The first comment is that this is only a partial list of the activities of the Fellows who worked on War related activities. The second is that there may have been a Fellow who appears in Figure 10.1 who would have appeared on a similar list had there been no War, simply because his work was of national or international significance. Accepting both those points, one would assume that the honours list during and just after a War would be heavily influenced by the wartime exploits of the individual. Wars do tend to focus the mind somewhat.

Figure 10.2 lists those Fellows whose work is briefly mentioned in earlier chapters who received the CBE.

Fellow	Honour
Bairstow (Sir Leonard)	CBE 1917; Kt 1952
Baker (Herbert Brereton)	CBE 1917
Baly (Edward Charles Cyril)	CBE 1918
Barcroft (Sir Joseph)	CBE 1918; Kt 1935
Bolton (Charles)	CBE 1920
Bragg (Sir William Henry)	CBE 1917; KBE 1920; OM 1931
Callendar (Hugh Longbourne)	CBE 1920
Crossley (Arthur William)	CMG 1917; CBE 1919
Dale (Sir Henry Hallett)	CBE 1919; Kt 1932; GBE 1943; OM 1944
Dixon (Harold Baily)	CBE 1918
Donnan (Frederick George)	CBE 1920
Dreyer (Georges)	CBE 1919
Duddell (William)	CBE 1917 (posthumously)

Fellow	Honour
Eve (Arthur Stewart)	CBE 1918
Frankland (Percy Faraday)	CBE 1920
Gordon (Mervyn Henry)	CMG 1917; CBE 1919
Herdman (Sir William Abbott)	Kt 1922; CBE 1920
Jenkin (Charles Frewen)	CBE 1919
Keeble (Sir Frederick William)	CBE 1917; Kt 1922
Lewis (Sir Thomas)	CBE 1920; Kt 1921
Raper (Henry Stanley)	CBE 1918
Wood (Thomas Barlow)	CBE 1918
Yule (George Udny)	CBE 1918

Figure 10.2. Some Fellows who received the CBE either during the War or shortly thereafter

Once again this list is restricted to those Fellows who appear in earlier chapters. Mention was made previously of the assumption that these honours were awarded for war-work. Some biographical memoirs, however, specifically mention this, Figure 10.3.

Fellow	Honour
Clerk (Sir Dugald)	He was created KBE largely for his work during the War as Director of Engineering Research at the Admiralty, as a member of the Advisory Committee for Aeronautics and as Chairman of the Internal Combustion Engine Committee for the Air Ministry. He was also a member of the Inventions Committee of the Board of Invention and Research.[2]
Dreyer (Georges)	He was created a CBE for this work.[3]
Fermor (Sir Lewis Leigh)	Investigated the coal resources of Korea State in Madhya Pradesh (1914-1915), acted as Mineral Adviser to the Indian Munitions Board (1916-1918). Here he worked out schemes for manufacturing calcium carbide and nitrogenous fertilisers in India. He also investigated the possibility of smelting aluminium ore in India as a War measure. At the end of the War he was awarded the OBE for his work on these two Boards.[4]
Fowler (Sir Ralph Howard)	Awarded OBE for war work.[5]

Fellow	Honour
Garrod (Sir Archibald Edward)	The War took him to Malta as consulting physician to the Forces there. He saw the patients evacuated from Gallipoli and later from Salonika. He was created KCMG for his services.[6]
Gibson (Charles Stanley)	In England he immediately rejoined Pope, and their work on the manufacture of mustard gas is only too well known to require detailed discussion. Unfortunately, during the course of this, owing to an accident in the works, Gibson suffered from gas poisoning and there is little doubt that he never fully recovered from this. His services to the country were recognised in 1919 by the award of the OBE and during the same year he was appointed Professor of Chemistry at the Egyptian Government School of Medicine in Cairo.[7]
Glazebrook (Sir Richard Tetley)	He had been made a CB in 1910 and a knighthood in 1917. He was created KCB in 1920.[8]
Hadcock (Sir Albert George)	Went to France several times personally to inspect the new guns and mountings in use at the Front, after the War he was a member of the commission sent to Germany on behalf of the Government to inspect the dismantling of arms factories there. He was created a KBE for his war-work.[9]
Rankine (Alexander Oliver)	His main personal research contribution was a device, called a Photophone, for transmitting speech by means of a beam of light, but also worked on acoustic and electromagnetic means of submarine detection. For his work in the War he received the OBE.[10]
Smiles (Samuel)	Chemist on the Small Arms Ammunition Committee of the Ministry of Munitions and carried out work on tracer bullets. For these services he was awarded the OBE.[11]
Threlfall (Sir Richard)	He threw himself with great ardour into the work of applying chemistry to the Army, Navy and Air Service. He served on the Board of Invention and Research under Lord Fisher, on the Advisory Council for Scientific and Industrial Research and on the Trench Warfare Committee .... His work on the preparation and use of phosphorous smoke screens and the tracer bomb were of vital importance to the War. For these services he was made a KBE in 1917 and a GBE in 1927.[12]

Fellow	Honour
Yule (George Udny)	Seconded from Cambridge (1915) and became statistician to the Director of Army Contracts, and on the formation of the Ministry of Food, he went over to that body eventually becoming Director of Requirements. For this work he was given the CBE.[13]

Figure 10.3. Comments in biographical memoirs to the award of honours

Perhaps the award to William Duddell FRS, mentioned in Figure 10.2, is worthy of comment. William Du Bois Duddell FRS was born on 1st July 1872 and died on 04th November 1917. He was an electrical engineer and received the Hughes Medal in 1912, having been elected Fellow of the Royal Society on 2nd May 1907, aged 35. More details are available in his biographical memoir.[14]

Duddell was busy, at least during the first part of the War. He served on the:

- Royal Society War Committee
- Physics Sub-Committee
- Engineering Sub-Committee
- Board of Invention and Research Panel member
- Department of Munitions Inventions main Panel and Instrument Committee Member

He also:

- was awarded at least one secret patent (with Sir Richard T. Glazebrook & Mr. F.E. Smith's number 2825/1915)
- wrote at least one report on submarine sound signalling (appears as Appendix IV)
- repaired and/or reconstructed various instruments recovered from wrecked enemy airships

Other Fellows were equally prolific in their work. For example:

Lord Rayleigh FRS was:

1. a member of the Royal Society War Committee
2. Chairman of the Royal Society Physics Committee
3. President of a Government Committee on Explosives for six years
4. Scientific Advisor to Trinity House (1896 to 1919)
5. Board of Invention and Research Panel Member and Member of the Section I. Airships Sub-Committee
6. President of the Advisory Committee on Aeronautics on its formation in 1909 and remained a Member until 1920
7. a former President of the Royal Society (1905-08)

He wrote many reports including the following:

1. Use of Liquid Hydrogen on airships
2. Detection of holes in fabric of an airship

3. Preliminary report on the Silicol Process for the production of hydrogen
4. Note on electrically heated garment for airship pilots
5. Note on the heating effect to be obtained from the exhaust of an airship, used to raise the inside temperature of the ship
6. Further model experiments on the temperature attainable from the exhaust gases in airships applied to heat the envelope

Sir Richard Glazebrook FRS was a member of:
1. The Royal Society War Committee
2. Royal Society Physics Sub-Committee
3. a Panel Member of the MID and also of the Instruments subcommittee
4. a Panel Member of the Air Inventions Committee and of the Aeronautics and Instruments Sub-Committees
5. a Member of the BIR Section II. (Submarines, mines, searchlights, wireless telegraphy and general electrical, electro-magnetic, optical and acoustic subjects)

He was also Director of National Physical Laboratory (NPL) during the War and wrote at least one Secret Patent (Mr. W. Duddell's, Sir Richard Glazebrook's & Mr. F.E. Smith's Invention No. C.P. Secret Patent 2825/1915).

Sir Dugald Clerk FRS was a member of the:
1. Engineering War Committee of the Royal Society
2. Physics War Committee of the Royal Society
3. Air Inventions Committee
4. Engine Sub-Committee (No 1)
5. Panel Member of the Board of Invention and Research
6. Internal Combustion Engine Sub-Committee of the BIR

Professor Sir J.E. Petavel FRS was a member of the:
1. Engineering War Committee of the Royal Society
2. Engine Sub-Committee (No 1), Aeronautics Sub-Committee (No 2) and Procedure Sub-Committee (No 5) of the Air Inventions Committee
3. Section I. Airships Sub-Committee of the Board of Invention and Research

Of course everyone in the first nine chapters played their part in the War effort. Some, as those above, played a significant part. Lord Rutherford FRS and Sir William Bragg FRS went on to the Presidency of the Royal Society, Figure 10.4.[15]

Name	Years as President
Sir Robert Robinson OM	1945-1950
Sir Henry (Hallett) Dale OM GBE	1940-1945
Sir William Henry Bragg OM KBE	1935-1940
Sir Frederick Gowland Hopkins OM	1930-1935
Ernest, Lord Rutherford of Nelson OM	1925-1930
Sir Charles Scott Sherrington OM GBE	1920-1925

Figure 10.4. Presidents of the Royal Society 1920-1950

Sadly Lord Rutherford died in Cambridge on the 19th October 1937 and Sir William in London on 12th March 1942. Interestingly all of the other Presidents listed in Figure 10.4 have been mentioned somewhere in the first nine chapters. Sir Charles Scott Sherrington and Sir Frederick Gowland Hopkins were members of the Royal Society Sectional Committee on Physiology. Sir Henry (Hallett) Dale was a member of the Sectional Chemical Committee and Sir Robert Robinson, Professor of Chemistry at Liverpool University where he helped in the preparation of pharmaceutical drugs.

All of the scientists in Figure 10.4 were awarded the Nobel Prize, Figure 10.6.

Year	Chemistry	Physics	Physiology or Medicine
1945	Artturi Ilmari Virtanen	Wolfgang Pauli	Sir Alexander Fleming, Ernst Boris Chain, Sir Howard Walter Florey
1944	Otto Hahn	Isidor Isaac Rabi	Joseph Erlanger, Herbert Spencer Gasser
1943	George de Hevesy	Otto Stern	Henrik Carl Peter Dam, Edward Adelbert Doisy
1942	Not awarded	Not awarded	Not awarded
1941	Not awarded	Not awarded	Not awarded
1940	Not awarded	Not awarded	Not awarded
1939	Adolf Friedrich Johann Butenandt, Leopold Ruzicka	Ernest Orlando Lawrence	Gerhard Domagk
1938	Richard Kuhn	Enrico Fermi	Corneille Jean François Heymans

Year	Chemistry	Physics	Physiology or Medicine
1937	Sir Walter Norman Haworth, Paul Karrer	Clinton Joseph Davisson, George Paget Thomson	Albert von Szent-Györgyi Nagyrápolt
1936	Petrus (Peter) Josephus Wilhelmus Debye	Victor Franz Hess, Carl David Anderson	Sir Henry Hallett Dale, Otto Loewi
1935	Frédéric Joliot, Irène Joliot-Curie	James Chadwick	Hans Spemann
1934	Harold Clayton Urey	Not awarded	George Hoyt Whipple, George Richards Minot, William Parry Murphy
1933	Not awarded	Erwin Schrödinger, Paul Adrien Maurice Dirac	Thomas Hunt Morgan
1932	Irving Langmuir	Werner Karl Heisenberg	Sir Charles Scott Sherrington, Edgar Douglas Adrian
1931	Carl Bosch, Friedrich Bergius	Not awarded	Otto Heinrich Warburg
1930	Hans Fischer	Sir Chandrasekhara Venkata Raman	Karl Landsteiner
1929	Sir Arthur Harden, Hans Karl August Simon von Euler-Chelpin	Prince Louis-Victor Pierre Raymond de Broglie	Christiaan Eijkman, Sir Frederick Gowland Hopkins
1928	Adolf Otto Reinhold Windaus	Sir Owen Willans Richardson	Charles Jules Henri Nicolle
1927	Heinrich Otto Wieland	Arthur Holly Compton, Charles Thomson Rees Wilson	Julius Wagner-Jauregg
1926	The (Theodor) Svedberg	Jean Baptiste Perrin	Johannes Andreas Grib Fibiger
1925	Richard Adolf Zsigmondy	James Franck, Gustav Ludwig Hertz	Not awarded
1924	Not awarded	Karl Manne Georg Siegbahn	Willem Einthoven
1923	Fritz Pregl	Robert Andrews Millikan	Sir Frederick Grant Banting, John James Rickard Macleod

Figure 10.5. Sir Henry (Hallett) Dale. (© Godfrey Argent Studio. Reproduced with permission)

Year	Chemistry	Physics	Physiology or Medicine
1922	Francis William Aston	Niels Henrik David Bohr	Archibald Vivian Hill, Otto Fritz Meyerhof
1921	Frederick Soddy	Albert Einstein	Not awarded
1920	Walther Hermann Nernst	Charles Edouard Guillaume	Schack August Steenberg Krogh

Figure 10.6. Science Nobel Laureates 1920-45.

There are also some other familiar names mentioned in Figure 10.6, for example Sir Alexander Fleming FRS.

Looking forward to the Second World War, which will be the subject of another book, Sir Henry (Hallett) Dale OM GBE, was to become one of the busiest Fellows, Figure 10.5. His entry in the Royal Society online database lists the following:[16]

Wellcome Physiological Research Laboratories, Brockwell Park, (1904); Director (1906); joined Central Research Institute of the Medical Research Committee which was to become the Medical Research Council (1914); Secretary of Royal Society's Shock Committee; Member, General Medical Council (1927-1937); served on National Institute for Medical Research (1928-1942); Trustee, Wellcome Trust; Trustee, British Museum (1940-1963);

Member, Medical Research Council (1942-1946); President, British Council (1950-1963); Chairman, Wellcome Trust (1938-1960); Director, Royal Institution.

Sir Henry was to play a large role in the activities of the Royal Society, as President, during World War II.

For some Fellows their involvement in World War II started much earlier.

A part time organisation was established by A.V. Hill FRS (Vice President), and Lord Ernest Rutherford FRS (President) called the Academic Assistance Council (AAC) (in 1933) with two Honorary Secretaries; William Beveridge, Director of the London School of Economics and C.S. Gibson, FRS, Professor of Chemistry at Guy's Hospital. The organisation was formed as part of the international effort to rescue refugee scholars from the increasingly hostile political situation in Europe.

In May 1933, Beveridge circulated a document announcing the creation of a council to assist refugees which was signed by (and others on 24 May):

A.V. Hill FRS
J.B.S. Haldane FRS
Lord Rayleigh FRS
Sir Charles Scott Sherrington FRS
Sir Frederick Gowland Hopkins FRS
Sir Joseph John Thomson FRS
Sir Robert Robinson FRS
Sir William Bragg FRS

Some three years later, on 13th June 1936, a permanent successor to the AAC was founded called the Society for the Protection of Science and Learning (SPSL). The Catalogue of the Archive of this Society, 1933-87 is housed in the Bodleian Library, University of Oxford.[17]

Appendix I[1]

Minutes of a Meeting of the War Cabinet, December 13th 1917

[This Document is the Property of His Britannic Majesty's Government]
Printed for the War Cabinet. December 1917
SECRET
WAR CABINET, 297

Minutes of a Meeting of the War Cabinet held at 10 Downing Street, S.W., on Thursday, December 13th, 1917, at 11 a.m.

Present:

THE PRIME MINISTER FRS (in the Chair).
The Right Hon. the Earl Curzon of Kedleston KG GCSI GCIE FRS
The Right Hon. G.N. Barnes MP
The Right Hon. A. Bonar Law MP
The Right Hon. the Viscount Milner GCB GCMG
The Right Hon. Sir E. Carson KC MP

The following were also present:-

The Right Hon. the Earl of Derby KG GCVO CB, Secretary of State for War
General Sir W. R. Robertson GCB KCVO DSO Chief of the Imperial General Staff (for minutes 23 to 29)
Lieutenant-General Sir C. F. N. Macready KGB KCMG, Adjutant-General to the Forces (for minutes 1 to 12)
The Right Hon W. Long MP FRS, Secretary of State for the Colonies (for minutes 1 to 18)
The Right Hon. C. Addison MD MP, Minister of Reconstruction (for minutes 1 to 18)
The Right Hon. R. Munro, KC MP, Secretary for Scotland (for minutes 1 to 18)
The Right Hon. H. E. Duke KC MP, Chief Secretary for Ireland (for

1 National Archives CAB 23/4_0071.

minutes 1 to 18)
Sir A. C. Geddes KCB MP, Minister of National Service (for minutes 1 to 18)
Professor W. G. Adams (for minutes 1 to 18)
Mr. J. F. Hope, M.P. (for minutes 1 to 17)
The Right Hon. Sir E. Geddes GBE KCB MP, First Lord of the Admiralty (for minutes 23 to 29)
Admiral Sir J. R. Jellicoe GCB OM GCVO, First Sea Lord and Chief of the Naval Staff (for minutes 19 to 29)
The Right Hon. W. Hayes Fisher MP, President, Local Government Board (for minutes 1 to 18)
The Right Hon. H. A. L. Fisher LLD MP, President, Board of Education (for minutes 1 to 18)
The Right Hon. Lord Rhondda, Food Controller (for minutes 1 to 18)
Mr. U. F. Wintour CB CMG, Permanent Secretary, Ministry of Food (for minutes 1 to 18)
Major the Hon. Waldorf Astor MP (for minutes 1 to 18)
Sir A. Lee, KCB MP, Director-General, Food Production Department (for minutes 1 to 18)
The Right Hon. Viscount Goschen, Food Production Department (for Minutes 1 to 18)
Lieutenant-Colonel W. Dally Jones CMG, Acting Secretary
Captain Clement Jones, Assistant Secretary
Mr. Thomas Jones, Assistant Secretary
Fleet Paymaster P. H. Row RN, Assistant Secretary

The food situation, finance:

1. The War Cabinet resumed the discussion of the food situation adjourned from yesterday's meeting (War Cabinet 296, minute 15) with special reference to Lord Rhondda's Memorandum (paper GT 180). The Prime Minister announced that the details of the financial arrangement come to with the American representatives yesterday morning would be settled at a conference that afternoon. The War Cabinet decided to request:

The Shipping Controller to give absolute priority to the Food Controller's requirements for tonnage necessary to carry out the program of food imports.

Meat and Cheese:

2. With reference to War Cabinet 283, minute 12, dealing with the proposed transfer of the organisation for the purchase of meat and cheese from the Board of Trade to the Ministry of Food, the War Cabinet were informed that the attempts to settle the matter had so far been unsuccessful. Mr. Long said it was important to bear in mind the Dominions' point of view, and suggested

that Sir Thomas McKenzie should be consulted. The War Cabinet decided to ask:

Lord Milner and Mr. Barnes to go into the matter that afternoon and if they failed to come to a final decision to bring up the matter before the Cabinet tomorrow.

Imports of Tea:

3. Lord Rhondda stated that the shortage of tea was an acute cause of popular discontent, which could be remedied by a relatively small expenditure of tonnage, and he would like the Shipping-Controller to be authorised to provide tonnage sufficient to raise at once the stock in bond to 60,000,000 lb. after the grocers' stocks had been replenished. Further, the restriction on the importation of Java and China tea should be removed. Mr. Long said that he understood that twelve liners were being diverted from the East to the Atlantic in order to bring corn to this country. Lord Derby stated that, under pressure from the Shipping Controller, he had undertaken not to recruit the full number of Chinese coolies. In that way about 100,000 tons of shipping would be saved between Vancouver and China, provided that France also stopped recruiting in China. The War Cabinet referred the question to Lord Milner and Mr. Barnes for decision that afternoon, in consultation with the Shipping Controller and Food Controller.

Protection of Labour:

4. Lord Rhondda urged that, in the interests of the food supply, it was essential that labour in flour mills and other food factories should be protected from military service. At present only temporary exemptions were granted. Sir Auckland Geddes said it was difficult to grant absolute protection, but his Department had already negotiated a large measure of protection, and would continue to do everything possible to meet the wishes of the Food Controller. No serious withdrawal of labour was taking place.

Accommodation and Staff for the Ministry of Food:

5. The War Cabinet instructed:

The Secretary to communicate to all the Departments concerned that in respect of accommodation, printing and staff the War Cabinet considered that the claims of the Ministry of Food should be treated as being of great urgency.

Inequalities of Distribution:

6. The attention of the War Cabinet was drawn to the inequality in the distribution of food as between one centre and another. A deputation which had waited on the Prime Minister on the previous day had alleged that in some districts there was an entire lack of butter, lard, margarine, and bacon,

it was suggested that greater use ought to be made of the local authorities in the work of distribution, and the administrative experience of Town Clerks and Councillors drawn upon. Further, the Ministry of Food might consider the desirability of making the Co-operative Wholesale Societies and the large private distributing agencies into 'controlled establishments' on the analogy of engineering works.

Lord Rhondda stated that at Birmingham and other centres local experiments were being tried with a view to improving distribution and getting rid of queues. He had set up nearly 2,000 local Food Committees, the personnel of which were largely drawn from the local authorities. With regard to local shortages, supplementary allowances had been made to a large number of towns, and steps were being taken to organise distribution schemes for bacon, butter, tea, &c, but they would necessarily take some time to put in motion. The War Cabinet decided to ask:

The Food Controller to prepare a report on the problem of distribution, with special reference to the points raised in the discussion.

Agricultural Program and Food Production:

7. The War Cabinet resumed the discussion of the agricultural program begun at the previous days' meeting (War Cabinet 295, minute 16), with special reference to Mr. Prothero's Memorandum (Paper G.T. 2767). Sir Arthur Lee, in the unavoidable absence of the President of the Board of Agriculture, informed the Cabinet that, at a meeting of Agricultural Commissioners, held the previous day, encouraging reports had been received as to the progress made with the agricultural program. He hoped that at least 80 per cent, of the 2,695,000 acres assigned to breadstuffs would be got ready. This would, roughly, be 2,000,000 acres above the 1916 area. No very reliable estimate could be given of the increased production by small growers, but it was conjectured that there had been an addition of 300,000 tons of potatoes, and 300,000 tons of other vegetables from that source in 1917, and it was hoped to increase this total to 1,000,0.00 tons in 1918. Mr. Munro dealt with the position in Scotland, where the aim was to plough by 1918, 350,000 acres above the 1916 area. Of this amount, 50,000 acres had been obtained in 1917. The realisation of the complete program was contingent on the supply of soldier labour of good quality, of superphosphates, and of an adequate staff at the Board of Agriculture. Mr. Duke said that in Ireland the output in 1917 above that of 1916 had been 1,750,000 tons of potatoes and 536,000 tons of cereals. The increase in acreage for these crops had been 600,000.

In 1918 it was hoped that the increase would be, at least, 1,200,000 acres. There were signs that the Sinn Feiners were turning from active rebellion to a policy of holding up crops, but, so far, this movement had not been serious except in two counties.

Labour Requirements:

8. Sir Arthur Lee said the agricultural program could only be carried out if the urgent minimum requirements specified in the Memorandum (GT 2767) were fully and promptly met. The most urgent need at the moment was for skilled ploughmen, of whom 8,500 in all were required. There were 1,000 in sight from the Army in France, and it was hoped to draw 1,000 from German prisoners now in this country. The Department could place 1,000 skilled ploughmen a week, as the horses and harness required were now in sight. He understood a second 1,000, withdrawn from the army in France would soon be available. Mr. Munro said it would not be possible in Scotland to return to the army any of the men lent to the farmers. As to additional labour, 1,000 men next spring would suffice. These should be, if possible, skilled agriculturists, and in any case they should be able bodied, Mr. Duke said that there was a constant flow from Ireland of from 500 to 1,000 labourers weekly, attracted by high wages on this side. They were, therefore, very near bedrock in Ireland, and had no skilled ploughmen to spare. Sir Auckland Geddes said there were perhaps 1,000 skilled ploughmen in the New Zealand Reserves, who could, he understood, be loaned for two and a half months. The New Zealand military authorities were willing to lend them on furlough. In Denmark there were from 3,000 to 5,000 deserters from the German Army now out of work. They were natives of Schleswig-Holstein, and among them were some of the best farmers in Europe. The War Office was raising no objection to their removal, nor was the Foreign Office, subject to the approval of the Danish Government, but it was necessary to arrange tonnage with the Shipping Controller, and to obtain particulars from the Food Production Department as to the farms to which these men could be sent. They would be under the Alien Restriction Act and Orders, and there would be no necessity to provide guards. In Denmark there were between 20,000 and 22,000 unemployed Danes. Probably many of these had had some experience of the land as small-holders; others were butter and margarine makers. He gathered from the Ministry of Labour that there would not be any Trade Union difficulties in connection with their employment in agriculture.

German Prisoners:

9. Sir Arthur Lee pointed out that it was essential that the War Office and the Prisoners of War Committee should agree to relax the regulations for guarding and accommodating German prisoners, if the maximum advantage was to be obtained from their employment. General Macready said the War Office was quite prepared to make the necessary relaxations, provided the War Cabinet was prepared to meet the criticism which always arose from the House of Commons and in the press when a prisoner escaped. Up to the present only one officer and two men had got away from the country. Lord Derby said he

was quite willing that the prisoners should go out in twos and threes to farmers, but it was impossible to have tiny camps all over the country. Surveillance could be left to the local police, and weekly reports could be obtained as to the conduct of the prisoners. Sir Auckland Geddes urged that there should be an industrial census taken of the German prisoners in France and this country similar to that which has been taken in the Home Forces, and that, as the ploughmen were discovered, they should be sent in batches to be employed on the land. Mr. Hope said that as far as the prisoners in the United Kingdom were concerned, instructions to this effect had been given months ago by the Prisoners of War Employment Committee, but they apparently had not been carried out. The War Cabinet decided that:

(a) The restrictions affecting German prisoners loaned to farmers could be relaxed as far as safely thought possible, the details to be arranged by the Departments concerned
(b) A trade index of the German prisoners should be made, and skilled ploughmen released in batches as discovered

Fertilisers:

10. Sir Arthur Lee stated that the consumption of sulphate of ammonia for munitions purposes was now expected to be greater than previously contemplated, and that there was a prospective deficiency of 40,000 tons in the supplies available for food production. As regards superphosphates, the Cabinet had decided that 50,000 tons per month of phosphate rock should be imported into this country for the five months 1st June to 31st October. Only 149,000 tons have so far been imported instead of 250,000 tons. Sir Arthur Lee pointed out the serious effect of these deficiencies on the future food supplies of the country.

Tractor Transport and Fuel:

11. Sir Arthur Lee called attention to the prolonged delays which have occurred in the delivery of tractors and other machinery ordered by the Department last spring, and to the importance of providing adequate supplies of fuel and spare parts for all agricultural machinery, whether privately owned or in the hands of the Department. Facilities for the provision of steam tackle and additional equipment were also urgently required. Mr. Long said that the oil situation had improved within the last week and was now somewhat more secure. He hoped it would be possible to supply all the oil required for agricultural purposes. The War Cabinet instructed:

The Secretary to call the attention of the Minister of Munitions and the Shipping Controller to the position as described by the Director-General of Food Production, and to the importance of expediting the shipment of machinery from America and of granting the other facilities to manufacturers of steam tackle and equipment now asked for.

Accommodation for the Food Production Department:

12. Sir Arthur Lee stated that his Department was in urgent need of further staff accommodation of about thirty to forty rooms. He did not press for a building in Whitehall, as he knew that the Office of Works had well-nigh exhausted the possibilities in that district. The War Cabinet decided that:

The First Commissioner of Works should be requested to provide the accommodation referred to as soon as possible, but in his efforts to meet the demands for new accommodation now being made, should inform Departments that they must be prepared, if necessary, to take offices at some distance from Whitehall.

Food Prices in 1918:

13. The War Cabinet requested:

The Food Controller to make an announcement at the earliest possible moment of the official prices for next year's grain, potatoes, and milk.

Departmental Expenditure on Food Production:

14. In response to a request from Sir Arthur Lee to be allowed by the Treasury a reasonable latitude in incurring minor expenditure on the Agricultural Program, the Chancellor of the Exchequer undertook to consider any representations made to him on the subject.

Staff of Board of Agriculture (Scotland):

15. The Chancellor of the Exchequer took note of representations made by Mr. Munro on behalf of the Scottish Board of Agriculture for an increase of staff.

Allotments:

16. Dr. Addison called attention to the insecurity felt over the country by the men who, in order to increase the food supply, had undertaken the cultivation of small patches of ground under the Cultivation of Land Act. It was not necessary to raise at this juncture questions of ownership or saleable interests, but only to safeguard the liberty to cultivate and provide security of tenure during the War. It was suggested that a public official statement might meet the case. (No decision was come to.)

Supply of Milk for Young Children and Mothers:

17. The War Cabinet had before them the following documents:-

Memorandum by the Food Controller (Paper GT 2861)

Second Interim Report of the Committee on the Production and Distribution of Milk (Paper GT 2877)

Report by the Food (War) Committee of the Royal Society (Paper GT 2899)

Notes on Lord Rhondda's Memorandum by the Chairman of the Committee on the Production and Distribution of Milk (Paper GT 2898)

Memorandum on Milk Production in 1918-19, by Major Waldorf Astor (Paper GT 2897)

Note by the Medical Department of the Board of Education (Paper GT 2955)

It was pointed out that there were serious objections to the principle of subsidising recommended by the Food Controller, and doubts were thrown on the extent and urgency of the need for cheap milk, in view of the high wages now so widely prevailing. Mr. Hayes Fisher said he would not object if the scheme were confined to necessitous children, and if suitable machinery was used to discover them.

Major Waldorf Astor said that there was no milk famine at present, but there undoubtedly was bad distribution. His Committee were in favour of any proposal to supply cheap or, if need be, free milk to necessitous children. They believed that this could be done by:

(a) Empowering the Sanitary Authorities to give, or sell at reduced prices, milk to necessitous children under school age, the necessary grants being made partly out of Exchequer grants and partly out of local rates;

(b) By the more general feeding of children of school age under the Provision of Meals Act, if and where this was necessary. Mr. Herbert Fisher said that his Department agreed with Major Astor's report.

The War Cabinet decided:

To accept the recommendations of the Committee on the Production and Distribution of Milk, as set forth above by the Chairman.

Oats for Horses Engaged in Winter Racing:

18. The War Cabinet had before them a memorandum by Lord Rhondda (GT 2929) in which he expressed his view that not a single pound of oats should be allowed to racing horses, having regard to the very grave shortage of cereals with which the country is threatened. Lord Rhondda drew attention to the serious effect that allowing a ration of oats to horses engaged in steeple-chasing would have upon public opinion in the United States of America. On the other hand, it was pointed out that it was impossible entirely to prevent racing in England if it were allowed to continue in Ireland, where it could not be stopped. It was also stated that horse-racing is still carried on in Germany.

The War Cabinet authorised:

The Food Controller to issue licences to allow horses engaged in fixtures, agreed by the Board of Trade, to receive a ration of oats; the ration to be 15 lb. a day each for a number of horses not exceeding 500, and the period of the ration not to extend beyond the middle of April.

Shelling of Funchal:

19. The First Sea Lord reported that 2 enemy submarines had shelled Funchal, Madeira, at daybreak on the 12th instant, 3 persons being killed and 17 wounded. Slight damage was done to the town.

Bombing Raid:

20. The First Sea Lord stated that a bombing raid had been carried out on the night of the 11-12th on Bruges Lock, 2½ tons of bombs being dropped. One of our machines is missing.

Submarines:

21 . The First Sea Lord informed the War Cabinet that:

(a) motor-launch ran over an enemy submarine, submerged in the vicinity of the Lizard, on the 12th instant. The submarine rose to the surface and the motor-launch attacked her with gunfire, but was unable to use depth charges owing to having carried away her propeller-shaft and rudder

(b) Explosions had occurred in the deep minefield in the vicinity of the Folkestone Gate, which indicated the possible loss of an enemy submarine

Enemy Naval Activity in the North Sea:

22. The First Sea Lord reported that information had been received that, on the 12th instant, enemy destroyers had attacked a Danish steamer off Longstone and a fishing vessel off the Tyne, the destroyers being accompanied by an airship. A report has since been received which indicated that it was possible that the enemy vessels were submarines and not destroyers. The presence of an airship was doubtful.

Attack on a Convoy:

23. The First Sea Lord informed the War Cabinet that a convoy of 6 ships, of which 1 was British, 2 Norwegian, 2 Swedish, and 1 Danish, under the escort of the destroyers 'Partridge' and 'Pellew' and 4 trawlers, had been attacked by 4 enemy destroyers about 34 miles off the coast of Norway at about 1 P.M. on the 12th instant. Full particulars of the action had not yet been received, but it was understood that the 'Partridge' had been sunk and that the 'Pellew' had reached Norwegian waters, being towed in by a Norwegian torpedo-boat, her engines being out of action. The convoy was stated by the commanding officer of the 'Pellew' to have scattered when the attack took place, but no news had yet been

received as to whether the convoy had arrived in Norwegian ports, although enquiries were being made to that end. The Admiral at Longhope had reported, however, that the convoy had been destroyed. The First Sea Lord indicated that there was a British force of two light cruisers and four destroyers 40 miles off when the action took place, also a light cruiser squadron to the southward, but they had been unable to intercept the enemy, who had presumably slipped through during the night.

As regards the protection of convoys in future, Admiral Jellicoe stated that there were two courses open to us: one was to send the convoys on a far northerly course, so that the enemy would not be able to take advantage of the dark hours to evade our patrols, but this would double the length of the voyage; the other was, to run the risk of having battle cruisers, cruisers or light cruisers in close touch with the convoy. If this latter course were adopted the enemy would obtain information of our movements and would undoubtedly concentrate submarines to attack them, and we had not a sufficient number of destroyers available to provide the requisite screen. The question was under consideration. The First Sea Lord indicated the very slight amount of help in the provision of destroyers which we might expect to receive from the United States in the near future.

The War Cabinet discussed the question of mentioning the engagement and possible loss, by the First Lord in the statement on shipping matters which he was to make to the House in the afternoon, and decided that as the information at present received was so uncertain, no particulars should be announced pending fuller data being forthcoming.

The Western Front:

24. The Chief of the Imperial General Staff informed the War Cabinet that two more German Divisions had been transferred from Flanders to the Cambrai region. He added that the fighting at Bullecourt had been severe. Two attacks had been made by the enemy at dawn, after heavy artillery preparation, but both attacks had been beaten off with heavy losses to the enemy, only a small portion of trench being lost by us.

The Invasion of Italy:

25 . The Chief of the Imperial General Staff stated that he had received information from General Plumer to the effect that the Italian commander was satisfied with the results of the recent fighting on the Italian Front.

The Italian Command:

26. The Chief of the Imperial General Staff stated that he had received a telegram from General Foch informing him that the Italians were raising the question of exercising more control over the French force in Italy, and asking

whether he was prepared to adopt the principle of complete Italian command over the French and British contingents. General Robertson read to the War Cabinet the original instructions given to General Plumer.

The War Cabinet held the view that, at this stage, it was unnecessary to consider the question, more particularly as General Diaz, who was in command of the Italian troops, was an untried man; but that if the Italians raised the question at a later date, after the abilities of General Diaz had been proved, the matter would be fully considered. They therefore authorised:

The Chief of the Imperial General Staff to inform General Foch that the War Cabinet did not at present propose to make any alteration in the existing instructions.

Palestine:

27. The Chief of the Imperial General Staff asked to be informed of the wishes of the War Cabinet in connection with the preparation of a report which he had been asked to make, relative to an advance in Palestine, based generally on the telegram that was sent to General Allenby in accordance with the Cabinet's directions (War Cabinet 296, minute 5). The War Cabinet decided that:

The General Staff should submit for consideration a project for carrying out the following alternative policies:

(a) Complete the conquest of the whole of Palestine, and hold the country for the remainder of the War

(b) Continue the advance through Palestine and Syria to the vicinity of Aleppo, so as permanently to interrupt railway communication with Mesopotamia

For the purposes of (a) Palestine to be considered as embracing the whole country between Beersheba and Dan.

Guns for Italy:

28. With reference to War Cabinet 294, minute 6, the Chief of the Imperial General Staff informed the War Cabinet that it had been his intention to send from Egypt to General Plumer two batteries of 6-inch howitzers out of those now in reserve at Alexandria, as he was of opinion that General Allenby had at his disposal at present more howitzers than he had occasion to use. As the weather on the Western Front may be expected in the near future to prevent any large offensive operations in that quarter, and also bearing in mind the difficulty of providing; the requisite shipping for the transfer of these batteries from Egypt, and the possible need of sending them back in the event of an extended advance in Palestine, the War Cabinet decided that:

Before the military authorities took any action for the removal of these guns, General Allenby should be asked if he will require the same in the event of his carrying out further operations.

Naval Allied Council:

29. In continuation of War Cabinet 290, minute 12, the War Cabinet had under further consideration the question of the publication of an abridged communication in regard to the Naval Allied Council.

The War Cabinet held the opinion that it was essential that the Permanent Military Advisors to the Supreme War Council should have for their assistance and their deliberations the services of an experienced naval officer, not necessarily of high rank, with the 'sea sense' who was fully acquainted with naval policy and the means by which it was best possible to carry out the same.

The War Cabinet were averse to the creation of a new and independent body to deal with naval matters only, and desired some organisation that would in any case act as a connecting link between the Military and Naval Councils, in view of the need for co-operation that frequently arises between the two services in the many operations of War.

It was mentioned that the Prime Minister had stated in the House of Commons that a British naval representative would be attached to General Wilson, and it was suggested that if we had a representative the French and Italians would also wish to appoint one of their naval officers.

The First Lord stated that the Admiralty had proposed to detail the British Naval Liaison Officer in Paris as Liaison Officer between the Admiralty and the Permanent Military Advisors to the Supreme War Council, and that General Wilson had been asked if such a course would be agreeable to him. Sir Eric Geddes added that the Military Council, through the Liaison Officer, would be able to acquire any further information or opinion that they might desire. The First Lord pointed out that, from a naval point of view, the efforts, &c, of the Allies were not comparable to those which prevailed from the military aspect. In the main theatre of naval warfare the Americans and ourselves provided the whole of the Allied force which was working under the British Admiralty, whilst in the Mediterranean the whole of the Allied naval force was under the command of the French Commander-in-Chief. The Allies had arranged that, as a general rule, the meetings of the Allied Naval Council would be held in London – not in France – under the presidency of the First Lord of the Admiralty, the permanent staff being located in London under Admiralty control.

The First Sea Lord stated that he had frequent conversations with the Chief of the Imperial General Staff, but that they nearly all related to the provision of escort, and he thought it possible that the Supreme Council needed a shipping expert even more than a naval expert, except for certain special operations. The War Cabinet requested:

The First Lord to confer with the First Sea Lord, and to report as to the practicability of appointing a suitable naval officer to the staff of the Permanent Military Advisers to the Supreme War Council, such officer being also associated with the Allied Naval Council.

The issue of the abridged statement to the press simultaneously with the other parties to the agreement was approved.

2, Whitehall Gardens, S.W.,
December 13, 1917.

Appendix II[1]

Members of the Board of Invention and Research, September 1917

Committee BIR
Office Memo 105

Board of Invention and Research
21st September 1917

Central Committee

Admiral of the Fleet the Lord Fisher of Kilverstone GCB OM GCVO LLD President
Professor Sir Joseph J. Thomson OM PRS[2]
The Hon. Sir Charles A. Parsons KCB FRS
Sir George T. Beilby FRS
Vice-Admiral Sir Richard H. Peirse KCB MVO

Panel

Professor H.B. Baker FRS
Professor Sir William H. Bragg CBE FRS
Sir Henry Carpenter FRS
Sir Dugald Clerk KBE FRS
Professor Sir William Crookes OM FRS
Professor Percy F. Frankland, FRS
Professor Bertram Hopkinson FRS
Sir Oliver Lodge FRS
Sir William Pope FRS
Lord Ernest Rutherford FRS
Mr. Gerald Stoney FRS
Lord Rayleigh FRS

1 National Archives ADM 293/9.
2 PRS denoted President of the Royal Society.

Sir Richard Threlfall KBE FRS

Secretariat

Commander R. Appleyard RNVR
Commander Gerald H. Brady RN
Wing-Commander F.A. Brock RN
Engineer-Lieutenant-Commander S.R. Dight RN
Mr. H.W. Hilliar
Engineer-Lieutenant S. Hunter RN
Lieutenant the Hon. Walker J. James RNVR
Mr. F.P. Johns
Commander A.A. Lovett-Cameron RN
Commander E.W. Nelson RNVR
Sir Richard A.S. Paget Bt
Mr. J.F. Phillips
Mr. E.L. Pickles
Lieutenant M. Heckstall Smith RNVR
Lieutenant A. Walker RNVR

Section I.
Airships

Lord Rayleigh FRS
Sir Richard Threlfall KBE FRS
Mr. G.S. Albright
Sir Horace Darwin FRS
Professor Sir Joseph Petavel FRS
Major F. Green
Secretaries Lieut. M. Heckstall Smith RNVR
Mr. E.L. Pickles

Section II.
Submarines, mines, searchlights, wireless telegraphy and general electrical, electro-magnetic, optical and acoustic subjects

The Duke of Buccleuch KT
Professor Sir William H. Bragg CBE FRS
Lord Ernest Rutherford FRS
Sir Richard Threlfall KBE FRS
Professor W.H. Eccles FRS
Sir Richard Glazebrook CB FRS
Mr. C.H. Merz
Secretaries Sir Richard A.S. Paget Bt
Commander A. Lovett-Cameron RN

Commander E.W. Nelson RNVR
Lieut. The Hon. Walter J. James RNVR
Mr. H.W. Hilliar

Section III.
Naval construction etc.
Rear-Admiral the Marquess of Bristol MVO
Professor Bertram Hopkinson FRS
Mr. John Smith
Marine Engineering
Mr. G. Stoney FRS
Sir Henry Carpenter FRS
Professor W.E. Dalby FRS
Mr. Alexander Gracie MVO
Sir Robert A. Hadfield Bt FRS
Professor F. Soddy FRS
Sir Alfred F. Yarrow Bt FRS
Internal combustion engines
Sir Dugald Clerk FRS
Professor Bertram Hopkinson FRS
Mr. A.E.L. Chorlton CBE
Professor W.E. Dalby FRS
Mr. R.P. Doxford
Mr. Summers Hunter
Mr. F.W. Lanchester FRS
Erosion and corrosion of propellers
The Hon. Sir Charles A. Parsons KCB FRS
Sir Henry Carpenter FRS
Mr. S.W. Barnaby
Mr. S.S. Cook FRS
Mr. J.H. Gibson
Oil Fuel
Sir Oliver Lodge FRS
Sir Boverton Redwood Bt FRSE
Secretaries, &c.:- Engr.-Lt.-Commdr. S.R. Dight RN
Commander R. Appleyard RNVR
Engr.-Lieut. S. Hunter RN
Lieut. A. Walker RNVR
Mr. F.P. Johns

Section IV.
Anti-aircraft apparatus of all kinds, primarily for use onboard ship

Admiral Sir Percy M. Scott Bt KCB KCVO LLD
Professor Sir William Crookes OM FRS
Professor H.F. Newall FRS
Secretary (acting):- Wing-Commander F.A. Brock RN

Section V.

Ordnance and ammunition

Admiral Sir Percy M. Scott Bt KCB KCVO LLD
Sir Henry Carpenter FRS
Rear-Admiral Sir Sydney M. Eardley-Wilmot
Mr. C.C. Mellstrom
Mr. Robert Redpath
Mr. Charles Wale

Explosives

Professor Sir William Crookes OM FRS
Professor H.B. Baker FRS
Sir William Pope FRS

Noxious Gases

Professor H.B. Baker FRS
Sir Henry Carpenter FRS
Professor P. F. Frankland FRS

Supply of Raw Materials for Explosives

Professor P. F. Frankland FRS
Sir William Pope FRS
Sir Martin Forster FRS
Secretary:- Commander Gerald H. Brady RN

Appendix III[1]

Report on methods of collecting sound from water and the determination of the direction of sound by Lord Rutherford FRS, September 1915

SECRET
This paper is the property of
HM Government and is subject to the
Provisions of the Official Secrets Act.
BIR 10064/16
30th September 1915

Report on methods of collecting sound from water and the determination of the direction of sound
by Lord Rutherford FRS

The problem of collection of sound from water has received very inadequate attention in the scientific journals, but has been the subject of considerable practical investigation by the authorities at Trinity House in connection with the system of bell signals, and by those interested in the commercial development of submarine signalling. In addition, many important experiments have been, and are being, made in the Navy not only on the general problem of signalling, but on the more difficult subject of detection of ships at a distance by their natural sounds communicated through water …

… a discussion of these questions naturally divides itself under three heads:

1. methods of generating sound waves of great intensity in water, and methods of detection of this sound at considerable distances – for signalling purposes
2. detection of ships in motion at a distance by the natural sounds due to their machinery etc. communicated through the hull to the water
3. detection of the direction of sound …

Rutherford goes on to discuss

- hydrophones

1 National Archives ADM 293/7.

- magnetophones
- the detection of submarines

Concluding with the following summary:

> ... in my opinion, it is important that experiments along these lines should be tried on a practical scale. If the receiving apparatus can be made sufficiently sensitive, it may prove possible to follow the course of a submerged submarine by means of a swift vessel which stops her engines at intervals to permit of sound-observations.

Mr. Duddell FRS has suggested that in the case of electro-magnetic methods it might even be possible to neutralise to a considerable extent the sounds due to a ship's own engines, viz., by methods analogous to those used in wireless technology. Sir Oliver Lodge FRS and Mr. Davies are making some preliminary experiments for the Committee, and are comparing the relative efficiency for this purpose of different forms and arrangements of receiving apparatus.

SUMMARY

An account has been given of the three chief methods of collecting sound from water and of the results so far obtained. Each of these methods has certain inherent advantages for special types of work. The first method, in which the sounds produced by the movements of a simple diaphragm are heard directly by the ear, has certain obvious advantages in its simplicity and constant sensibility. By the use of these diaphragms the actual sound produced by the submarine should be heard without serious complication from natural modes of vibration of the instrument. By the choice of suitable vibrators arranged in parallel, I have been able to increase the intensity of the sound by at least 20 times that given by the Broca tube, and I am hopeful that the sensibility can be still further increased by these methods. This type of collector should, under certain conditions, have a range of detection of sound comparable with that of a hydrophone.

The submerged buoyed hydrophone, devised by Commander Ryan, is a sensitive instrument for detection of sound, and has already reached a practical stage of development. A system of hydrophones, connected with a central listening station on shore, has obvious advantages for detecting the approach of a submarine or other ship to the hydrophone area, and by suitable spacing the hydrophones should also give valuable information as to the position of the submarine at any moment. The hydrophone is probably the best instrument for this purpose; obviously the direct method cannot be used. For more general purposes, however, the hydrophone would probably not prove so suitable as one of the other types of collectors on account of capricious variations of its sensibility. The magnetophone, like the simple sound-collector, has the advantage of constant sensibility and reliability. No definite information is yet available of its sensitiveness as a sound-detector compared with the hydrophone, but special apparatus is under construction to test this point definitely. It has certain advantages for special kinds of work, e.g., the combination of magnetophone and mine as devised by Commander Ryan.

Each of these methods of detecting sound in water has sufficient promise of practical importance to justify a very complete investigation of its possibilities and tests on a practical scale.

A discussion has been given of the various methods that might be utilised for determining the direction of sound from an observing ship. It is concluded that observation of the difference of intensity of the sound produced in two collectors of constant sensibility fixed on opposite sides of a ship offers the best chances of success.

In conclusion, I am of the opinion that it is of great importance that the Committee should arrange promptly for investigations along the following lines:-

1. improvements in the existing methods and apparatus for the detection of submarine sound
2. a comparison under various conditions on a practical scale of the relative advantages and disadvantages of the different methods of collection of sound
3. examination of the best methods of transmitting external sounds in water to observing tanks fixed inside a ship
4. methods of reducing sound-disturbances due to motion of ship engines, &c., to a minimum
5. effect of motion of a ship on the range of detection of submarines, &c.
6. practical methods for determining the direction of ships by the sound transmitted through water
7. investigation of the 'spectrum' of the sound-vibrations emitted by submarines

Appendix IV[1]

Report on submarine sound signalling, October 1915

SECRET
This paper is the property of
H.M. Government and is subject to the
Provisions of the Official Secrets Act
Board of invention and Research
Victory House Cockspur Street, S.W.
BIR 10067/16

Report on submarine sound signalling

On Monday October 11th, Sir Richard Paget and the writer visited Portsmouth in order to see some experiments in submarine sound signalling by means of a Fessenden apparatus.

The apparatus was set up on two submarines, the H9 and the H8. Two sets of apparatus were fitted on each submarine, one on each side, about 10 feet back from the bows, submerged in the water tanks. The positions of the diaphragms of the two apparatus on each submarine were not identical. On the H9 the apparatus on the port side had its diaphragm flush with the hull of the ship, and on the starboard side the diaphragm was let in by about 3 inches.

The same apparatus, as far as the diaphragm and coils are concerned, is used for transmitting and receiving. The diaphragm, stated to be 30 inches in diameter, of which about 20 inches was active, supports a copper tube in which alternating currents are induced when the apparatus is used as a transmitter; this causes the diaphragm to vibrate vigorously. When used as a receiver the vibration of the diaphragm moves the copper tube in a constant magnetic field, causing currents to be produced in the tube, which react on a coil connected to a telephone receiver.

Preliminary experiments indicate that there is a frequency of vibration which seems to suit the diaphragm better than any other, giving a better note and taking less power. The following readings were taken.

1 National Archives ADM 293/2.

Frequency	Volts	Ampères
510	150	12
548	162	2-5
560	180	12

Frequency 548 seemed to be best for this transmitter.

Object of experiments: the object of our experiments was to observe to what extent the direction of the source of sound could be located by the comparison of the sounds received on the two sides of the ship, and also the strength and regularity of the signals.

It was arranged that submarine H8 should anchor in a convenient position and transmit signals when required. Sir Richard Paget, a representative of the Fessenden Company, and the writer, were on the H9, which it was arranged should manoeuvre in circles at a distance of 1 mile from submarine H8, in order to make observations on direction. This arrangement was not found to be very convenient, and the scheme was changed to submarine H9 going a distance about 3 miles from H8, and then approaching her slowly on a zigzag course so that H8 was alternately a few points to the port and then on the starboard of H9. This proved to be a much more satisfactory arrangement.

The signals in all cases were strong; they could be heard through the hull of the ship with ease in nearly every part, except the engine-room when the engines were running. The signals on the receivers were hardly any stronger than those heard through the hull. The main advantage of the receivers being the exclusion of all external noises, due to the machinery, &c. The signals were heard over a distance of from half a mile to 3 miles, and in all cases good. The speed of the signalling was not very high, and there seemed to be a slight tendency for the dots and dashes to run into one another if the speed was increased. The law of decrease in the strength of a signal with distance could not be measured, as no apparatus was available. If one can judge anything by ear, the strength did not seem to fall off as rapidly as the square of the distance.

The experiments on detecting the direction, using the Fessenden receivers, were carried out by quickly switching over from the port to the starboard receiver, and comparing the strengths of the two.

When the H9 was heading direct for the transmitting submarine, there appeared to be a slight bias in favour of the port receiver, which had a distinctly stronger and better note; this is the receiver which is flush with the hull.

When the H9 made zigzags, observations were made on the receivers, and the observer noted which direction he thought the submarine occupied; the course of the ship was then determined and the results compared. These results at first were somewhat irregular, but after a little practice it was found to be possible to determine whether the transmitting submarine was on the port or the starboard bow, when the amount was greater than two, or three points. If the transmitting submarine is abeam, then the signals in the receiver facing the transmitting submarine are very much louder than on the opposite side. The intermediary positions between the beam and the end-on were more indefinite owing to the difficulty of estimating relative strengths of sounds. These seemed also to be a slight indefiniteness in the variations of the strength of the signals when they are nearly equal with the submarine heading almost direct for the transmitter.

This may be due to the difference between the positions of the two receivers.

Experiments were made without receivers; listening to the sound coming through the hull in a position 20 to 25 feet from the bows.

As the H9 zigzagged going towards the transmitter, there was no difficulty whatever in telling by the sound when the transmitter changed over from the port to the starboard. In fact, the accuracy of detection seemed to be somewhat higher on the hull with the human ears and no collecting device, than on the receivers. This is probably due to the more favourable position of the observers, being father away from the bow than the receivers. The diameter of the hull at the position of the Fessenden diaphragms was approximately 8 feet, and at a position where we made observations on the hull 10 feet. With regard, however, to any estimate of the position of the transmitter, other than just passing through the end-on position, indications appear to be indefinite. One knew perfectly well whether the H8 was on the port side or starboard, and also felt pretty certain when she was nearly abeam, but the intermediary positions seems very difficult to estimate.

A noticeable effect was the great weakening of the signals when the submarine was reversed and the wash of the propellers passed along the side of the ship.

Other experiments were made, with the engines running, motors running, neither running, and with wireless apparatus working and in no cases were the signals blocked out; they could be quite easily read on the hull and on the receivers. No attempts were made to signal over long distances.

Although a fair number of ships were constantly passing, no effects of sound shadows of echoes were observed. The propellers were heard at times, when the ships were close.

Conclusions: There seems no doubt that the apparatus generates powerful signals, which are extremely easy to receive over short distances, and would probably be obtainable over much longer distances. The experiments seem to indicate that the present position and arrangement of the receivers is not the most satisfactory for determining accurately the direction, and steps should be taken to find out whether there is not a better position, as the receivers appear to be too far forward. It is to be noted that it is possible to get some directional effect with so small a boat as a submarine.

Signed W. Duddell FRS October 15th 1915

Appendix V[1]

"Some Special War Work"

Written and presented by Sir Alfred Ewing to the Edinburgh Philosophical Society 13th December 1927

When the War broke out in 1914, it happened that I was a civil servant in the Admiralty. From being Professor of Applied Mechanics at Cambridge I had suffered a sea change nearly twelve years before, by accepting an invitation to become Director of Naval Education. Lord Selbourne and Admiral Fisher had just launched what was called the New Scheme, under which all naval cadets were to receive, as an essential part of their training, a serious grounding in the principles and techniques of engineering. My duties were those of adviser and inspector of the work in training establishments, the dockyards and the Fleet. With headquarters in the Admiralty, I became familiar with the atmosphere of a great Government Department. I learnt the uses as well as the abuses of red tape. By visits to the ports and occasional cruises I imbibed something of the naval spirits and traditions. I met many members of the silent service, in their less silent moments, on terms which bred intimacy and, on my part, a warm admiration. A civilian adviser was a being whose place in the chain of naval responsibility could not easily be assigned. In the Navy, orders and the obedience to orders are Heaven's law; but advice, if it is to serve any useful purpose, must balance itself tactfully on the edge of a back seat. However, I was generally tolerated, even by the younger officers, and made friends, among the seniors, with some whose distinction in naval service has become well known.

Looking back now, the tremendous personality of Fisher stands out in memory, towering above all others. It was a privilege to know that great man in the period when his genius had the fullest scope. On his beloved Navy he threw himself with the reforming zeal of a Luther or a Knox, convinced of the rightness of his ideas, a foe to complacency, ruthless, volcanic, defiant of opposition. In this spirit he made all things new – the training of officers and men, the motive power, the guns, the ships, the organisation of squadrons. One by one the products of Fisher's brain took practical shape: his imagination,

1 National Archives ADM 1/23899.

sagacity, knowledge, were the servants of an indomitable will and a tireless driving force. The magnificent fleet which assembled at Spithead just before the War was Fisher's fleet: if he felt the pride of parenthood he had reason.

But such things are not done without a struggle. That a reformer should tread on corns is inevitable; that he should sometimes be tempted to stamp on them is regrettable. I saw Fisher in the zenith of unchallenged power: I saw him also fighting with his back to the wall, opposed, hated, almost overcome. I saw him retire in 1910, to the undisguised delight of some who were strangely blind to everything but his faults. I saw him brought back by Sir Winston Churchill when we were in the throes of War, his powers scarcely impaired, his authority almost untrammelled, and at once the Admiralty seemed to glow with an intenser life. In force, vision, courage, these two – Churchill and Fisher – were well mated: their co-operation, brief though it was, had lasting results. Its impetus gave us a building program which enabled the country, more than two years later, to withstand the close and desperate menace of unrestricted submarine attack. When the storm broke in 1914 and before it broke, we were fortunate in having the office of First Lord held by a man with the initiative and the strength of Sir Winston Churchill.

It was in these surroundings that I was called on very unexpectedly to undertake the special work now to be described. On the fateful 4th of August my friend Admiral Oliver, then Director of the Naval Intelligence Division of the War Staff, showed me a number of telegrams. They were intercepts of wireless cipher, sent from ships or land stations which belonged to the Navy, the Post Office and the Marconi Company. He knew me to be interested in cipher, for we had talked a year or two before about mechanical methods of ciphering and deciphering despatches in connection with a rather futile machine which I had devised. He said he had no one to deal with these intercepts: would I take the matter up and see if I could make anything of them? Of course I said I should try: it was a moment when one grasped at even the most unpromising chance of being useful. So he said he would give orders to have all the enemy intercepts sent direct to me. From then they began to arrive, a continually increasing stream. Later, when we had set up special intercepting stations, the stream swelled till the number of messages that came addressed to 'Ewing, Admiralty' sometimes exceeded 2000 a day.

It was at once evident from inspection of the early intercepts that they fell into four or five distinct classes. One set were clearly transposition ciphers, where the letters composing the original message had been rearranged to form unintelligible groups. These, presumably, were military messages, for a transposition cipher is suitable for use in the field, where a code-book cannot be safely carried – the risk of its falling into enemy hands would be too great. A code-book means a book in which the needful words or phrases are printed as in a dictionary, and against each is set an arbitrary group of letters or of figures.

The sender must have the book to select the appropriate group of letters or figures; the receiver must also have the book in order to interpret them. In the use of any code-book additional secrecy may be obtained by resorting to what is called a 'key', which means some prearranged way of altering the letters or figures in the groups. The receiver must of course know the key, besides having the book. Several different keys may be in use at the same time on the same book, to keep the messages addressed to one correspondent secret from other correspondents. Thus the Germans used one and the same Naval Signal Book not only for ordinary fleet signals on one key, but also for highly confidential orders to Admirals and so forth, on other keys.

Such, in brief, was the problem as it first presented itself. I quickly secured the help of a few friends: they formed the nucleus of what afterwards became a large staff. Included in the number were two or three masters from the Cadets' Colleges who had a good working knowledge of German. That was an essential for any member of the staff; another essential was discretion. In the next five days I visited Lloyds', the General Post Office and the British Museum to see their collections of code-books, and was everywhere received with a delightful readiness to place at my disposal any information that could be given. It was a time of enthusiasm, of eagerness to be of service. Official barriers were broken down. That I came on War business from the Admiralty was an 'open sesame' to the most secluded arcana. Admitted into the great Library behind the British Museum Reading-room, conducted to the most appropriate shelves and left to prowl among dusty code-books, I was able to glean from them certain general notions as to how codes might be built up. I also got in touch with the Manager of the Marconi Company to arrange for more systematic interception of the enemy wireless. The messages were coming on a great variety of wave-lengths; it was therefore necessary to increase the number of watchers and of watching stations. Later, as the work developed, more and more stations were opened for the purpose, some by the Marconi Company and others by ourselves; but all acting as official eavesdroppers to bring grist to the mill of the deciphering staff, intent night and day that not a whisper of the enemy might be missed. As it was clear that some of the messages were of military origin, I went to the War Office to find out what steps, if any, were being taken to deal with them. We were still in the first days of the War (it was August 9th) and these intercepts had not yet come to the notice of the War Office authorities. On my pointing out their military character it was decided to send for Brigadier-General Anderson, an officer of the Royal Engineers who, I was told, had done good work in cipher reading during the Boer War. He came, and for some time we co-operated in attacking the military cipher – each with a small staff of assistants. A little later the other ciphers required all my attention and we then agreed to part, General Anderson's bureau in the War Office taking charge of the military cipher ad mine in the Admiralty taking charge of the naval and diplomatic ciphers.

Among the visits which I paid in the early days of the War was one to the Eastern Telegraph Company to confer with them about watching the German Wireless Stations in Africa to which signals were being sent from Nauen near Berlin, and also to get authentic material which should facilitate discovery of the cipher. From their files they were able to extract old messages from Berlin to the German Colonies or ships abroad, in ciphers of the kind we were now intercepting. These formed a useful supplement to the current material, especially as they were free of errors to which the intercepted wireless was liable. Of the German high-power stations in Africa, Windhuk in the south survived until May 1915. Long before it was captured by the British forces we were systematically listening to, and fully understanding, the cipher messages which passed through it between Berlin and the Governor of German South-West Africa. At the end of January, for example, we heard him report that the rising of the Boers had been 'almost totally shipwrecked' notwithstanding the support it had received in arms, ammunition and money.

But that is anticipating. What, from the outset, we in the Admiralty were most concerned with was to obtain a clue to the enemy's naval cipher, used in communicating information and orders by wireless from ship to ship or from shore stations, often in fact conveying the orders of the Commander in Chief or of the German Admiralty. In this we had two amazing pieces of good fortune.

Towards the end of August, when the War was less than a month old, a German light cruiser – the Magdeburg – stranded on an island in the Gulf of Finland and was destroyed by two Russian vessels. The Russians found the body of a drowned signalman still clasping in his arms the confidential signal-book of the German Navy. To save the book from the enemy was, one may conjecture, the impulse of a gallant man facing death; but, if that was his purpose, it was frustrated. The sea gave up its dead, and, with the dead, it gave up the book so loyally preserved.

Here was a priceless acquisition. The Russian Admiralty realised that it would be used to the best advantage if it were placed at the disposal of the British Naval authorities. A Russian officer conveyed the precious volume to London: it was brought to the Admiralty on October 17th by Captain Wolcoff, the Naval Attaché, and was put into my hands.

By this time we had accumulated much material: the watching staff of telegraphists, who were systematically taking in the enemy wireless, had become pretty familiar with their work; the number of intercepting stations had been increased, their program more or less arranged, and the apparatus improved. The types of cipher had been analysed. By comparing the same messages taken in at different stations one could be sure of their general accuracy. But at first, when we applied the new-found book to them, they were disappointing. Only a few messages, and these not important, could be read directly from the book; most were unintelligible. This was because they were keyed, and the key or keys had still to be discovered.

The book from the Magdeburg, which was the chief signal-book of the German Navy, continued in use till about May 1917. Its code consisted of groups of letters, commonly three letters in a group. The usual process of keying, as was presently discovered, consisted of substituting for each letter another letter, according to a prescribed plan. Occasionally, however, for communications which were intended to be ultra secret and confined to particular correspondents, more complicated methods of keying were employed, especially in later stages of the War. These gave my staff of solvers some interesting nuts to crack.

As time went on, much practice made the staff so skilful that the nuts, however hard, were cracked with scarcely an exception.

Associated with the signal book were charts in which the North Sea Area was parcelled out into hundreds of little numbered squares; they supplied a quick and secret means of indication position. You had simply to state the number of the square instead of giving latitude and longitude. The Germans, I should add, continued to use the signal-book with no apparent suspicion of its having become compromised. According to their Official History, it was only after the War that they learnt from Russia that the secret papers of the Magdeburg had been picked up and given to the British Admiralty, with the result that we were reading their cipher.

Among the first intercepts to be read, after the signal-book came into our possession, were some that showed a German auxiliary ship had been ordered to search for missing torpedo boats in a particular area. I took them to Admiral Oliver, who, by that time, had succeeded Admiral Sturdee as Chief of the Staff. He at once sent a cruiser to the place indicated, and sure enough found the ship there. This gave confidence in our new organ of information: it was a first success, small indeed, but encouraging. The next step was to find the key in which most of the messages were ciphered, and also another key which was the more private cipher of the Commander in Chief. Fleet-Paymaster Rotter, who combined a thorough knowledge of German with a remarkable talent for solving such conundrums, was lent to me from the Intelligence Division. He undertook an intensive study of the book and the messages and in a few days discovered both these keys.

Thus, from an early date in November 1914, we were over-hearing a host of secret naval orders and instructions of the enemy, and interpreting them as fast as they came in. From listening stations the message was telegraphed over a private wire to the Admiralty and delivered to my office. There it was deciphered and translated and, if the contents were of importance, they were at once brought to the notice of the War Staff. Not infrequently they gave information which led to orders for immediate action on the part of the British

Fleet.

As everybody knows, the Germans generally kept their High Sea Fleet in the safe-guarded river estuaries of the Heligoland Bight, behind a defensive mine-field, and only brought the ships out from time to time for a raid or excursion in the more open waters of the North Sea. The first of these raids took place on November 3rd, when our reading of their naval signals had barely begun. But after that no further sortie of the High Sea Fleet was made without our knowing beforehand that it was about to occur. Whenever a move was imminent the wireless intercepts showed it without fail. There would be orders for minesweepers to clear certain channels through the field; orders to lighthouses and the outer lightships of the Jade and the Elbe to show lights for a certain period; orders that barrier booms should be opened; orders for aerial reconnaissance and so on. These indications, taken together, were plain enough; but besides them we would sometimes overhear the orders of the German Commander in Chief to squadrons and flotillas, issued a day before the event, from which we learnt the composition of the force and its time of departure.

All this had its first demonstration in December 1914 when German cruisers bombarded Scarborough and Hartlepool. On the afternoon of the 14th we had clear evidence from several wireless intercepts that a part at least of the German fleet was to come out the following day. Sir Winston Churchill who was from the beginning keenly alive to the value of this source of information, has told the story in his book 'The World Crisis'. He has described how our Admiralty took measures to cut off the enemy forces by getting between them and their base. These measures, together with the movements of the German ships, had the effect that, on December 15th, the North Sea became a mighty chess-board with the pieces disposed for a great game. The game after all did not come off. Effective contact was never established. A curtain of invisibility fell upon the waters, and the returning enemy slipped past, not even aware of what he had escaped. On both sides, as is now known, it was a day of crooked purposes and disappointed hopes. But to our authorities it gave the assurance that the wireless eavesdropping and deciphering could be trusted. What was foretold had come to pass. Let me quote here a passage from Sir Winston Churchill:-

... 'Naturally there was much indignation at the failure of the Navy to prevent, or at least to avenge, such an attack upon our shores. What was the Admiralty doing? Were they all asleep? ... However, we could not say a word in explanation. We had to beat in silence the censures of our countrymen. We could never admit, for fear of compromising our secret information, where our squadrons were nor how near the German raiding cruisers had been to their destruction. One comfort we had. The indications upon which we had acted had been confirmed by events. The sources of information upon which we relied were evidently trustworthy' ...

Here indeed was a secret to be closely guarded. Any suspicion of it on the part of the enemy would be disastrous: the supply would be cut off at its source. At home, among friends, a thing of such extraordinary interest was only too likely to be the subject of heedless gossip. But its very importance saved it. Beyond the cryptographers themselves and a very few responsible officials, there was no knowledge that work of this kind was going on. Even Admirals at sea, who were carrying out orders based on it, were scarcely aware how the news came. In some quarters the idea got about, and was not discouraged, that the British were served by particularly intelligent and active spies in Germany. The small ring of people who knew the real source of information were too conscious of its value to run the risk of giving it away. From time to time we were on tenterhooks lest the enemy should guess: could they possibly treat it as a mere coincidence that, when they made a move, the British ships should make one too? But yes, they continued to broadcast plans and orders, in codes every one of which was compromised. Their messages were overheard and deciphered while they, it would seem, were untroubled by any thought of our listening ears. One fancies that the British reputation for stupidity was an invaluable asset. The profoundly important secret that we were systematically reading and deciphering the German wireless – that secret remained undiscovered by the enemy and undisclosed at home. It was, perhaps, the best-kept secret of the War.

Within the small circle of initiated persons the mysterious agency thus set up was called 'Room 40'. The origin of the name was that, when the staff of decipherers first overflowed the tiny limits of my private room, a large room numbered 40 in the old building of the Admiralty was assigned to us. Later, as the work grew bigger, and the workers much more numerous, we moved to more spacious quarters and room after room was added; but the original title stuck – a title that suggested nothing and stirred nobody's curiosity. Lord Balfour, after he took office as First Lord, sometimes used another piece of camouflage by calling us 'the Japanese' – perhaps in tribute to the impenetrability of the oriental mind. Sir Winston Churchill has told how, while he was having a fateful interview with the Prime Minister in the political crisis of 1915 he was summoned by a telephone message from his secretary to come back to the Admiralty at once because 'very important news of the kind that never fails' had just come in. It was an agreeable periphrasis, 'news of this kind that never fails'.

I have said that we had two marvellous pieces of good fortune. The second came soon after the first. On December 3rd, 1914, a parcel of books was given me which had just arrived from Lowestoft. A fisherman had found them in his trawl and had the good sense to see that they might be of value. It was an incredible stroke of luck. For here were precisely the papers still needed to make our mastery of the enemy's naval signals complete, a conversation book of the German Admiralty, which, like the other, was subject to a process of keying. But before it could be used, we had to find the current key. That was done the same afternoon while the water-sodden volume was beginning to dry before my fire. It happened that there had been intercepted, some days earlier, two versions of a wireless message, sent out independently from separate German stations. In one version the whole was given in the naval signal-book code, and all of it was therefore easily read. The second version was identical, except that a few words of it were given in the other code. I had noticed the parallelism and had put the messages aside for further study. It is never wise to mix your ciphers: like mixing drinks it may lead to self-betrayal. The sender of the mixed version, in his effort after special secrecy, had given us an instant means of discovering the key of the new book; one had simply to compare the mixed version with the plain.

It was on this code-book, and with the same key, that, on August 2nd, the German Admiralty had communicated with its scattered warships, informing them that hostilities had begun against Russia: that War with France was 'certain' and with Great Britain 'very probable'. It was on the same book but with another and more confidential key, that a wireless message to the Goeben, in the Mediterranean, on August 3rd, gave her the news that an alliance had been concluded with Turkey, and directed her – with her consort the Breslau – to proceed immediately to Constantinople. These and many more early messages of no small interest were duly intercepted, and were stored up till we could read them: by the time we could do so, however, the War with Germany was fully three months old.

The current applications of the new code-book were numerous and highly important. Besides its directly naval use, it was a medium of colonial, consular and some diplomatic correspondence. There were many different keys: gradually we succeeded in deciphering them all. As the War went on the methods of ciphering were changed from time to time; but there was little difficulty in following up these changes.

The parcel from the trawler included a copy of another code-book of secondary importance, the H.V.B. or Handelschiffsverkehrsbuch, which served as the official instrument of correspondence with the German mercantile marine. The Germans knew it to be already compromised – a copy had been captured in Australia early in the War. Nevertheless they continued, by means of various ciphering keys, to employ it in official correspondence for special purposes. It was used, for instance, by their ships in the Baltic, and also by the zeppelins when they intended a raid on England.

When these naval code-books first came into our hands we were intensely engaged for a time in discovering the various keys which were then in use. One after another they yielded to treatment. Some of the staff developed an uncanny degree of skill. I recall an exciting week when every day witnessed the solution of a previously unread cipher. Just after that, on December 20th, 1914, I was able to go to Lord Fisher and tell him we could now, confidently and accurately, read all the German naval signals. This happy condition lasted, substantially without a break, during all of 1915 and 1916, covering the period of enemy fleet movements.

For naval purposes the most important use of Room 40 was the watch it enabled us to keep on the composition of the German fleet and its intended activities. As I have said, the enemy squadrons never made a sortie without unwittingly giving us notice of their intention and with this information the British Admiralty tried, on every possible occasion, to bring about a meeting with our ships. Confidence became gradually established that the enemy would make no move without giving notice. This confidence, which was well founded, had an immense effect on the naval strategy of the War. Our ships could stay at their various bases, with no perpetual scouring of the sea in order to meet and counter an unexpected raid. They could lie in safety until the warning came which caused them to be summoned out. Try to imagine what this meant in sparing crews from exhaustion and machinery from wear, in saving fuel, above all in avoiding loss of ships and men through mines and torpedo attack. Imagine also the definitely planned response when the alarm signal was received – what it meant to substitute positive knowledge for the chance of an accidental meeting. 'Without the cryptographers' department', says Sir Winston Churchill, 'there would have been no battle of Jutland'. And it is equally true to say that a year earlier there would have been no Battle of the Dogger Bank.

That action put our ability to penetrate the mind of the enemy to a striking test. On the morning of Saturday, January 23rd, 1915, we intercepted a cipher message from the German Commander in Chief to the Admiral of the First Cruiser Squadron (Rear-Admiral von Hipper) ordering him to take the First and Second Scouting Groups, with two destroyer flotillas, to scout on the Dogger Bank. They were to proceed to sea that night and to return the next evening after dark.

This was quickly followed by a reply from the German Admiral naming the flotillas he selected, and by orders to them; also by directions for the lighting up of buoys and the showing of lights at certain hours, and by orders for an aerial reconnaissance. Thus it came about that we knew what enemy ships were coming out, when they were coming, by what channel they would clear their own minefield and whither they were bound, namely to the Dogger Bank, and extensive shoal off the Yorkshire coast. Sir Winston Churchill has told them how, with these deciphered messages before them, the Admiralty sent orders to Admiral Jellicoe and the Grand Fleet at Scapa, to Admiral Beatty with the battle Cruisers at Rosyth, and to Commodore Tyrwhitt with the Light Cruisers and Destroyers at Harwich. The battle cruisers, light cruisers, and destroyers were to meet at seven o'clock in the morning at a point where, it was calculated, they would lie between the Germans and the safe waters of the Heligoland Bight. But unfortunately the German ships had started later or steamed more slowly than was reckoned on, with the result that when, in the Sabbath dawn, they discovered the presence of British forces, they were still somewhat to the south-eastward. At once they turned and fled for home, hotly pursued by Beatty and his cruisers. As you will recall, the Blücher, the rear ship of their line, was sunk by gun-fire: their flag-ship, the Seydlitz, was severely damaged. German gunfire put the Lion out of action at a critical period of the engagement, with the result that the pursuit was brought to a premature end.

All the while, from 7.30a.m. when the ships first sighted one another, there was pouring into Room 40 a stream of German messages, each overheard at our listening stations, telegraphed to the Admiralty, and there deciphered within less than half an hour of the time of origin. These messages from the German Admiral told of his flight south eastward pursued by British battle cruisers, of his being in action and of his urgent need of support; this to the German Commander in Chief, who, with his battleships, was still at their sheltered anchorage. Then, a few minutes later, we heard the reply: 'Our main fleet and flotillas coming out'. This reassuring statement was made in clear, that is to say, in unciphered German, but there was a significant addition – a cipher group which we knew to mean 'as soon as possible'. The intention, so it appeared, was that the clear part of the message should be read by the British Admiral, and discourage him from the chase, the all-important qualifying phrase being concealed. A ciphered order to get up steam in all boilers came later, too late to make effective the succour for which Admiral von Hipper had called. Shortly after noon it was reported that the Blücher had fallen out, and half an hour later that she was lost and that the action was broken off.

These are only a few of the many signals we overheard that strange Sunday morning. In the War Room of the Admiralty were assembled Sir Winston Churchill, Lord Fisher, Admiral Wilson and Admiral Oliver. As each German message was deciphered I took it in, putting it silently before them and noting the reflection of the news in their intent faces. At the same time every British signal received from the Admiral or over-heard by the listening operators of the Admiralty, was brought in too. Together the German and the British messages gave a marvellous contemporary picture of the action from its beginning to its close. There were gaps indeed, to be filled in later. But the main phases of the action stood out clear, almost at the instant of happening, before the group of watchers hundreds of miles from the scene. Such a panorama was never unrolled before: one may doubt if such a panorama will ever be unrolled again. Even in the greater Battle of Jutland, more than a year later, though we could still read all the German naval cipher, there was no sensation comparable to this. There the curtain was lifted only fitfully: we had no more than rare and partial glimpses of a vast dim stage.

But on that memorable Sunday of the Dogger Bank action we, who in this strange way were spectators, were left in no uncertainty as to the progress and the issues of the drama. When it was over, the workers of Room 40 could reflect with satisfaction on the contribution they had made. Naturally, however, there was keen disappointment that so promising a beginning should have so unsatisfying a finish. I will remember Sir Winston Churchill's gesture when he read the telegram announcing that our ships had given up the chase. It was about the time that people were leaving the churches after morning prayers.

That afternoon, and in the days that followed, we had intercepts which revealed the damage our guns had done. One message had a very human touch. As the surviving ships approached their anchorage the German Commander in Chief made a wireless signal that the passing cruisers were to be given three hurrahs. Beyond any question these cheers were well deserved. A few days later the Kaiser paid a complimentary visit and we duly heard beforehand of the arrangements to be made for his reception – even directions about uniform for officers and men. The officers were to wear undress uniform with orders, overcoats, dirks, and brown gloves. Little fishes as well as big ones were landed by the Room 40 nets.

Besides letting us keep a close watch on the movements of German ships, the intercepted naval messages, when carefully studied and compared, allowed important inferences to be drawn regarding such things as the composition of the enemy squadrons, the presence of new ships, the position of minefields and of the swept channels through them. To deduce such information required technical knowledge as well as quick perception; the task was entrusted to a very able naval officer, now Rear-Admiral Herbert Hope, who was lent by the Intelligence Division to Room 40 for this purpose, and served as a member of the staff from November 1914 onwards. It would be difficult to overstate the value of what he did in that capacity.

The Zeppelins, especially in their early raids, were remarkably loquacious. When they came out of their sheds in the morning they would report themselves to Headquarters by wireless, sometimes adding the words 'only H.V.B. on Board'. We came to know that these words were invariably the prelude to a raid. They mean the more confidential naval signal book was left behind: that they were taking a book, already compromised, whose capture, should the airship be wrecked or shot down over enemy country, would not be nearly so serious. Sometimes, too, the destination was plainly stated. While returning they would send in advance wireless reports of their exploits – not always accurate. I recall one which used a curious phrase: it described itself as having successfully bombarded 'the fortress of London'! Another was at least franker. It reported that a Midland town and the neighbouring industrial establishments had been attacked with explosive and incendiary bombs, claiming good results, as there were no defences.

The submarines, too, though they seldom used wireless transmissions when far from their base, would report freely as they approached it on their way home. Thus on May 12th, 1915, we caught at more than one listening station, messages from the German submarine, U.20, detailing her bag: she had sunk on the south coast of Ireland a sailing-ship, two steamers, and 'Lusitania'. Another message gave the latitude and longitude, and added the words 'by one torpedo'. Copies of these messages in the original cipher were made and certified as correct by the receiving operators, in case they should ever be required for use as evidence. They were not required. The Commander of U.20, after being much complimented on his achievement, met his fate in another submarine which was sunk by one of our Q boats in 1917.

After the action of the Dogger Bank a long time passed before the German ships again came out, except for excursions so brief and limited as to give our ships no chance to attack. One such excursion took place during the political crisis of May 1915. The advance indications were so serious that it was thought 'The Day' so long expected was at hand. All the Grand Fleet was accordingly called out. But before the contact could be established the Germans had gone home. It was not till the spring of 1916, after the command of the German Fleet had passed to Admiral Scheer, that a bolder policy was initiated. On April 25, the day after the Easter rebellion in Ireland, the Germans brought off a hurried bombardment of Lowestoft, returning to their base before our forces from the North could reach them. This was followed by other activities which culminated in the Battle of Jutland. Enemy signals, intercepted on May 30th, made it clear that the German Fleet was about to put to sea in force. Orders were accordingly issued by the Admiralty with the result that, on the afternoon of the 31st, Admiral von Hipper's squadron, forming the van of the German Fleet, encountered, to their surprise, the battle cruisers under Beatty, and the battle of Jutland began. On that I need not dwell: the story has been told and retold, discussed and re-discussed. It is not for me, nor have I any wish, to touch on points round which controversy has centred. As I have already said, the wireless watchers learnt very little of what was going on during the action. There was, for the most part, a puzzling silence, rarely broken. As night fell a few important signals were caught, each of which was promptly deciphered and passed on without delay to the War Staff.

Apart from the naval signals, which were our first concern, we intercepted an immense number of cipher communications between Berlin and places abroad. The isolated position of Germany, for her cables were cut directly the War began, obliged her to resort to wireless and, when our listening stations got into their stride, little of it escaped. There were messages to Constantinople, Sofia, Athens, Teheran; correspondence both by telegrams and letters with agents in North and South America. Of some remarkable messages to Washington I shall speak later. I recall an early message from von Jagow, the Secretary of State for Foreign Affairs, to somebody who was reputed to have the ear of the Japanese, instructing him to seize an opportunity of pointing out that Japan had 'put her money on the wrong horse' and that her interest demanded she should not shut herself out from an understanding with Germany. With Madrid especially there was a continuous exchange of messages. German representatives there made use of a wireless station from which a voluminous stream of information daily poured into Berlin. It was all in cipher, of various sorts, most of which we could read. It retailed the reports of spies, it told of intrigues in Morocco, of ships passing Algeciras, of arrangements for the reception of submarines on the Spanish coast, and a host of other things that are too numerous to recall. One curious item I remember very well. Soon after Portugal had entered the War, on the side of the Allies, an indefatigable German agent in Madrid sent a wireless message to Berlin suggesting that the rivers flowing from Spain into Portugal should be contaminated at the frontier with cholera bacillus. For this purpose he requested that two glass phials of pure culture should be sent him at the first safe opportunity. One ought to add that a prompt reply came from Berlin declining the proposal. There was nothing to show whether the refusal sprang from a higher standard of chivalry in War, or from a better knowledge of the difficulties which would attend this remarkable application of bacteriology.

I want to say a little more about the wireless listening stations. Besides those which the Marconi Company provided, we had a group set up and admirably managed by two amateurs. In the first month of the War a former pupil of mine, the late Mr. Russell Clarke, then a barrister and a wireless enthusiast, came to me to see if he could be useful. He had an idea that there might be surreptitious signalling from England to Germany, and that he could detect it if he had permission to try. By that time all wireless, other than official, had been rigorously stopped. The permission and appliances he needed were at once given and I told him that when he had satisfied himself he was to come back for another job, one more likely to be productive. In a few weeks he returned, having found no trace of the thing he was looking for. Then I asked him to go along with his friend Colonel Hippisley – also a keen wireless amateur – to open an Admiralty station at Hunstanton for catching enemy cipher. These two gentlemen did most admirable and important service. They made the Hunstanton's station so effective a listening place that, as the work grew, they were instructed to add mast after mast, each mast carrying a separate aerial, in order to increase the capacity for reception; and then to start more stations in other places.

In all our intercepting stations each listening aerial had an assigned range of wave-lengths, over which the operators kept watch. For greater security the program was so arranged that every message should be taken at not less than two places. Each place was connected by wire to the Admiralty, in the basement of which there was a telegraph office. From there the messages passed by pneumatic tube to Room 40, where the decipherers on duty became painfully familiar, by night and day, with the incessant thus of the pneumatic carrier as it fell into the waiting basket. The night watch was no sinecure, especially when the Germans contracted the habit – as they did in 1916 – of changing the cipher key of the principal naval signals every night at twelve o'clock. At first they used to stick to one key for weeks or even months; in those days a change of key was a dreaded and exciting event, and frequent changes might have been rather baffling; but by the time the nightly changes began, the staff were so quick at the game that the new key was usually discovered two or three hours later. There were many messages of an almost routine kind which provided easy material for the solution.

The work of the telegraph operators who were taking in the cipher at listening stations well deserves a tribute. It was tiresome and exacting. Imagine the patience needed to record, with meticulous correctness, groups of figures or symbols of whose meaning the operator had not the slightest idea. For these workers there was none of the compensating thrill of discovery; they had not even any clear understanding of the nature of the service they were doing to the State. That was hidden under a veil of secrecy which nobody dared to lift. You may judge of their skill in a highly specialised task from this, that when, as sometimes happened, the call-signs of the enemy ships were all simultaneously changed and we were left to puzzle out the identity of each new sign, the telegraphic helped greatly by recognising the personal style of the senders. What they were listening to was not the spoken voice (there was no wireless transmission of speech) but only the dot and dash of Morse. Nevertheless the mannerism, the manual accent, so to say, of the individual enemy telegraphist revealed him to their alert and sensitive ears. These operators, young men for the most part, doing invaluable service, were harassed by the taunts of girls who asked them why they were not at the Front. When this grievance came to our notion it was quickly remedied. The stroke of an Admiralty pen converted them into members of the Royal Naval Volunteer Reserve. They were put in uniform, and after that the most patriotic girl felt no call to flourish a white feather in their faces.

There was still another group of stations also in constant communication with Room 40 – the special observing stations for directional wireless. Their function was to determine the direction from which an enemy signal came and thereby enable us to fix the place of origin. Captain Round, a clever engineer of the Marconi Company, gave practical shape to a method of doing this and was instructed to put up three directional stations: one at Lowestoft, one near York, and one at Murcar on the coast of Aberdeenshire. Later there was a fourth at Lerwick. When, for example, an enemy ship somewhere in the North Sea made a signal, no matter what, its bearing would be taken by each of the directional stations and telegraphed to Room 40 where corresponding lines were quickly laid down on a big chart. The intersection of these lines gave the place of the ship when she made the signal. We brought this process into systematic use early in the War; the Germans (as Admiral Scheer says in his book) followed a good deal later. They set up directional stations which served to find out where their own airships were, so that they could pass on the information by wireless to the airship itself. An airship is so much at the mercy of the winds that it cannot find its position by dead-reckoning with any certainty. So, when a Zeppelin was out over the sea, it would occasionally make a signal in order that the German directional stations should be able to tell it where it was. We picked up the same signal at our directional stations. In a few minutes the position of the Zeppelin was marked on our chart. Presently we would catch a cipher message from a German shore station giving the Zeppelin their reckoning, which generally confirmed ours.

No secret was made of the fact that we used directional wireless to find the positions of enemy ships. This gave it camouflage value as a means of hiding the fact that we were reading their cipher. People were allowed to ascribe to directional wireless the information which had come to us in quite another way. It diverted suspicion from the essential secret.

I have spoken of the initial luck that attended the naval side of our cryptographic work: we had scarcely less on the diplomatic side. In the summer of 1915 there came to the Admiralty, through the India Office, two German consular code-books which had been captured in the East. A study of them showed that they had a strong family resemblance; one might be derived from the other by a sort of shuffling process. This led to the obvious conjecture that they were members of a considerable family, related to one another in the same way. We soon found that much of the enemy's correspondence could be read, not indeed on these books, but on others which, though we never saw them, we were able to reconstruct from their resemblance to the two in our possession. Hence we had a starting point from which to penetrate several of the German consular and diplomatic ciphers and so to read, not only wireless intercepts, but ciphered documents which were occasionally got from other sources.

Early in February 1916 a despatch from the German Embassy in America summarised a report by a confidential agent on the position in Ireland in which the decision was announced to begin action on Easter Eve, with the expectation of immediate German help. Part of the German help, as you may remember, was to send Sir Roger Casement in a submarine to the Irish coast at Tralee Bay and a disguised tramp steamer with a cargo of arms to the same place. Casement was arrested on landing and the gun-running steamer was duly met and taken in charge by the British patrol.

Another enterprise, on which our work also threw useful and restraining light, was a German intrigue in Persia which had Afghanistan and India for its goal. In the second half of 1915 we were able, thanks largely to the efforts of an accomplished member of my staff, Mr. George Young, to decipher, during its progress, a long telegraphic correspondence between Berlin and Teheran which revealed the terms of a secret treaty and plans of the enemy campaign. While the plans were being matured they were upset: the Russians invaded Persia and advanced towards Teheran. Though not in the secrets of the Foreign Office, I think the workers of Room 40 are justified in believing that this timely counterstroke was not a mere coincidence.

The power to read various diplomatic German ciphers was acquired only gradually and as a reward of persistent effort on the part of certain specially capable members of the staff. Given enough material and cryptographers so expert as they became, few, if any, ciphers will escape penetration. The detection of new keys used with an already known book does not, as a rule, present great difficulty. The process of building up a code-book which the reader has never seen is less easy: it is necessarily slow, but it is surprisingly possible, especially when some related correspondence is at the same time passing in other codes which the cryptographer is able to read. Then, if he is watchful, he may have an occasional stroke of luck – a message may be found that has been sent in two codes, perhaps for the information of two correspondents who are provided with different books. So, if he can read one of the two, he gets all the words of the other version as nuggets in his mining operation into the other code. What he must, in any case, have, is lots of material on which to work. At the best it is a long game of trial and error; but, provided the book continues in use and many messages are sent on it, one by one the bits of the puzzle fit into their places. The fact that Germany was shut off from conveying new code-books to her distant correspondents compelled the continued employment, over long periods, of the same books. She was also driven to use channels of correspondence which it was possible to tap. Count von Bernstorff, the German Ambassador at Washington, in giving evidence about ciphers to a Committee of Enquiry of the German National Assembly after the War, justly emphasises this point. Speaking of the correspondence with Washington he says: 'The cipher was not changed as often as would have been the case under normal conditions ... To the extent that it was possible to do so, we operated the existing ciphers by means of keys; but I learnt later that the British decoded all our telegrams.'

That statement is exaggerated. But one may admit that the degree of observation which Room 40 was able to keep on the Count's correspondence was sufficient to yield some moment of intense interest. We read, for instance, in September 1916, a telegram from the German Chancellor to von Bernstorff instructing him to discuss the projected submarine warfare cautiously with Colonel House, with a view to President Wilson's making a peace move 'which should ostensibly appear spontaneous'. And a few months later, when, after the amazing episode of the Zimmermann telegrams which has been made public through the issue (in 1925) of the third volume of Mr. Page's Life And Letters.

Speaking in Edinburgh after that publication, Lord Balfour said it had untied his tongue regarding the work which is the subject of this lecture. His remarks then and the kind letter from him which has been read by the Chairman will, I hope, be held to excuse some untying of mine.

Let me repeat in outline the strange story. On January 16th 1917 a telegram was despatched by Zimmermann, the German Secretary of State for Foreign Affairs, to von Eckhardt, the German Minister in Mexico City, instructing him to offer the President of Mexico an alliance against the United States, with a prospect of recovering the lost territory of Texas, New Mexico and Arizona. All this was conditional on the United Sates ceasing to be neutral as a result of the coming U-boat campaign. It was also to be suggested to the President of Mexico that he invite Japan to join Germany and Mexico in an alliance against the United States. This cheerful proposal to arrange, conditionally, for stabbing in the back the power whose good offices as a peacemaker the Germans were still seeking, was made even more remarkable by the method of its transmission. To ensure its reaching Mexico, the German Foreign Office sent it across the Atlantic by several routes. It was wirelessed direct from Nauen to Seyville in Long Island, as a ciphered despatch to Bernstorff for his information, and to be passed on by him to the German representative in Mexico. The same message was also handed, in cipher, to the Swedish Minister in Berlin, to be sent by him to Stockholm, from which city it was cabled to Buenos Aires and thence to Washington. This route caused it to pass over British cables, ostensibly as a Swedish cipher message, but it did not escape detection. Finally, the Germans (as they have themselves revealed) used yet a third and a stranger way of getting it across. By the courtesy of the American State Department and under the orders, it was said, of President Wilson himself, messages between Bernstorff and the German Government were sometimes allowed to pass in cipher through the American Ambassador in Berlin. A long cipher telegram from Berlin to Washington, nominally American but really from the German Chancellor to Bernstorff, which purported to relate to the peace efforts of Wilson, was being despatched in that way on the same day (January 16), and to it the Zimmermann message for Mexico was actually attached. Was it cynical humour that led the Germans to employ the American State Department and its Embassy in Berlin as a channel for such a communication?

The Zimmermann message was sent in a difficult cipher of which one of my staff, Mr. Nigel de Grey, had made a special study. Though the first version was imperfect, the general sense was clear enough to make him instantly appreciate its immense political importance. Later he succeeded in making out the full text. You will find it in the Page volume, along with a series of subsequent messages on the same subject, all of which we also intercepted and deciphered.

Here was highly explosive material. No one could read the Zimmermann telegram without realising that, if made public in America, it would set the country aflame. Wilson was hesitating on the brink of War – reluctant to plunge – clinging painfully to the idea of neutrality which seemed to be almost a part of his religion. The threat to Texas, New Mexico and Arizona would stir even the apathy of the Middle West. But how to make it public without betraying the precious, the vital, secret of Room 40? For answer you must turn to the Page letters. You will see there how Lord Balfour, then Foreign Minister, told the essential parts of our secret to Mr. Page for communication under the strictest confidence to President Wilson; how Wilson, after carefully verifying the authenticity of the Zimmermann message, gave it to the American press, which published it on March 1st; how there was a German tumult of enquiry and recrimination as to responsibility for the leakage. The effect on American opinion was decisive: it prepared the way for a declaration of war. But the curtain which hid Room 40 remained wholly undisturbed. From behind it we listened to the storm with serenity, especially to the caustic comments of some newspapers on the superiority of the American intelligence service over ours. The cryptographic machine continued to function as silently as before.

By the date of the Zimmermann telegrams Room 40 had become a big affair. It was still a separate branch of the Admiralty under my direction, occupying many rooms, with a staff which had swelled to near fifty, including a ladies' section that did good service on the political side. I was always on the lookout for recruits, for the work grew faster than fit people could be found to cope with it. The first ladies to join were personal and family friends whose intelligence I knew and on whose discretion I could count. They, no less than the men, justified the confidence to the full. Among the men, temporarily brought together for a common purpose, there was wide diversity in age, temperament, habits, state. There were peers, professors, and college dons or doctors; civil servants from other Government offices; one or two publishers, a parson, lawyers, schoolmasters, officers disabled from War service of a different sort; men of other trades or of none. To them all cryptography was a new task: to most it became surprisingly congenial, developing unsuspected gifts, or fits which, had found expression only in the guessing of acrostics. Our fellowship in a great secret was no negligible bond. From its mustard-seed beginning Room 40 had indeed grown. It was an organism full of vitality, and the best way to organise an organism is to encourage it to grow. My function beyond that of recruiting officer and official spokesman, was mainly to group the units and link together the various subsections, which, engrossed each in its own portion of the work, might know little of what the others were doing. The conscientious watcher of a plant's growth must sometimes prune, yet very rarely had I the unpleasant duty of suggesting, even to a newcomer, that he had better find some other means of contributing to win the War.

The achievements of Room 40 were achievements of the staff. It would be invidious to single out names when all worked so hard and so well. If there were diversities of gifts there was the same spirit. From day to day there was much to be done requiring no special cryptographic talent, tasks of an almost routine kind, needing only intelligence, assiduity, patience, care. From time to time there were problems which in addition demanded a rate aptitude for research, amounting, one may say, to genius. Fortunately a few members of the staff possessed that incommunicable faculty for inspired guessing. To a good many there would come flashes, sometimes brilliant flashes; but two or three, when they had acquired experience, seemed to live in an atmosphere of continuous light. They would leap or fly to conclusions with an agility incomprehensible to my own pedestrian wits.

Of the dead, one may speak. Six at least of that band have gone: W.H. Anstie, a Naval College master who joined almost at the beginning and did admirable service to the end; Charles Godfrey, Headmaster at Osbourne College, who gave what time he could spare from other duty, bringing the discernment and cold logic of the mathematician to bear with excellent effort; E.C. Quiggin, University Lecturer in German at Cambridge, a specially accomplished linguist – the latest of the recruits I enrolled; Bertram Hopkinson, who in the early days of key-finding, when we were in a fever of discovery, let us profit for a while by his splendid intelligence before he became absorbed in work for the Flying Corps which cost him his life; Russell Clarke, by temperament something of a freelance and intellectual rebel, original, resourceful and immensely energetic, whose unsparing efforts in setting up and running wireless intercepting stations probably impaired his health and brought about a far too early death; Benjamin Faudel Phillips, no less devoted, whom we loved, whose imperturbable geniality lubricated any little grit that might get into the wheels of an overworked machine, and kept us from realising how gravely his own strength was being taxed. After the War he kept an open door for old colleagues, and until his death a year ago his beautiful house in Hertfordshire was a rallying point of the Room 40 Club.

Ten years have passed, and Room 40 has long ago gone the way of so many War establishments, hastily extemporised, intensely active while the need lasted, and serving the urgent purpose of the moment astonishingly well. I believe the scattered units who composed the staff still recall their period of secret service as having provided the most fascinating employment of their lives. I, for one, do so. The topsy-turveydom of War, which makes it virtuous to kill and destroy, caused us to embrace without a qualm the stealthy occupation of the eavesdropper, usually so ignoble. We accepted it as a high vocation, to be obeyed with enthusiasm and pursued with holy zeal. Now that the work is done, we may I think, look back upon it with satisfaction and even pride.

My own share in all this came to an end before the War was over. I was invited, greatly to my surprise, to be Principal of the University of Edinburgh. At first I declined the offer on the ground of a War job which I should not leave. But the electors pressed it, urging that for a time the Edinburgh duties would be so light that I might undertake them too. Lord Balfour was appealed to, in his double capacity as Chancellor of the University and First Lord of the Admiralty. He advised me to accept, but on the basis of my continued direction of Room 40. An arrangement for this was made, and so long as I could live in London it was easy. When, some months later, I had to take up residence in Edinburgh it became scarcely practicable, and, on May 31st 1917, by their Lordships' order, I hauled down my flag and handed over the command to Admiral Hall. As Director of the Intelligence Division of the War Staff he had been for long in touch with our work, had supplied material from time to time for us to decipher, and had been the channel through which the political results reached the Foreign Office. The department was transferred as a going concern, well able to do without me, with all its staff and its voluminous records. Through the accident, one may say, of its creation, it had, up till then, been an independent branch of the Admiralty, placed definitely in my charge by order of the Board. From June 1917, for the remainder of the War, it was carried on as a section of the Intelligence Division. During that final period I had no official relations but it was pleasant, in one or two visits to the old rooms, to be greeted by familiar faces and be assured that the work continued to thrive.

Here these reminiscences close. The story now told, I need scarcely add, is not in its essential facts a revelation of secrets. For a time after the War the facts did remain concealed, but since then they have been disclosed in various ways. They have been publicly referred to by Sir Winston Churchill, under whom, as First Lord, the work of Room 40 was begun, and by Lord Balfour, under whom it was continued. These gentlemen have written and spoken, not only with the authority of office, but with fundamental knowledge of the work and its significance. The supplementary details now presented may have some interest in the conduct of the War. In any case they give, for what it is worth, a first-hand record of a personal experience, in its way unique, the memory of which does not grow dim.

Appendix VI[1]

Some work of the Anti-Aircraft Experimental Section of the MID 1916

Aeroplane Sub-Committee of Section 1
Board of Invention and Research
A – Problems set by the Admiralty

Helicopter and direct lift flying machines: The practicability of the helicopter type flying machine has been considered in connection with a combined aeroplane and helicopter, invented by Mr. H.D. Lister. It was decided that although a direct lift machine is theoretically possible, the practical difficulties appear to be insuperable at the present time. Further, the difficulties are enormously increased when the horizontal propulsion apparatus is fitted. A representative of Section 1 is a member of a Sub-Committee of the Department of Munitions Inventions, which is examining the helicopter in question.

Research on dopes for aeroplanes: This research commenced in May, with a view (1) to the standardisation of the cellulose acetate used as a dope constituent, and (2) to the elimination of acetone as a solvent for cellulose acetate. The two subjects are intimately connected, for the present cellulose acetates vary in composition and properties, and especially in solubility, according to the mode of preparation.

The investigation has been carried out for the Sub-Committee by Dr. H.J.H. Fenton FRS, and is still proceeding. The results up to the present time point to the necessity for a standard method of analysis of the acetates, and to creosote and cyclohexanone as useful dope constituents. No practical substitute for acetone has yet been discovered, although it has been found possible to replace at least 50 percent of the acetone formerly employed by a mixture of methyl acetone and methyl ethyl ketone.

A request, dated 31st October 1916, has been received from the Secretary of the Admiralty for the investigation of a dope not containing acetone, and in view of the urgency of the problem an independent investigation is being carried out by Mr. J. Huebner at the Municipal School of Technology in

1 National Archives ADM 293/7.

Manchester.

B – Original research carried out by the Sub-Committee

Night flying of aeroplanes:

(a) landing ground and guide lights – the Sub-Committee has examined the practical problems and difficulties associated with night flying in its various aspects. The requirements of the night pilot for guidance and safe landing were first considered, and a report was put forward recommending to the Admiralty that landing grounds allowing a clear run of half a mile and properly illuminated should be provided at intervals of 50 miles, and a system of guide lights should be stationed at regular intervals in the part of the country likely to be flown over. It is understood that the recommendations of the Sub-Committee have, in the main, been carried out.

(b) lighting of aerodromes – a large number of inventions connected with the illumination of night landing grounds has been considered. Some of these are already incorporated in existing systems, but in many cases they are impractical on account of either the glare from lights or the obstruction of the aerodrome. Various systems of fixing lamps to the aeroplane in order to facilitate landing have also been considered. It is found difficult to select a satisfactory position on the machine for the lamp, so as to avoid the glare which tends to dazzle the pilot and obscure the ground.

(c) detection of enemy aircraft – in order to render hostile aircraft visible to patrol aeroplanes at a higher altitude, a scheme put forward by Mr. Lanchester FRS has been experimented with. According to the proposal, the patrolled area of country is to be fitted with searchlights, giving a plane horizontal beam of light, so that the lower stratum of the atmosphere is illuminated. The intensity of the illumination required was determined by experiments at the National Physical Laboratory.

A simple form of searchlight consisting of a mirror, formed of a sheet of nickel plated steel bent approximately to the form of a parabola, and having a tungsten arc lamp arranged on the focus line of the mirror, has been invented by Mr. Lanchester FRS.

The papers relating to the scheme were transferred to the Director-General of Military Aeronautics when the anti-aircraft defences of the country were taken over by the army.

Air brakes for aeroplanes – information of various experiments on this question had been collated. A device for lowering both the wing flaps for braking is now being tried on experimental machines.

Aeroplane gun – a gun designed by Mr. Lanchester FRS, loaded with cartridges containing 16 pellets of about ¼ oz. weight each, and intended to make up for inaccuracy of aim by the spread of the pellets, has been referred to the Royal Aircraft Factory for test. The Superintendent reported that the value of scattering the shot is considerable in view of the character of the aim from one aeroplane at another. The gun has not been proceeded with.

Altimeter – experimental work on the production of an altimeter using a hard steel, free from hysteresis, is being carried out in conjunction with the Air Department.

Use of aircraft for gun-laying and spotting in Naval Actions. A paper by Mr. Lanchester FRS on this subject is still under consideration.

C – Proposals put forward by Inventors and other members of the General Public

Numerous inventions have been considered and, where necessary, have been referred to the Director of Air Services for his information. The following are among the more important:-

Chlorinated India rubber obtained by the exhaustive chlorination of plantation crape in trichloroethylene was submitted by Mr. Peachey. The substance gives very tough films, but is useless as an aeroplane dope owing to its non-contractile property and its tendency to decompose by weathering.

Paraffin flare for illuminating landing grounds – invented by Mr. Money. A perforated asbestos drum containing an absorbent material is soaked with paraffin. After lighting, the paraffin is vapourised and passes through the holes. The tests show the apparatus to be satisfactory, and it has been referred to the Director of Air Services, with a recommendation that it be adopted in place of petrol flares.

Samples of cellulose acetate submitted by Mr. W. G. Stephenson have been examined and appeared to be very satisfactory. The further consideration was deferred pending the arrangement for its manufacture by Mr. Stephenson. This has not yet materialised.

An earth speed indicator for aeroplanes – invented by Captain C. W. Wheatley, has been investigated. The invention is based on the deflection of an electrically charged fibre as it passed through the earth's magnetic field. The practical difficulties of accurately measuring the minute forces which arise make the success of the instrument very doubtful.

Visibility of aeroplanes – transparent 'cellon' sheet proposed by Dr. Masterman (possibly FRS), as a covering for aeroplane wings and bodies, to render them less visible, has been investigated. Strength and weathering tests were carried out at the National Physical Laboratory, and the material was subsequently brought to the notice of the Air Department. It is understood that experimental wings covered in this material have been made by Messrs. Short Brothers.

Parachutes – a parachute designed by Mr. E.R. Calthrop and developed by the Airships Sub-Committee has been tried for dropping weights from aeroplanes. Difficulties were experienced in getting the parachute clear of the aeroplane without fouling, and after several mishaps further trials were abandoned.

Metal propellers – the possibility of using metal propellers was examined in connection with a proposal by Mr. H. Leitner, for a hollow propeller built up of thin sheet steel. It was found that past experiments showed that metal propellers rapidly developed fatigue and broke up, and the proposal was not proceeded with. A full size propeller according to this scheme has, however, been built for the Department of Munitions Inventions.

Notes

Chapter 1

1 Letter from Sir William Turner Thiselton-Dyer FRS, National Archives FD 5/57.
2 Royal Society website: http://royalsociety.org/.
3 Royal Society War Committee Minute Book CMB/36.
4 National Archives DSIR 10/127.
5 Royal Society War Committee Minute Book CMB/36.
6 *Who Was Who* 1941-50 (London, 1967), p.52.
7 *Who Was Who* 1929-40 (London, 1967), p.57.
8 http://royalsociety.org/library/collections/.
9 *Who Was Who* 1929-40 (London, 1967), p.235.
10 *Who Was Who* 1961-1970 (London, 1967), p.206.
11 http://royalsociety.org/library/collections/.
12 *Who Was Who* 1941-50 (London, 1967), p.280.
13 *Who Was Who* 1929-40 (London, 1967), p.449.
14 *Who Was Who* 1961-1970 (London, 1967), p.486.
15 *Burke's Peerage, Baronetage and Knightage* (London, 107th ed 2003), p.956.
16 *Who Was Who* 1916-28 (London, 1967), p.689.
17 *Who Was Who* 1929-40 (London, 1967), p.851.
18 *Who Was Who* 1916-28 (London, 1967), p.754.
19 *Who Was Who* 1941-50 (London, 1967), p.1075.
20 National Archives CAB 23/1 0033, CAB 23/1 0059, CAB 23/1 0080 and CAB 23/4 0071.
21 *Obituary Notices of Fellows of the Royal Society* Vol 4 1942-1944, p.240.
22 *Obituary Notices of Fellows of the Royal Society* Vol 3 1939-1941, p.412.
23 *Obituary Notices of Fellows of the Royal Society* Vol 5 1945-1948, p.38.
24 *Obituary Notices of Fellows of the Royal Society* Vol 3 1939-1941, p.34.
25 *Biographical Memoirs of Fellows of the Royal Society* Vol 48 2002, p.293.
26 *Obituary Notices of Fellows of the Royal Society* Vol 5 1945-1948, p.640.
27 http://www.nobelprize.org/nobel_prizes/physics/laureates/1917/barkla.html.
28 *Obituary Notices of Fellows of the Royal Society* Vol 4 1942-1944, p.284.
29 http://www.nobelprize.org/nobel_prizes/chemistry/laureates/1907/buchner.html.
30 *Biographical Memoirs of Fellows of the Royal Society* Vol 44 1998, p.80.
31 *Who Was Who* 1961-1970 (London, 1967), p.206.
32 http://www.nobelprize.org/nobel_prizes/medicine/laureates/1936/dale.html.
33 http://www.nobelprize.org/nobel_prizes/physics/laureates/1921/einstein.html.
34 *Biographical Memoirs of Fellows of the Royal Society* Vol 2 1956, pp.117-127.
35 *Biographical Memoirs of Fellows of the Royal* Society Vol 16 1970, p.286.
36 *Obituary Notices of Fellows of the Royal Society 1942-1944* Vol 4, p.12.
37 *Obituary Notices of Fellows of the Royal Society* 1950-1951 Vol 7, p.374.
38 *Biographical Memoirs of Fellows of the Royal Society* Vol 13 1967, p.132.
39 *Biographical Memoirs of Fellows of the Royal Society* Vol 13 1967, p.168.
40 http://www.nobelprize.org/nobel_prizes/medicine/laureates/1922/hill.html.
41 http://www.nobelprize.org/nobel_prizes/medicine/laureates/1929/hopkins.html.
42 http://www.nobelprize.org/nobel_prizes/medicine/laureates/1930/landsteiner.html.

43 http://www.nobelprize.org/nobel_prizes/medicine/laureates/1922/meyerhof.html.
44 http://www.nobelprize.org/nobel_prizes/physics/laureates/1923/millikan.html.
45 *Obituary Notices of Fellows of the Royal Society* Vol 4 1942-1944, p.102.
46 *Obituary Notices of Fellows of the Royal Society* Vol 4 1942-1944, p.304.
47 http://www.nobelprize.org/nobel_prizes/chemistry/laureates/1904/ramsay.html.
48 http://www.nobelprize.org/nobel_prizes/physics/laureates/1904/strutt.html.
49 http://www.nobelprize.org/nobel_prizes/physics/laureates/1928/richardson.html.
50 *Biographical Memoirs of Fellows of the Royal Society* Vol 22 1976, p.420.
51 *Obituary Notices of Fellows of the Royal Society* Vol 2 1936-1938, p.409.
52 http://www.nobelprize.org/nobel_prizes/medicine/laureates/1932/sherrington.html.
53 http://www.nobelprize.org/nobel_prizes/chemistry/laureates/1921/soddy.html, the Royal Society Chemical War Committee minutes and *Biographical Memoirs of Fellows of the Royal Society* Vol 3 1957, p.210.
54 *Obituary Notices of Fellows of the Royal Society* Vol 3 1939-1941, p.595.
55 *Biographical Memoirs of Fellows of the Royal Society* Vol 29 1983, pp.623, 641, 643.
56 http://www.nobelprize.org/nobel_prizes/chemistry/laureates/1915/willstatter.html.
57 http://www.nobelprize.org/nobel_prizes/physics/laureates/1927/wilson.html.
58 *Biographical Memoirs of Fellows of the Royal Society* Vol 4 1958, pp.308-9.
59 *Obituary Notices of Fellows of the Royal Society* Vol 8 1952-1953, p.332.
60 *Obituary Notices of Fellows of the Royal Society* Vol 4 1942-1944, p.431.
61 *Obituary Notices of Fellows of the Royal Society* Vol 3 1939-1941, p.548.
62 *Biographical Memoirs of Fellows of the Royal Society* Vol 1 1955, p.16.
63 *Obituary Notices of Fellows of the Royal Society* Vol 7 1950-1951, p.342.
64 *Biographical Memoirs of Fellows of the Royal Society* Vol 6 1960, p.43.
65 *Biographical Memoirs of Fellows of the Royal Society* Vol 3 1957, p.45.
66 *Obituary Notices of Fellows of the Royal Society* Vol 7 1950-1951, p.358.
67 *Obituary Notices of Fellows of the Royal Society* Vol 7 1950-1951, pp.171-2.
68 *Obituary Notices of Fellows of the Royal Society* Vol 7 1950-1951, pp.421-422.
69 Comment in Donnan's obituary – *Biographical Memoirs of Fellows of the Royal Society* Vol 3 1957, p.26.
70 *Obituary Notices of Fellows of the Royal Society* Vol 6 1948-1949, p.483.
71 *Obituary Notices of Fellows of the Royal Society* Vol 7 1950-1951, pp.470-471.
72 *Biographical Memoirs of Fellows of the Royal Society* Vol 7 1961, p.255.
73 *Obituary Notices of Fellows of the Royal Society* Vol 4 1942-1944, p.84.
74 *Obituary Notices of Fellows of the Royal Society* Vol 8 1952-1953, p.311.
75 National Archives WO 297/1489.
76 *Obituary Notices of Fellows of the Royal Society* Vol 4 1942-1944, pp.795-809.
77 *Obituary Notices of Fellows of the Royal Society* Vol 5 1945-1948, p.221.
78 National Archives DSIR 37/139.
79 *Obituary Notices of Fellows of the Royal Society* vol 7 1950-1951, pp.323, 325.
80 National Archives MUN 7/332.

Chapter 2

1 Minutes of the Sectional Chemical Committee held on 25th February 1916.
2 Minutes of the Sectional Chemical Committee held on 13th May 1916.
3 *Biographical Memoirs of Fellows of the Royal Society* Vol 2 1956, p.158.
4 *Obituary Notices of Fellows of the Royal Society* Vol 1 1932-1935, p.506.
5 Letters to Mr Anderson and Professor Irvine are mentioned in the Sectional Chemical Committee Minutes 20th July 1916.
6 *Biographical Memoirs of Fellows of the Royal Society* Vol 22 1976, pp.415-527, Sir Robert Robinson OM PRS p.425.
7 item 8 from minutes of the Sectional Chemical Committee 20th July 1916.
8 See the *Royal Society Sectional Chemical Committee Minute Book* CMB/28/24.
9 An organic chemical, known as dope, covered aircraft fabric to strengthen and make it water proof.
10 Minutes of the Sectional Chemical Committee held on 17th June 1915.
11 Minutes of the Sectional Chemical Committee held on 7th July 1915.

12 Minutes of the Sectional Chemical Committee held on 29th July 1915.
13 Arthur G. Green, "The History of Mustard Gas", *Journal of the Society of Chemical Industry* 1919, Vol XXXVIII, p.363.
14 Minutes of the Sectional Chemical Committee held on 25th February 1916.
15 Cellulose acetate was used in the preparation of aircraft dope and in photography.
16 Minutes of the Sectional Chemical Committee held on 16th April 1916.
17 Minutes of the Sectional Chemical Committee held on 22nd November 1916.
18 National Archives DSIR 10/127.
19 Correspondence between Sir Richard Glazebrook and William Ernest Dalby can be found in the Royal Society Archives by searching the Past Fellows database.
20 National Archives DSIR 10/127.
21 Royal Society Archives MS/525/6/4.
22 Minutes of the Royal Society Natural Products (War) Committee CMB/38.
23 National Archives DSIR 10/127.
24 Royal Society Archives – The National Physical Laboratory 1913-19 CD/6.
25 National Archives DSIR 10/127.
26 National Archives DSIR 10/127.
27 National Archives DSIR 10/127.
28 National Archives DSIR 10/127.
29 National Archives T 1/12145.
30 The Royal Society Sectional Committee on Physiology CMB/36/36.
31 National Archives FD 5/57.
32 National Archives WO 142/299.

Chapter 3

1 National Archives ADM 293/7.
2 http://royalsociety.org/library/collections/#fellowship.
3 National Archives ADM 293.
4 National Archives ADM 293/2.
5 National Archives ADM 293/5.
6 National Archives ADM 293/9.
7 National Archives ADM 293/4.
8 National Archives ADM 293/2.
9 National Archives ADM 293/2 document 38164/17.
10 National Archives ADM 293/9, p.29.
11 National Archives MUN5/118.
12 National Archives MUN 5/117.
13 National Archives MUN 7/290.
14 National Archives MUN 7/277.
15 National Archives MUN 7/317.
16 *Obituary Notices of Fellows of the Royal Society* Vol 3 1939-1941, p.218.
17 National Archives MUN 7/314.
18 http://royalsociety.org/library/collections/#fellowship.
19 National Archives MUN 7/314.
20 National Archives DSIR 37/24.
21 http://www.nobelprize.org/nobel_prizes/physics/laureates/1928/richardson.html.
22 National Archives DSIR 37/24 minutes of the meeting October 2nd 1916.
23 National Archives WO 142/53.
24 National Archives WO 142/59.
25 http://royalsociety.org/library/collections/#fellowship.
26 National Archives WO 142/53.
27 *Obituary Notices of Fellows of the Royal Society* Vol 8 1952-1953, p.571.
28 *Obituary Notices of Fellows of the Royal Society* Vol 1 1932-1935, p.597.
29 National Archives MUN 4/6911.
30 *Biographical Memoirs of Fellows of the Royal Society* Vol 3 1957, pp.274-275.

Chapter 4

1 *Obituary Notices of Fellows of the Royal Society* Vol 1 1932-1935, pp.45-53.
2 *Obituary Notices of Fellows of the Royal Society* Vol 6 1948-1949, p.402.
3 *Obituary Notices of Fellows of the Royal Society* Vol 1 1932-1935, p.84.
4 *Obituary Notices of Fellows of the Royal Society* Vol 3 1939-1941, p.706.
5 *Obituary Notices of Fellows of the Royal Society* Vol 2 1936-1938, p.368.
6 *Obituary Notices of Fellows of the Royal Society* Vol 3 1939-1941, p.499.
7 *London Gazette* 21st June 1916, issue 29633, p.6191.
8 *London Gazette* 15th May 1917, issue 30070, p.4725.
9 *London Gazette* 10 June 1921, issue 32353, p.4694.
10 *Who Was Who* 1951-60 (London, 1967), p.1006.
11 *Biographical Memoirs of Fellows of the Royal Society* Vol 2 1956, pp.269-290.
12 http://www.army.mod.uk/rlc/history/355.aspx.
13 *London Gazette* 15th May 1917, issue 30070, p.4725.
14 http://www.army.mod.uk/structure/4140.aspx.
15 *Obituary Notices of Fellows of the Royal Society* Vol 4 1942-1944, p.21.
16 *Obituary Notices of Fellows of the Royal Society* Vol 9 1954, p.69.
17 *Biographical Memoirs of Fellows of the Royal Society* Vol 4 1958, p.74.
18 *Biographical Memoirs of Fellows of the Royal Society* Vol 2 1956, p.20.
19 *Obituary Notices of Fellows of the Royal Society* Vol 8 1952-1953, pp.504-505.
20 *Biographical Memoirs of Fellows of the Royal Society* Vol 1 1955, p.163.
21 *Obituary Notices of Fellows of the Royal Society* Vol 4 1942-1944, p.577.
22 *Obituary Notices of Fellows of the Royal Society* Vol 3 1939-1941, p.89.
23 *Obituary Notices of Fellows of the Royal Society* Vol 1 1932-1935, p.534.
24 *Obituary Notices of Fellows of the Royal Society* Vol 5 1945-1948, p.410.
25 *Obituary Notices of Fellows of the Royal Society* Vol 9 1954, p.37.
26 *Obituary Notices of Fellows of the Royal Society* Vol 2 1936-1938, p.177.
27 *Biographical Memoirs of Fellows of the Royal Society* Vol 2 1956, p.118.
28 *Obituary Notices of Fellows of the Royal Society* Vol 9 1954, p.158.
29 *Obituary Notices of Fellows of the Royal Society* Vol 8 1952-1953, p.421.
30 *Obituary Notices of Fellows of the Royal Society* Vol 3 1939-1941, p.44.
31 *Obituary Notices of Fellows of the Royal Society* Vol 5 1945-1948, p.770.
32 *Obituary Notices of Fellows of the Royal Society* Vol 7 1950-1951, p.456.
33 *Obituary Notices of Fellows of the Royal Society* Vol 1 1932-1935, p.112.
34 *Biographical Memoirs of Fellows of the Royal Society* Vol 1 1955, p.242.
35 *Obituary Notices of Fellows of the Royal Society* Vol 7 1950-1951, p.511.
36 *Obituary Notices of Fellows of the Royal Society* Vol 7 1950-1951, p.283.
37 *Obituary Notices of Fellows of the Royal Society* Vol 6 1948-1949, p.302.
38 http://www.npl.co.uk/about/history/.
39 *Obituary Notices of Fellows of the Royal Society* Vol 5 1945-1948, p.171.
40 *Obituary Notices of Fellows of the Royal Society* Vol 8 1952-1953, p.111.
41 *Obituary Notices of Fellows of the Royal Society* Vol 8 1952-1953, p.172.
42 *Biographical Memoirs of Fellows of the Royal Society* Vol 1 1955, p.175.
43 *Biographical Memoirs of Fellows of the Royal Society* Vol 3 1957, p.265.
44 National Archives MUN 5/118.
45 *Obituary Notices of Fellows of the Royal Society* Vol 6 1948-1949, p.43.
46 *Obituary Notices of Fellows of the Royal Society* Vol 4 1942-1944, p.631.
47 *Obituary Notices of Fellows of the Royal Society* Vol 2 1936-1938, p.504.
48 *Obituary Notices of Fellows of the Royal Society* Vol 7 1950-1951, p.142.
49 *Obituary Notices of Fellows of the Royal Society* Vol 3 1939-1941, p.884.
50 *Obituary Notices of Fellows of the Royal Society* Vol 4 1942-1944, p.801.
51 *Obituary Notices of Fellows of the Royal Society* Vol 1 1932-1935, p.96.
52 *Biographical Memoirs of Fellows of the Royal Society* Vol 51 2005, p.294.
53 *Obituary Notices of Fellows of the Royal Society* Vol 9 1954, p.219.
54 *Obituary Notices of Fellows of the Royal Society* Vol 8 1952-1953, p.7.

55 *Obituary Notices of Fellows of the Royal Society* Vol 8 1952-1953, p.159.
56 *Biographical Memoirs of Fellows of the Royal Society* Vol 6 1960, p.65.
57 *Biographical Memoirs of Fellows of the Royal Society* Vol 1 1955, p.83.
58 *Biographical Memoirs of Fellows of the Royal Society* 1917, pp.xxii-xxiii.
59 *Biographical Memoirs of Fellows of the Royal Society* Vol 1 1955, p.223.
60 *Biographical Memoirs of Fellows of the Royal Society* Vol 3 1957, p.218.
61 *Obituary Notices of Fellows of the Royal Society* Vol 8 1952-1953, p.301.
62 *Biographical Memoirs of Fellows of the Royal Society* Vol 7 1961, p.288.

Chapter 5

1 National Archives MUN 5/18.
2 Royal Society Archives MDA/A/27/29/21.
3 Royal Society Archives CMB/39.
4 http://royalsociety.org/library/collections/.
5 Royal Society reference numbers CMB/39/1, CMB/39/2, CMB/39/3, CMB/39/4, CMB/39/5, CMB/39/6, CMB/39/7, CNB/39/2.
6 *Obituary Notices of Fellows of the Royal Society* Vol 2 1936-1938, p.229.
7 http://royalsociety.org/library/collections/#fellowship.
8 *Obituary Notices of Fellows of the Royal Society* Vol 5 1945-1948, p.426.
9 *Obituary Notices of Fellows of the Royal Society* Vol 3 1939-1941, pp.761-2.
10 *Biographical Memoirs of Fellows of the Royal Society* Vol 1 1955, p.7.
11 *Obituary Notices of Fellows of the Royal Society* Vol 5 1945-1948, p.165.
12 *Obituary Notices of Fellows of the Royal Society* Vol 9 1954, p.31.
13 *Obituary Notices of Fellows of the Royal Society* Vol 8 1952-1953, pp.262-363.
14 *Obituary Notices of Fellows of the Royal Society* Vol 9 1954, p.81.
15 *Obituary Notices of Fellows of the Royal Society* Vol 1 1932-1935, p.75.
16 *Obituary Notices of Fellows of the Royal Society* Vol 3 1939-1941, pp.164-5.
17 *Obituary Notices of Fellows of the Royal Society* Vol 5 1945-1948, p.116.
18 *Obituary Notices of Fellows of the Royal Society* Vol 3 1939-1941, p.955.
19 *Obituary Notices of Fellows of the Royal Society* Vol 9 1954, p.134.
20 *Obituary Notices of Fellows of the Royal Society* Vol 5 1945-1948, p.478.
21 *Obituary Notices of Fellows of the Royal Society* Vol 7 1950-1951, p.362.
22 *Biographical Memoirs of Fellows of the Royal Society* Vol 5 1959, p.97.
23 *Biographical Memoirs of Fellows of the Royal Society* Vol 1 1955, p.147.
24 *Obituary Notices of Fellows of the Royal Society* Vol 2 1936-1938, p.301.
25 *Obituary Notices of Fellows of the Royal Society* Vol 3 1939-1941, p.433.
26 *Obituary Notices of Fellows of the Royal Society* Vol 1 1932-1935, p.5.
27 *Obituary Notices of Fellows of the Royal Society* Vol 5 1945-1948, p.782.
28 *Obituary Notices of Fellows of the Royal Society* Vol 2 1936-1938, p.151.
29 *Obituary Notices of Fellows of the Royal Society* Vol 4 1942-1944, p.413.
30 *Obituary Notices of Fellows of the Royal Society* Vol 4 1942-1944, p.427.
31 *Obituary Notices of Fellows of the Royal Society* Vol 3 1939-1941, p.225.
32 *Obituary Notices of Fellows of the Royal Society* Vol 3 1939-1941, pp.632-3.
33 *Biographical Memoirs of Fellows of the Royal Society* Vol 2 1956 pp 291-298.
34 *Obituary Notices of Fellows of the Royal Society* Vol 4 1942-1944, p.699.
35 *Obituary Notices of Fellows of the Royal Society* Vol 4 1942-1944, p.176.
36 *Obituary Notices of Fellows of the Royal Society* Vol 6 1948-1949 pp 503-538.
37 *Biographical Memoirs of Fellows of the Royal Society* Vol 3 1957, p.10.
38 *Obituary Notices of Fellows of the Royal Society* Vol 5 1945-1948, p.247.
39 *Obituary Notices of Fellows of the Royal Society* Vol 2 1936-1938 pp.19-24 and the *Encyclopaedia Britannica Ultimate Reference Suite.*
40 *Obituary Notices of Fellows of the Royal Society* Vol 4 1942-1944, p.687.
41 *Obituary Notices of Fellows of the Royal Society* Vol 6 1948-1949, p.232.
42 *Obituary Notices of Fellows of the Royal Society* Vol 2 1936-1938, p.365.
43 *Biographical Memoirs of Fellows of the Royal Society* Vol 5 1959, p.273.
44 *Obituary Notices of Fellows of the Royal Society* Vol 1 1932-1935, p.558.

45 *Obituary Notices of Fellows of the Royal Society* Vol 1 1932-1935, p.321.
46 *Obituary Notices of Fellows of the Royal Society* Vol 1 1932-1935, p.299.
47 *Biographical Memoirs of Fellows of the Royal Society* Vol 2 1956, p.259.
48 *Biographical Memoirs of Fellows of the Royal Society* Vol 3 1957, p.234.
49 *Obituary Notices of Fellows of the Royal Society* Vol 5 1945-1948, p.235.
50 *Obituary Notices of Fellows of the Royal Society* Vol 5 1945-1948, p.12.
51 *Obituary Notices of Fellows of the Royal Society* Vol 1 1932-1935, p.140.
52 *Obituary Notices of Fellows of the Royal Society* Vol 2 1936-1938, p.169.
53 *Obituary Notices of Fellows of the Royal Society* Vol 1 1932-1935, p.189.
54 *Obituary Notices of Fellows of the Royal Society* Vol 4 1942-1944, p.221.
55 *Biographical Memoirs of Fellows of the Royal Society* Vol 2 1956, p.150.
56 *Obituary Notices of Fellows of the Royal Society* Vol 2 1936-1938, p.307.
57 *Obituary Notices of Fellows of the Royal Society* Vol 1 1932-1935, p.266.
58 *Obituary Notices of Fellows of the Royal Society* Vol 8 1952-1953, p.525.
59 *Obituary Notices of Fellows of the Royal Society* Vol 7 1950-1951, p.240.
60 *Obituary Notices of Fellows of the Royal Society* Vol 4 1942-1944, p.374.
61 *Obituary Notices of Fellows of the Royal Society* Vol 4 1942-1944, p.727.
62 *Biographical Memoirs of Fellows of the Royal Society* Vol 2 1956, p.209.
63 *Obituary Notices of Fellows of the Royal Society* Vol 8 1952-1953, p.231.
64 *Obituary Notices of Fellows of the Royal Society* Vol 2 1936-1938, p.446.
65 *Obituary Notices of Fellows of the Royal Society* Vol 4 1942-1944, p.657.
66 *Obituary Notices of Fellows of the Royal Society* Vol 3 1939-1941, p.872.
67 *Obituary Notices of Fellows of the Royal Society* Vol 2 1936-1938, p.329.
68 *Obituary Notices of Fellows of the Royal Society* Vol 2 1936-1938, p.266.
69 *Obituary Notices of Fellows of the Royal Society* Vol 6 1948-1949, p.266.
70 *Biographical Memoirs of Fellows of the Royal Society* Vol 2 1956, p.300.
71 *Obituary Notices of Fellows of the Royal Society* Vol 7 1950-1951, pp.520-521.
72 *Obituary Notices of Fellows of the Royal Society* Vol 8 1952-1953, p.14.
73 *Obituary Notices of Fellows of the Royal Society* Vol 8 1952-1953, p.25.
74 *Obituary Notices of Fellows of the Royal Society* Vol 7 1950-1951, p.294.
75 *Obituary Notices of Fellows of the Royal Society* Vol 4 1942-1944, p.462.
76 *Obituary Notices of Fellows of the Royal Society* Vol 8 1952-1953, p.71.
77 *Obituary Notices of Fellows of the Royal Society* Vol 6 1948-1949, p.386.
78 *Obituary Notices of Fellows of the Royal Society* Vol 1 1932-1935, p.131.
79 *Obituary Notices of Fellows of the Royal Society* Vol 1 1932-1935, p.71.
80 *Biographical Memoirs of Fellows of the Royal Society* Vol 2 1956, p.223.
81 *Obituary Notices of Fellows of the Royal Society* Vol 4 1942-1944, p.74.
82 *Obituary Notices of Fellows of the Royal Society* Vol 1 1932-1935, p.202.
83 *Obituary Notices of Fellows of the Royal Society* Vol 8 1952-1953 pp 275-296.
84 *Obituary Notices of Fellows of the Royal Society* Vol 1 1932-1935, p.149.
85 *Biographical Memoirs of Fellows of the Royal Society* Vol 4 1958, p.353.
86 *Biographical Memoirs of Fellows of the Royal Society* Vol 2 1956, p.328.
87 *Obituary Notices of Fellows of the Royal Society* Vol 4 1942-1944, p.310.
88 *Obituary Notices of Fellows of the Royal Society* Vol 1 1932-1935, p.173.
89 *Obituary Notices of Fellows of the Royal Society* Vol 1 1932-1935, p.399.
90 *Obituary Notices of Fellows of the Royal Society* Vol 1 1932-1935, p.235.

Chapter 6

1 National Archives HW 3/4.
2 National Archives ADM 1/23899.
3 National Archives ADM 1/23899.
4 http://royalsociety.org/library/collections/.
5 National Archives HW3/6.
6 National Archives ADM 223/768.
7 National Archives HW 3/170.

8 National Archives ADM 293/4.
9 *Biographical Memoirs of Fellows of the Royal Society* Vol 2 1956, p.249.
10 National Archives ADM 293/7.
11 http://royalsociety.org/library/collections/.
12 *Obituary Notices of Fellows of the Royal Society* Vol 5 1945-1948, p.65.
13 http://collectionsonline.nmsi.ac.uk/.
14 National Archives PDF file GB 0069 MS2019.
15 *Biographical Memoirs of Fellows of the Royal Society* Vol 3 1957, pp.163, 165.
16 http://www.nobelprize.org/nobel_prizes/physics/laureates/1926/perrin.html.
17 *Obituary Notices of Fellows of the Royal Society* Vol 4 1942-1944, p.304.
18 National Archives ADM 293/7.
19 *Obituary Notices of Fellows of the Royal Society* Vol 7 1950-1951, pp. 470-471.
20 *Encyclopaedia Britannica Ultimate Reference Edition.*

Chapter 7

1 http://royalsociety.org/library/collections/.
2 *Obituary Notices of Fellows of the Royal Society* Vol 3 1939-1941, p.792.
3 *Obituary Notices of Fellows of the Royal Society* Vol 3 1939-1941, p.784.
4 National Archives ADM 293/7.
5 National Archives miscellaneous report filed in ADM 293/6.
6 *Obituary Notices of Fellows of the Royal Society* Vol 3 1939-1941, pp.291-324.
7 National Archives WO 142/69.
8 Unfortunately the original minutes do not contain initials. There were few Professors active in during World War I with the surnames of these Professors, so it is a reasonable assumption to assign initials and designations of FRS where appropriate. Three of the Colonels, namely Crossley, Smithells and Starling, may also have been Fellows as the Royal Society database has entries matching these surnames with the relevant experience. With no confirmation, however, the decision has been taken to add this comment.
9 Hannah Gay, *History of Imperial College London 1907-2007* (London 2007), p.142.
10 National Archives WO 142/6.
11 These Minutes have no year associated with them (in fact most of the minutes from this Committee have no year). However, 1916 is the only year when 28th November fell on a Tuesday. The minutes are shown below as such.
12 National Archives WO 142/59.
13 *Obituary Notices of Fellows of the Royal Society* Vol 9 1954, p.6.
14 *Obituary Notices of Fellows of the Royal Society* Vol 1 1932-1935, p.525.
15 *Obituary Notices of Fellows of the Royal Society* Vol 6 1948-1949, p.320.
16 *Obituary Notices of Fellows of the Royal Society* Vol 1 1932-1935, p.597.
17 *Obituary Notices of Fellows of the Royal Society* Vol 4 1942-1944, p.29.
18 *Obituary Notices of Fellows of the Royal Society* Vol 7 1950-1951, p.117.
19 *Obituary Notices of Fellows of the Royal Society* Vol 8 1952-1953, p.436.
20 *Biographical Memoirs of Fellows of the Royal Society* Vol 35 1990, p.330.
21 *Obituary Notices of Fellows of the Royal Society* Vol 8 1952-1953, p.571.
22 *Biographical Memoirs of Fellows of the Royal Society* Vol 4 1958, p.226.
23 *Obituary Notices of Fellows of the Royal Society* Vol 3 1939-1941, pp.104-5.
24 *Biographical Memoirs of Fellows of the Royal Society* Vol 4 1958, p.329.
25 *Obituary Notices of Fellows of the Royal Society* Vol 8 1952-1953, p.611.
26 *Whitaker's Almanac 1916*, London, pp. 223-5.
27 *Whitaker's Almanac 1916*, London, p.273.
28 http://royalsociety.org/library/collections/#fellowship.
29 *Obituary Notices of Fellows of the Royal Society* Vol 6 1948-1949, pp.546-549.
30 *Obituary Notices of Fellows of the Royal Society* Vol 2 1936-1938, p.590, also *Obituary Notices of Fellows of the Royal Society* Vol 3 1939-1941, p.103.
31 *Biographical Memoirs of Fellows of the Royal Society* Vol 7 1961, p.85.
32 *Obituary Notices of Fellows of the Royal Society* Vol 8 1952-1953, p.596.
33 *Obituary Notices of Fellows of the Royal Society* Vol 7 1950-1951, p.493.

34 National Archives MUN 7/412.
35 Sir William Kershaw Slater was born in 1893 and therefore a young man in World War I. He was knighted in 1951 and elected to Fellowship in 1957, which explains his humble salary and duties.
36 *Obituary Notices of Fellows of the Royal Society* Vol 6 1948-1949, p.8.
37 *Obituary Notices of Fellows of the Royal Society* Vol 4 1942-1944, p.598.
38 *Obituary Notices of Fellows of the Royal Society* Vol 4 1942-1944, p.771.
39 *Biographical Memoirs of Fellows of the Royal Society* Vol 46 2000, pp.72-73.
40 See the citation for Sir Ralph 's election to Fellowship in http://royalsociety.org/library/collections/#fellowship.
41 *Biographical Memoirs of Fellows of the Royal Society* Vol 4 1958, p.108, and http://royalsociety.org/library/collections/.
42 http://royalsociety.org/library/collections/#fellowship.
43 *Biographical Memoirs of Fellows of the Royal Society* Vol 46 2000, pp.269-283.
44 *Biographical Memoirs of Fellows of the Royal Society* Vol 24 1978, pp.323-367.
45 *Obituary Notices of Fellows of the Royal Society* Vol 3 1939-1941, p.479.
46 *Obituary Notices of Fellows of the Royal Society* Vol 7 1950-1951, pp.421- 422.
47 *Obituary Notices of Fellows of the Royal Society* Vol 2 1936-1938, p.78.
48 *Obituary Notices of Fellows of the Royal Society* Vol 9 1954, p.243.
49 *Obituary Notices of Fellows of the Royal Society* Vol 1 1932-1935, p.346.
50 *Obituary Notices of Fellows of the Royal Society* Vol 2 1936-1938, p.222.
51 http://www.barrandstroud.com/company.php.
52 *Obituary Notices of Fellows of the Royal Society* Vol 1 1932-1935, pp.545-546.
53 *Obituary Notices of Fellows of the Royal Society* Vol 2 1936-1938, p.143.

Chapter 8

1 *Whitaker's Almanac* 1916, p.105.
2 National Archives ADM 116/3486.
3 *Whitaker's Almanac*, 1916, pp.254-257.
4 Maurice Cocker, *Destroyers of the Royal Navy 1893-1981* (London, 1981).
5 David Lyon, *The First Destroyers* (London, 2001).
6 Randal Gray and Przemyslaw Budzbon, *Conway's All the World's Fighting Ships, 1906-1921, Volume 2* (Annapolis MD, 1985).
7 National Archives MUN 7/322.
8 *Biographical Memoirs of Fellows of the Royal Society* Vol 4 1958, p.216.
9 *Biographical Memoirs of Fellows of the Royal Society* Vol 1 1955, p.248.
10 *Biographical Memoirs of Fellows of the Royal Society* Vol 3 1957, p.183.
11 *Biographical Memoirs of Fellows of the Royal Society* Vol 5 1959, p.3.
12 *Biographical Memoirs of Fellows of the Royal Society* Vol 5 1959, p.195.
13 *Obituary Notices of Fellows of the Royal Society* Vol 3 1939-1941, p.579.
14 *Biographical Memoirs of Fellows of the Royal Society* Vol 6 1960, p.34.
15 *Obituary Notices of Fellows of the Royal Society* Vol 1 1932-1935, p.391.
16 *Obituary Notices of Fellows of the Royal Society* Vol 8 1952-1953, p.123.
17 *Obituary Notices of Fellows of the Royal Society* Vol 1 1932-1935, p.607.
18 *Obituary Notices of Fellows of the Royal Society* Vol 5 1945-1948, p.765.
19 *Biographical Memoirs of Fellows of the Royal Society* Vol 5 1959, p.77.
20 *Obituary Notices of Fellows of the Royal Society* Vol 8 1952-1953, p.449.
21 *Obituary Notices of Fellows of the Royal Society* Vol 4 1942-1944, p.618.
22 *Obituary Notices of Fellows of the Royal Society* Vol 4 1942-1944, p.382.
23 *Obituary Notices of Fellows of the Royal Society* Vol 4 1942-1944, p.519.
24 *Obituary Notices of Fellows of the Royal Society* Vol 1 1932-1935, p.498.
25 *Biographical Memoirs of Fellows of the Royal Society* Vol 2 1956, p.106.
26 *Obituary Notices of Fellows of the Royal Society* Vol 4 1942-1944, p.273.
27 *Obituary Notices of Fellows of the Royal Society* Vol 6 1948-1949, p.51.
28 *Obituary Notices of Fellows of the Royal Society* Vol 1 1932-1935, p.54.
29 *Biographical Memoirs of Fellows of the Royal Society* Vol 2 1956, p.139.

30 *Obituary Notices of Fellows of the Royal Society* Vol 8 1952-1953, p.199.
31 *Biographical Memoirs of Fellows of the Royal Society* Vol 3 1957, p.134.
32 *Obituary Notices of Fellows of the Royal Society* Vol 5 1945-1948, p.795.
33 *Obituary Notices of Fellows of the Royal Society* Vol 4 1942-1944, p.431.
34 *Obituary Notices of Fellows of the Royal Society* Vol 1 1932-1935, p.593.
35 *Obituary Notices of Fellows of the Royal Society* Vol 3 1939-1941, p.622.
36 *Obituary Notices of Fellows of the Royal Society* Vol 3 1939-1941, p.218.

Chapter 9

1 *Whitaker's Almanac*, 1916, p.104.
2 *Whitaker's Almanac*, 1916, p.495.
3 The Royal Society Archives. CMB/36/33. Report on the work of the Grain Pests (War) Committee.
4 Royal Society Archives, Food (War) Committee Minutes CMB/73.
5 National Archives, CAB/24/3_0008.
6 National Archives, CAB/24/7_0096.
7 Figures furnished by the Canadian Government; see Supplement to Crop Report, Int. Inst. Agric, Rome, February, 1917.
8 *Milling*, 3rd March 1917, p. 198, and *Economist*, 3rd March 1917, p. 455.
9 *Journal*, Board of Agriculture, January 1917, p.956.
10 *Board of Trade Journal*, 15th February 1917, and *Corn Trade News*, 22nd January 1917.
11 E.g., *Milling*, 3rd March 1917, p. 199.
12 The continuity of the processes of marketing and milling, including delivery, involves the presence of an irreducible quantity of material passing through those processes at any given time.
13 Annual Report of the Liverpool Steam Ship Owners' Association for 1916, p. 32.
14 Board of Trade Report on " Cost of Living in the United Kingdom," 1906. Compare the collections of workmen's budgets by Mr. Charles Booth, the Economic Club, and Mr. Rowntree. From a physiological point of view, of course, the importance of bread to the population is far larger than these figures of money expenditure might suggest, and it is much greater to the working classes than to the middle classes. See paragraph 11 above.
15 National Archives, CAB/24/14_0067.
16 National Archives, CAB/24/34_0089.
17 National Archives CAB/24/34_0077.
18 *Obituary Notices of Fellows of the Royal Society* Vol 1 1932-1935, p.41.
19 *Obituary Notices of Fellows of the Royal Society* Vol 1 1932-1935, p.30.
20 *Obituary Notices of Fellows of the Royal Society* Vol 7 1950-1951, pp.38-9.
21 *Obituary Notices of Fellows of the Royal Society* Vol 1 1932-1935, p.570.
22 *Obituary Notices of Fellows of the Royal Society* Vol 3 1939-1941, p.752.
23 *Obituary Notices of Fellows of the Royal Society* Vol 3 1939-1941, p.816.
24 *Obituary Notices of Fellows of the Royal Society* Vol 4 1942-1944, p.565.
25 *Obituary Notices of Fellows of the Royal Society* Vol 8 1952-1953, p.550.
26 *Obituary Notices of Fellows of the Royal Society* Vol 1 1932-1935, p.565.
27 *Obituary Notices of Fellows of the Royal Society* Vol 4 1942-1944, p.17.
28 *Biographical Memoirs of Fellows of the Royal Society* Vol 4 1958, p.283.
29 *Obituary Notices of Fellows of the Royal Society* Vol 3 1939-1941, p.336.
30 *Obituary Notices of Fellows of the Royal Society* Vol 8 1952-1953, p.132.
31 *Obituary Notices of Fellows of the Royal Society* Vol 7 1950-1951, p.87.
32 *Obituary Notices of Fellows of the Royal Society* Vol 3 1939-1941, p.266.
33 *Obituary Notices of Fellows of the Royal Society* Vol 3 1939-1941, p.278.
34 *Obituary Notices of Fellows of the Royal Society* Vol 1 1932-1935, p.66.
35 *Obituary Notices of Fellows of the Royal Society* Vol 6 1948-1949, p.25.
36 *Obituary Notices of Fellows of the Royal Society* Vol 1 1932-1935, p.466.
37 *Obituary Notices of Fellows of the Royal Society* Vol 1 1932-1935, pp.159-160.
38 *Obituary Notices of Fellows of the Royal Society* Vol 1 1932-1935, p.330.
39 *Obituary Notices of Fellows of the Royal Society* Vol 6 1948-1949, p.134.
40 Sir Charles Scott Sherrington OM FRS is mentioned in Figure 1.8. as a Nobel Laureate, in

Chapter 2 as a member of The Royal Society Sectional Committee on Physiology and in Chapter 10 as a future President of the Royal Society (1920-1925).
41 *Obituary Notices of Fellows of the Royal Society* Vol 3 1939-1941, p.854.
42 *Obituary Notices of Fellows of the Royal Society* Vol 1 1932-1935, p.586.
43 *Biographical Memoirs of Fellows of the Royal Society* Vol 1 1955, p.200.
44 *Obituary Notices of Fellows of the Royal Society* Vol 7 1950-1951, p.447.
45 *Obituary Notices of Fellows of the Royal Society* Vol 1 1932-1935, p.516.
46 *Who Was Who 1916-1928* A. & C. Black Limited (1929).
47 *Proceedings of the Royal Society* Series B Vol 101 1927, pp.i-v.
48 *Obituary Notices of Fellows of the Royal Society* Vol 7 1950-1951, p.20.
49 *Obituary Notices of Fellows of the Royal Society* Vol 8 1952-1953 pp 342.
50 *Obituary Notices of Fellows of the Royal Society* Vol 2 1936-1938 pp 468.
51 *Obituary Notices of Fellows of the Royal Society* Vol 6 1948-1949, p.464.
52 *Obituary Notices of Fellows of the Royal Society* Vol 8 1952-1953, p.494.
53 *Biographical Memoirs of Fellows of the Royal Society* Vol 3 1957, p.110.
54 *Obituary Notices of Fellows of the Royal Society* Vol 7 1950-1951, p.478.
55 *Biographical Memoirs of Fellows of the Royal Society* Vol 3 1957, pp 193-202.
56 *Biographical Memoirs of Fellows of the Royal Society* Vol 3 1957, p.54.
57 *Obituary Notices of Fellows of the Royal Society* Vol 3 1939-1941, p.743.
58 *Obituary Notices of Fellows of the Royal Society* Vol 6 1948-1949, p.565.
59 *Obituary Notices of Fellows of the Royal Society* Vol 1 1932-1935, p.340.
60 *Obituary Notices of Fellows of the Royal Society* Vol 9 1954, p.56.

Chapter 10

1 https://www.gov.uk/honours/overview.
2 *Obituary Notices of Fellows of the Royal Society* Vol 1 1932-1935, pp.101-102.
3 *Obituary Notices of Fellows of the Royal Society* Vol 1 1932-1935, pp.569-576.
4 *Biographical Memoirs of Fellows of the Royal Society* Vol 2 1956, pp.101-113.
5 *Obituary Notices of Fellows of the Royal Society* Vol 5 1945-1948, pp.61-78.
6 *Obituary Notices of Fellows of the Royal Society* Vol 2 1936-1938, pp.225-228.
7 *Obituary Notices of Fellows of the Royal Society* Vol 7 1950-1951, pp.115-137.
8 *Obituary Notices of Fellows of the Royal Society* Vol 2 1936-1938, pp.29-56.
9 *Obituary Notices of Fellows of the Royal Society* Vol 2 1936-1938, pp.141-143.
10 *Biographical Memoirs of Fellows of the Royal Society* Vol 2 1956, pp.249-255.
11 *Obituary Notices of Fellows of the Royal Society* Vol 8 1952-1953, pp.583-600.
12 *Obituary Notices of Fellows of the Royal Society* Vol 1 1932-1935, pp.45-53.
13 *Obituary Notices of Fellows of the Royal Society* Vol 8 1952-1953, pp.309-323.
14 *Proceedings of the Royal Society* Series A Vol 94 1917-1918, pp.xxxiv-xxxv.
15 Royal Society website: http://royalsociety.org/.
16 http://royalsociety.org/library/collections/.
17 http://www.rsl.ox.ac.uk/dept/scwmss/wmss/online/modern/spsl/spsl.html.

Bibliography

Archive documents

National Archives: ADM 1/23899, ADM 116/3486, ADM 223/768, ADM 293, ADM 293/2, ADM 293/4, ADM 293/5, ADM 293/6, ADM 293/7, ADM 293/9, CAB 23/1 0033, CAB 23/1 0059, CAB 23/1 0080, CAB 23/4 0071, CAB 24/14_0067, CAB 24/3_0008, CAB 24/34_0077, CAB 24/34_0089, CAB 24/7_0096, DSIR 10/127, DSIR 37/139, DSIR 37/24, FD 5/57, GB 0069 MS2019, HW 3/170, HW 3/4, HW3/6, MUN 4/6911, MUN 5/117, MUN 5/118, MUN 5/18, MUN 7/277, MUN 7/290, MUN 7/314, MUN 7/317, MUN 7/322, MUN 7/412, MUN5/118, T 1/12145, WO 142/299, WO 142/53, WO 142/59, WO 142/6, WO 142/69 and WO 297/1489.

Royal Society Archives: CD/6, CMB/28/24, CMB/36, CMB/36/33, CMB/36/36, CMB/38, CMB/39, CMB/39/1, CMB/39/2, CMB/39/3, CMB/39/4, CMB/39/5, CMB/39/6, CMB/39/7, CMB/73, CNB/39/2, MDA/A/27/29/21 and MS/525/6/4.

Printed books

Board of Trade Report "Cost of Living in the United Kingdom" (London, 1906)
Burke's Peerage, Baronetage and Knightage (London, 2003, 107th ed.)
Cocker, Maurice, *Destroyers of the Royal Navy 1893-1981* (London, 1981)
Encyclopaedia Britannica Ultimate Reference Edition (London, 2011)
Gay, Hannah, *History of Imperial College London 1907-2007* (London, 2007)
Lyon, David, *The First Destroyers*, (London, 2001)
Randall, Ian, *Conway's All the World's Fighting Ships 1906-1921*, (London, 1997)
Whitaker's Almanac 1916 (London, 1916)
Who was Who 1916-28 (London, 1967 ed.)
Who was Who 1929-40 (London, 1967 ed.)
Who was Who 1941-50 (London, 1967 ed.)
Who was Who 1951-60 (London, 1967 ed.)
Who was Who 1961-70 (London, 1967 ed.)

Royal Society publications

Biographical Memoirs of Fellows of the Royal Society 1917
Biographical Memoirs of Fellows of the Royal Society Vol 1 1955

Biographical Memoirs of Fellows of the Royal Society Vol 2 1956
Biographical Memoirs of Fellows of the Royal Society Vol 3 1957
Biographical Memoirs of Fellows of the Royal Society Vol 4 1958
Biographical Memoirs of Fellows of the Royal Society Vol 5 1959
Biographical Memoirs of Fellows of the Royal Society Vol 6 1960
Biographical Memoirs of Fellows of the Royal Society Vol 7 1961
Biographical Memoirs of Fellows of the Royal Society Vol 13 1967
Biographical Memoirs of Fellows of the Royal Society Vol 16 1970
Biographical Memoirs of Fellows of the Royal Society Vol 22 1976
Biographical Memoirs of Fellows of the Royal Society Vol 24 1978
Biographical Memoirs of Fellows of the Royal Society Vol 29 1983
Biographical Memoirs of Fellows of the Royal Society Vol 35 1990
Biographical Memoirs of Fellows of the Royal Society Vol 44 1998
Biographical Memoirs of Fellows of the Royal Society Vol 46 2000
Biographical Memoirs of Fellows of the Royal Society Vol 48 2002
Biographical Memoirs of Fellows of the Royal Society Vol 51 2005
Obituary Notices of Fellows of the Royal Society Vol 1 1932-1935
Obituary Notices of Fellows of the Royal Society Vol 2 1936-1938
Obituary Notices of Fellows of the Royal Society Vol 3 1939-1941
Obituary Notices of Fellows of the Royal Society Vol 4 1942-1944
Obituary Notices of Fellows of the Royal Society Vol 5 1945-1948.
Obituary Notices of Fellows of the Royal Society Vol 6 1948-1949
Obituary Notices of Fellows of the Royal Society Vol 7 1950-1951
Obituary Notices of Fellows of the Royal Society Vol 8 1952-1953
Obituary Notices of Fellows of the Royal Society Vol 9 1954
Proceedings of the Royal Society Series A Vol 94 1917-1918
Proceedings of the Royal Society Series B Vol 101 1927

Journals

Annual Report of the Liverpool Steam Ship Owners' Association 1916
Board of Trade Journal 1917
Corn Trade News 1917
Economist 1917
International Institute of Agriculture 1917
Journal of the Board of Agriculture 1917
Journal of the Society of Chemical Industry 1919
Milling 1917

Websites

http://collectionsonline.nmsi.ac.uk/.
http://royalsociety.org/.
http://royalsociety.org/library/collections/#fellowship.

http://royalsociety.org/library/collections/#fellowship.
http://royalsociety.org/library/collections/.
http://www.army.mod.uk/rlc/history/355.aspx.
http://www.army.mod.uk/structure/4140.aspx.
http://www.barrandstroud.com/company.php.
http://www.london-gazette.co.uk/ 21st June 1916, page 29633, 15th May 1917, page 4725, 15th May 1917, page 4725 and 10th June 1921, page 4694.
http://www.nobelprize.org/nobel_prizes/chemistry/laureates/1904/ramsay.html.
http://www.nobelprize.org/nobel_prizes/chemistry/laureates/1907/buchner.html.
http://www.nobelprize.org/nobel_prizes/chemistry/laureates/1915/willstatter.html.
http://www.nobelprize.org/nobel_prizes/chemistry/laureates/1921/soddy.html.
http://www.nobelprize.org/nobel_prizes/medicine/laureates/1922/hill.html.
http://www.nobelprize.org/nobel_prizes/medicine/laureates/1922/meyerhof.html.
http://www.nobelprize.org/nobel_prizes/medicine/laureates/1929/hopkins.html.
http://www.nobelprize.org/nobel_prizes/medicine/laureates/1930/landsteiner.html.
http://www.nobelprize.org/nobel_prizes/medicine/laureates/1932/sherrington.html.
http://www.nobelprize.org/nobel_prizes/medicine/laureates/1936/dale.html.
http://www.nobelprize.org/nobel_prizes/physics/laureates/1904/strutt.html.
http://www.nobelprize.org/nobel_prizes/physics/laureates/1917/barkla.html.
http://www.nobelprize.org/nobel_prizes/physics/laureates/1921/einstein.html.
http://www.nobelprize.org/nobel_prizes/physics/laureates/1923/millikan.html.
http://www.nobelprize.org/nobel_prizes/physics/laureates/1926/perrin.html.
http://www.nobelprize.org/nobel_prizes/physics/laureates/1927/wilson.html.
http://www.nobelprize.org/nobel_prizes/physics/laureates/1928/richardson.html.
http://www.npl.co.uk/about/history/.
http://www.rsl.ox.ac.uk/dept/scwmss/wmss/online/modern/spsl/spsl.html.
https://www.gov.uk/honours/overview.

Index

Related titles published by Helion & Company

Muddling Through. The Organisation of British Army Chaplaincy in World War One
Peter Howson
ISBN 978-1-909384-20-0

Most Unfavourable Ground. The Battle of Loos 1915
Niall Cherry
ISBN 978-1-906033-21-7

The Other Side of the Wire Volume 1. With The German XIV Reserve Corps On The Somme, September 1914-June 1916
Ralph J. Whitehead
ISBN 978-1-908916-89-1

The Other Side of the Wire Volume 2. The Battle of the Somme. With the German XIV Reserve Corps, 1 July 1916
Ralph J. Whitehead
ISBN 978-1-907677-12-0

Ice, Steel and Fire. British Explorers in Peace and War 1921–45
Linda Parker
ISBN 978-1-908916-49-5

HELION & COMPANY
26 Willow Road, Solihull, West Midlands B91 1UE, England
Telephone 0121 705 3393 Fax 0121 711 4075
Website: http://www.helion.co.uk